Management Engineering

A Guide to Best Practices for
Industrial Engineering in Health Care

Management Engineering

A Guide to Best Practices for
Industrial Engineering in Health Care

Edited by
Dr. Jean Ann Larson,
FACHE, FHIMSS, DSHS

CRC Press
Taylor & Francis Group
Boca Raton London New York

CRC Press is an imprint of the
Taylor & Francis Group, an **informa** business

A PRODUCTIVITY PRESS BOOK

CRC Press
Taylor & Francis Group
6000 Broken Sound Parkway NW, Suite 300
Boca Raton, FL 33487-2742

© 2014 by Taylor & Francis Group, LLC
CRC Press is an imprint of Taylor & Francis Group, an Informa business

Printed on acid-free paper
Version Date: 20140813

International Standard Book Number-13: 978-1-4665-7990-3 (Paperback)

Library of Congress Cataloging-in-Publication Data

Management engineering : a guide to best practices for industrial engineering in health care / editor, Jean Ann Larson.
    p. ; cm.
    Includes bibliographical references and index.
    ISBN 978-1-4665-7990-3 (paperback : alk. paper)
    I. Larson, Jean Ann, editor of compilation.
    [DNLM: 1. Health Care Sector--organization & administration--United States. 2. Health Services Administration--United States. 3. Process Assessment (Health Care)--organization & administration--United States. W 84 AA1]

RA971
362.1068--dc23   2013036988

Visit the Taylor & Francis Web site at
http://www.taylorandfrancis.com

and the CRC Press Web site at
http://www.crcpress.com

Contents

SECTION I INTRODUCTION

SECTION II HOW DO MANAGEMENT ENGINEERS FUNCTION?

SECTION III WHAT DO MANAGEMENT ENGINEERS DO?

SECTION IV DECISION-MAKING SUPPORT

SECTION V FUNDAMENTAL TOOLS AND METHODS OF THE MANAGEMENT ENGINEER

SECTION VI ADDRESSING CURRENT CHALLENGES

SECTION VII LOOKING TO THE FUTURE

About the Editor

Jean Ann Larson, PhD, is a healthcare executive with a deep background in performance improvement, organization change, learning, and leadership. She holds a BS in industrial engineering from Wichita State University, an MBA from the Thunderbird Graduate School of International Management, and a doctorate in organization change from Pepperdine University. Jean Ann heads her own business and executive development consultancy, and has authored and edited several books and articles including the 2002 predecessor to this book, *Effective Guidebook for Management Engineering* (HIMSS Guidebook Series, ISBN 0-9704287-1-5).

Prior to starting her own firm, she was the vice president of clinical and quality services and the EPMO at Children's Medical Center Dallas and chief learning officer for Beaumont Hospitals in the Detroit area. She has also worked as an assistant hospital director, the director of management systems, an operations analyst, and a management engineer. She is active in several of her professional organizations and is the immediate past-president of the Society for Health Systems of the Institute of Industrial Engineers.

About the Editor

About the Contributors

Kelly Arnold has worked in the healthcare industry for thirty-six years and approximately nine of those years were spent as a bedside RN in a major teaching hospital in the Southeast. Half of that time was in a medical–surgical unit caring for pulmonary medicine and post-op open heart and thoracic surgery patients. The remaining time at the bedside was spent in a general medical–surgical ICU. Kelly has also worked as a management engineer for the past twenty-seven years. This time has been divided between Emory University Hospital and DeKalb Medical Center, both located in Atlanta, Georgia. Kelly has been an active member of Georgia and National HIMSS and is a past president in the Georgia chapter. Kelly has a bachelor of science in industrial engineering from Georgia Tech and a master's degree in health systems also from the Georgia Tech. As Kelly views the end of a long career in healthcare approaching, he sees continued expanding opportunities for application of that systems thinking, analytical skills, and technical expertise that MEs can bring to bear in the complex healthcare industry.

Dean Athanassiades is senior director of Software Customer Services at Philips Healthcare. He has thirty years experience in the information technology sector. Dean is a member of the faculty at the University of Phoenix in the healthcare informatics program and a fellow of HIMSS, a diplomate of the Society for Health System, and a senior member of IIE. He holds the CPHIMS and the PMP certifications, and is a Six Sigma black belt. Dean received a bachelor's degree in industrial engineering from Georgia Tech and an MBA from Georgia State University. He is currently pursuing his doctorate in industrial–organizational psychology.

Alexander Bohn is a transformation engineer with Care Logistics, a healthcare consulting and technology firm in Alpharetta, Georgia. Alexander has a bachelor of science degree in industrial engineering from Kettering University. Prior to Care Logistics, Alexander worked for Beaumont Health System (Troy, Michigan). Alexander is the 2013 president of the Young Professionals division of the Institute of Industrial Engineers. Alexander presented at the 2011 IIE Annual Conference and was published in *IE* magazine for his work in project management simulation.

David Z. Cowan has thirty years of experience in healthcare planning and management. He is currently senior research scientist in the Health Systems Institute, a multidisciplinary research center at the Georgia Institute of Technology. He led the Masters of Science in Health Systems, a specialty program in the School of Industrial Engineering at Georgia Tech, for many years. He is now a senior research scientist and focuses on the integration of healthcare facilities, information technology, and processes to improve safety, clinical outcomes, quality, and efficiency in the science of healthcare delivery. He has broad expertise in the areas of healthcare information technology, facilities planning, financial turnarounds, and strategic planning.

Cristina Daccarett is a healthcare professional with extensive experience in Lean Six Sigma. Cristina has a bachelor of science degree in industrial engineering from Purdue University and a master's in health services administration from the University of Michigan. Cristina has worked for Cardinal Health (McGaw Park, Illinois), Beaumont Hospital (Troy, Michigan), the University of Iowa Hospitals and Clinics (Iowa City, Iowa), Froedtert Hospital (Milwaukee, Wisconsin), and St. Luke's Hospital (Boise, Idaho). Although at times challenging, Cristina finds it extremely rewarding to have a career focused on improving the delivery of healthcare.

Adrienne Dickerson has, throughout her career, focused on working with hospitals and other organizations to expand the use of proven industrial and systems engineering tools and techniques in the healthcare setting. Adrienne graduated with honors from the Georgia Institute of Technology with a bachelor's degree in industrial engineering and a master of science in health systems. She is the current president of Cadence Health, Inc.

Adrienne has extensive experience in hospital operations including patient throughput, managed care contracting, revenue cycle, technology implementation, decision support, and facility-wide process improvement. She was on the board of the Georgia HIMSS chapter for nine years, is also a senior member of the Institute for Industrial Engineers (IIE), and a diplomate with the Society for Health Systems (SHS).

Lawrence (Larry) Dux is currently the director of Clinical Information Systems and Process Improvement at Froedtert Health Community Memorial Hospital, Menomonee Falls, Wisconsin. He holds a bachelor of science degree in industrial engineering and a master's degree in business administration from the University of Wisconsin-Madison. He is a senior member of the Institute of Industrial Engineers and a diplomate of the Society for Health Systems, a senior member of the American Society for Quality, and a Fellow/CPHIMS member of the Healthcare Information and Management Systems Society. He has extensive experience teaching and applying process improvement tools and techniques. He has served as a Wisconsin Forward Award (WFA) Examiner since 2004 and has participated in eight WFA site visits. He was a member of the team that wrote and edited the WFA application for Community Memorial Hospital in 2006. Larry has served on the Pewaukee School District Board of Education, which received the 2010 Wisconsin Governor's Forward Award of Excellence.

Steven R. Escamilla is director of the California Quality Collaborative, the healthcare improvement partner of the Pacific Business Group on Health. He is also co-founder of the Bay Area Performance Improvement Network, dedicated to bridging healthcare improvement professionals in the San Francisco region. Steven has an extensive background in performance management and operational improvement with a variety of healthcare organizations. He is the former executive director of clinical performance improvement for John Muir Health, and has contributed to organizations including Brigham and Women's Hospital, Boston Medical Center, Fairview Health Services, and CEP America Medical Group. With a bachelor of science in industrial engineering from Stanford University, and a master of science in industrial engineering and health systems engineering from the University of Wisconsin in Madison, he is a former president of the Society for Health Systems, has served on the Annual Conference and Education Committee for the Healthcare Information and Management Systems Society, and has served as the vice president for technical networking for the Institute of Industrial Engineers. Additionally, Steven is a fellow of HIMSS and the American College of Healthcare Executives, and a diplomate of the Society for Health Systems.

Deborah D. Flint has more than twenty years of experience analyzing and improving processes pertinent to the delivery of healthcare. Deborah has a bachelor's degree in industrial engineering from Auburn University, a master of business administration from the University of Alabama in Birmingham, and is a registered professional engineer in the state of Alabama. Deborah has worked at the University of Alabama at Birmingham (UAB) Health System as both a management engineer and as a hospital business manager. For the past two years, Deborah has worked at the Kirklin Clinic (ambulatory clinic affiliated with the UAB Health System) where she currently leads clinicwide projects to reduce patient waiting time and optimize efficiency of workflow to ultimately improve patient and staff satisfaction. Deborah is Lean Six Sigma Black Belt certified.

Alyn Ford, vice president of marketing and business development for Care Logistics®, has more than twenty-five years of experience in healthcare, commercializing innovative solution offerings, and is responsible for market awareness and demand generation for the Care Logistics Hospital Operating System™ Solution. Most recently, he was the vice president of product management during the establishment of the first seven hospital sites and the inception of the Care Logistics Order Logistics module. Alyn was one of the initial contributors who established the commercial PACS market in Canada, and in cooperation with Deloitte & Touche Healthcare, was the co-creator of the AGFAPath Solution for Diagnostic Imaging using PACS technology. He holds an associate degree with advanced certification in medical radiation technology from the Northern Alberta Institute of Technology where he achieved the highest national academic and clinical standing in Canada for his year of certification as a medical radiation technologist. Alyn also holds a certificate in business administration from the University of Saskatchewan.

Roger Gruneisen is a healthcare professional and consultant with extensive experience in Lean Six Sigma and operations research. Roger has a bachelor of science degree in operations research from the United States Military Academy. After service in the U.S. Army, Roger worked for General Electric, University of Kentucky Healthcare, Johns Hopkins University APL, and QHR. Roger finds it extremely rewarding to have a career focused on improving the delivery of healthcare and improving the decision-making process.

John T. Hansmann is a healthcare management engineer with more than twenty-five years experience in productivity management, benchmarking, and operations consulting. John has both a bachelor's of science and a master's of science degree in industrial engineering from North Dakota State University. John previously worked for Midwest Health Services, Inc. (Peoria, Illinois) and Intermountain Health Care (Salt Lake City, Utah). He currently works for Tenet Health Care (Dallas, Texas) as the senior director for labor management and productivity, responsible for Tenet's Labor Management program.

Richard Herring, as the national director for Perkins+Will's Healthcare Planning and Strategies practice, has led and participated in some of the firm's most complex planning and design projects. Richard's extensive experience with healthcare clients across the country has produced many innovative solutions, leading to his nomination as one of the most influential professionals in the healthcare design profession in 2009 by the Center for Health Design. He has planned projects for all sectors of the healthcare market including large regional systems, academic medical centers, community hospitals, governmental agencies, and large for-profit systems. This broad experience in best practice concepts serves as an invaluable resource for his clients. During his nineteen-year tenure at Perkins+Will, Richard has played a key role in building and leading the internationally respected facility planning, programming, and operational planning practices for the firm. Richard is a licensed architect, member of the American Institute of Architects, and is an Accredited Professional of Leadership in Energy and Environmental Design through the United States Green Building Council. Richard is also an Institute of Industrial Engineers Certified Lean Black Belt.

Dutch Holland has been a pilot, a full-time NASA consultant, a university professor, and the founder of a regional consulting firm that focuses on managing organizational changes—on target, on time, and on budget. He holds a BS in math and physics, an MBA, and a PhD in management, operations research and statistics.

Karl Kraebber is a project manager in the Operational Improvement Group at Indiana University Health in Indianapolis, Indiana. Karl has extensive experience facilitating service line value stream improvement teams, conducting departmental rapid improvement events, mentoring frontline staff and training leadership on Lean healthcare principles and applications. Karl has a master of science degree in organizational leadership and a bachelor of science in general health science from Purdue University. Karl has worked for Purdue University Healthcare Technical Assistance Program (West Lafayette, Indiana), Franciscan St. Elizabeth Health (Lafayette, Indiana) and St. John's Hospital (Springfield, Illinois). Karl is a champion of change and a diligent promoter of organizational transformation. Karl thoroughly enjoys working with hospital leaders to break down traditional silos and think of the hospital as a complex system with the patient as the primary focus.

Tarun Mohan Lal is a healthcare professional specializing in healthcare delivery science. Tarun has a bachelor of science in industrial engineering from the Manipal University, India, and a master of science in industrial engineering from Texas A&M University and is currently pursuing his PhD from the State University of New York. Tarun has experience working for manufacturing companies and ERP implementation in the past and is currently working for the Internal Business Consulting group of the Mayo Clinic in Rochester, Minnesota.

Amanda Mewborn's passion is improving efficiency in healthcare operations. An industrial and systems engineer as well as a registered nurse, Amanda has a master of science degree in health systems and a bachelor of science degree in industrial and systems engineering from Georgia Institute of Technology, as well as a bachelor of science degree in nursing from Georgia State University. Amanda is a registered nurse and is certified in pediatric nursing. She is Pragmatic Marketing certified in product management, a certified professional of healthcare information management systems, and a certified Lean Black Belt. Amanda is a diplomate in the Society for Health Systems, an active member of Healthcare Information Management Systems Society, and senior member in the Institute for Industrial Engineers. Amanda has worked for DeKalb Medical (Decatur, Georgia), Children's Healthcare of Atlanta (Atlanta, Georgia), Care Logistics (Alpharetta, Georgia), Johns Hopkins University Applied Physics Lab (Laurel, Maryland), and Perkins+Will (Atlanta, Georgia). She has diverse experience in healthcare operations, focusing on areas such as facility design, Lean, process improvement, clinical operations improvement, patient experience and satisfaction, nursing, revenue enhancement, managed care contracting, decision support, benchmarking, finance, and cost accounting.

Bridget O'Hare is a healthcare professional with extensive experience in human factors engineering. She currently is working to improve the usability of healthcare informatics and she was one of the project leaders for cardiac alarm communication research at William Beaumont Hospital in Royal Oak, Michigan and also for the Never Means Never initiative at Banner Health in Mesa, Arizona. She has more than two decades of operational experience in large multihospital settings and has worked in the field of human factors engineering in healthcare for more than a decade. Bridget is an ASQ certified Six Sigma black belt and holds certification in Just Culture. Bridget holds an MS in operations management from Michigan Technological University and a BS in hospital administration and planning from Mercy College of Detroit. Bridget is passionate about using human factors engineering practices and principles to improve patient safety.

Roque Perez-Velez, PE, DSHS, is a senior engineer with Management Engineering Consulting Services, an internal industrial engineering consulting group serving the University of Florida Health (formerly UF&Shands) academic health system in Gainesville, Florida. Roque has more than twenty years of experience as an industrial and management engineer with extensive experience in healthcare and manufacturing operations, financial and cost–benefit analysis, stochastic simulation, process improvement methodologies, project management and statistical analysis.

In addition to his role at the University of Florida, Roque is an adjunct faculty member for the University of Florida's MHA program and a US Army reserve officer. Roque holds a bachelor's degree in industrial engineering from the University of Puerto Rico, and a master's degree in industrial and systems engineering from the University of Florida. Roque is a senior member of the Institute of Industrial Engineers, a diplomate in the Society for Health Systems, and a licensed professional engineer.

Bennetta R. Raby, PMP, MS, is a project management and strategy expert of twenty-three years. Her work spans more than twelve industries and ranges from not-for-profit to international operations. Bennetta is a writer, national speaker, consultant, and presenter. Raising your Project Management I.Q. and Project Management for leaders are two initiatives geared toward encouraging everyone at all levels to embrace the discipline as a way of life.

Thomas Roh is a healthcare professional specializing in operations research. Thomas has a bachelor of science degree in industrial engineering from the University of Nebraska and a master of science in health systems from Georgia Tech. Thomas has worked for Becton-Dickinson, Emory Healthcare, and is currently working for the Mayo Clinic in Rochester, Minnesota.

Duke Rohe is a quality improvement education consultant at the University of Texas MD Anderson Cancer Center. Duke has a bachelor of science in industrial engineering from Lamar University. Duke has worked at MD Anderson Cancer Center for fifteen years, as an organizational change consulting firm Holland & Davis for 1 year, and at St. Luke's Episcopal Hospital for twenty-two years. Duke enjoys contributing tools and insights to the healthcare and creativity professionals through tool sites and listservs.

Rudolph (Rudy) Santacroce, PE, PMP, DSHS, is the director of Management Engineering Consulting Services, an internal industrial engineering consulting group serving the University of Florida academic health system in Gainesville, Florida. Rudy has more than nineteen years of experience as an industrial and management engineer with extensive consulting experience in healthcare operations, financial and cost–benefit analysis, Lean process improvement methodologies, and engineering analytics. Rudy holds a bachelor's degree in industrial and systems engineering and a master's degree from the University of Florida. Rudy is senior member of the Institute of Industrial Engineers, a board member and diplomate in the Society for Health Systems, a board member for the University of Florida's Center for Supply Chain Management, a licensed professional engineer, and a certified Project Management Professional.

Ben Sawyer, current executive vice president of Care Logistics®, has taken a lead role in developing the industry's first Hospital Operating System™ solution, a logistical control system for the movement of patients throughout their stay in a hospital. This innovation has cleared the way for hospitals to achieve total hospital efficiency and effectiveness. With more than twenty-five years experience in managing healthcare operations, he served as the quality and performance improvement executive at St. Mary's Health System, personally leading many Lean initiatives and Kaizen events, and has developed innovative approaches to healthcare delivery. Earlier in his career, Ben served as a service line executive for two other health systems. Ben's hospital operational and quality/PI leadership experience gives him a unique and practical approach when addressing the operational challenges hospitals and health systems face today.

Bart Sellers has more than twenty-five years of experience working in process improvement in the aerospace, aircraft maintenance, and healthcare industries. Bart has been leading a multihospital Lean implementation in healthcare for the last six years. Bart has a bachelor of science in mechanical engineering from Brigham Young University and an MBA from Utah State University. He is a diplomate and former board member of the IIE Society for Health Systems.

Joyce T. Siegele is the productivity improvement manager at Northside Hospital in Atlanta, Georgia. She has a bachelor of science in Industrial and systems engineering and a master of science in industrial and systems engineering with a specialization in engineering management from the University of Florida. Joyce recently achieved Fellow status with ACHE (American College of Healthcare Executives). She is currently on the board of directors of SHS (Society of Health Systems) as well as a diplomate in SHS. She has held several conference positions including conference chair within SHS over the past several years. Joyce enjoys the ever-changing challenge of working on productivity and operations improvement in healthcare.

Mary Ellen Skeens leads the Solutions Consulting team for Philips Healthcare Clinical Informatics. She has fifteen years of experience in healthcare information technology and process improvement. Mary Ellen holds professional certifications as an ASQ Certified Six Sigma Black Belt, Project Management Professional, and Certified Professional in Healthcare Information and Management Systems. She is a Society of Health Systems diplomate and Healthcare Information and Management Systems Society Fellow and has served in various leadership roles in both organizations. Mary Ellen was trained as an industrial engineer at the Georgia Institute of Technology and holds a master's degree in health systems.

Sue Ann Te is the director of transformation engineering with Care Logistics,® a healthcare consulting and technology firm based in Alpharetta, Georgia. Prior to Care Logistics,® Sue worked for DeKalb Medical Center (Decatur, Georgia) and Children's Healthcare of Atlanta (Atlanta, Georgia) leading process improvement efforts in the areas of operations, revenue cycle, and human resources. Sue has a bachelor of science in industrial engineering and a master of science in health systems from Georgia Tech.

John L. Templin, Jr., FACHE, LFHIMSS, FAAHC, DSHS, has more than forty years health-care management consulting experience. He has consulted with more than 200 hospitals and related entities. John has a bachelor of science in management engineering and a master of science in management degree from Rensselaer Polytechnic Institute in Troy, New York. He started his career with the shared management engineering program of the Healthcare Association of New York State. For the past 26 years he has been president of Templin Management Associates, Inc., a healthcare management consulting company. John has been extremely involved in and honored by healthcare professional organizations. He currently serves as treasurer of the Society for Healthcare Systems. John finds it extremely rewarding to continue volunteering with his professional societies.

Phil Troy, PhD, is a quantitative process and decision support systems analyst. He earned a bachelor of science degree in engineering science and a master of science degree in quantitative business analysis at the Pennsylvania State University, and a doctorate in operations research from Yale University. His analytical skills include queuing theory, Monte Carlo simulation (including discrete event simulation), optimization, systems analysis, and software development. For the last several years, Dr. Troy has focused his efforts on analyzing and simulating perioperative hospital processes, including an analysis of surgical bed needs for an intensive care unit, the development of a simulation-based optimization model for a proposed presurgery screening clinic, and the development (in progress) of an enterprise simulation model of the hospital's perioperative processes.

Michael L. Washington, PhD, is a health scientist with extensive experience in evaluating and improving public health systems. Dr. Washington has a bachelor of science in industrial and systems engineering from the University of Florida, and a master's and PhD in industrial engineering focusing on health systems from the University of South Florida. He has worked for the Centers for Disease Control and Prevention and the Department of Navy. Dr. Washington uses his industrial engineering tools to improve public health all over the world, including working with the World Health Organization and numerous ministries of health.

Marvina Williams is a registered nurse and a member of the Healthcare Planning and Strategies Division of Perkins+Will in Atlanta, Georgia, where she specializes in healthcare design and operational planning. She has more than thirty years of management experience in hospital environments. Marvina's contributions at Perkins+Will consist of operational studies including workflow, workload calculations, patient care procedures, support services, simulation modeling and design validation of process improvement initiatives, and staffing efficiencies. She graduated magna cum laude with a bachelor of science degree in nursing from Olivet Nazarene University in Illinois. She understands the changes and demands that healthcare providers are facing and seeks opportunities to streamline processes to improve client and staff satisfaction.

Ryan Elizabeth Wood, MBA, BASc, CSSBB, is the coordinator in management engineering at Beaumont Health System, in Troy, Michigan. At Beaumont, Ryan is a project manager, facilitator, and coach, working with a variety of service lines on process improvement, system implementation, strategic planning, program development, building design, and problem solving. Wood earned a bachelor of applied science degree in industrial and manufacturing systems engineering, a master's in business administration, and a Canadian Operational Research Society diploma, all from the University of Windsor in Ontario, Canada. She is a Certified Six Sigma Black Belt through the American Society for Quality.

About the Reviewers

Leroy Baker has more than thirty-five years of experience in the healthcare industry. Leroy has broad experience in project management, system selection, system implementation, analysis of business and technical needs, process improvement, budgeting, policy development, and management training. A graduate of Virginia Tech Leroy earned a degree in industrial engineering and operations research. He has worked for many healthcare organizations, both providers and consulting firms, including the University of Wisconsin Hospital and Clinics, VHA, Health Central (Minnesota), and Roanoke Memorial Hospital. Leroy is a life member and fellow of the Healthcare Information and Management Systems Society, a senior member of the Institute of Industrial Engineers, and a diplomate in the Society for Health Systems. Leroy earned recognition as a Certified Professional in Healthcare Information and Management Systems (CPHIMS) in 2002.

Brian Compas, FHIMSS, is an industrial engineer who has worked in healthcare for more than twenty-five years. He was the director of a Management Engineering Department at Abington Memorial Hospital (Abington, Pennsylvania), a logistics consultant for Owens & Minor (Allentown, Pennsylvania), a principal consultant for Healthlink (Houston, Texas) and IBM (Armonk, New York), and a strategic consultant for Siemens Healthcare (Malvern, Pennsylvania). He is a past HIMSS board member and fellow, and has volunteered on various committees and task forces for the past twenty-five years.

Danielle Larson-Jaramillo graduated from Western Michigan University with both her bachelor's and master's degrees in industrial engineering. She has experience in healthcare through several internships and research opportunities, including William Beaumont Hospital in Royal Oak, Michigan, Bronson Hospital in Battlecreek, Michigan, Children's Medical Center of Michigan, and Pfizer. Danielle is also a member of the Institute of Industrial Engineers and Alpha Pi Mu.

Jerry Macks has spent more than four decades in various capacities in the healthcare management engineering arena: consultant, in-house staff, and corporate office staff. A hallmark of his career was the coordination of the specification, installation, and evaluation of the first hospitalwide computerized medical information system in a research center. He also has performed productivity and other analyses in virtually every hospital department. Jerry earned a bachelor of engineering science degree in industrial engineering from Johns Hopkins University and a master of science in personnel administration from George Washington University. After he left a twenty-six-year career at the NIH Clinical Center, he joined MedStar's Performance Improvement

Department. In that setting, he coordinates efforts to use and appreciate clinical data. He is a long-time member of the MedStar Institutional Review Board. Jerry has been the podium speaker at numerous annual meetings of SHS, HIMSS, and their predecessor organizations and served in leadership roles in those groups as well. His professional affiliations include the American College of Healthcare Executives (fellow), Hospital Information and Management Systems Society (honorary fellow and life member), and Institute of Industrial Engineers (life member), and he is part of the founding group of the Society for Health Systems.

Ron McDade, CPHQ, DSHS, is an industrial engineer with more than twenty-five years in healthcare improvement. His healthcare experience has spanned the continuum of care with MedStar Health (Columbia, Maryland), Sinai Hospital (Baltimore, Maryland), and Georgetown University Hospital (Washington, DC). Ron earned a BS degree in industrial engineering from the University of Pennsylvania and an MBA from the University of Maryland. He is president-elect and a board member of the Society for Health Systems and a senior member of IIE. He emphasizes the integration of cost, quality, and service improvements in his work.

INTRODUCTION

1

Chapter 1

Management Engineering: A Best Practices Guide to Industrial Engineering in Healthcare

Jean Ann Larson

Contents

Introduction

The use of industrial engineering (IE) in healthcare by Frank Gilbreth and others can be traced back as early as 1908; yet opportunities for IEs in healthcare or management engineers have never been greater. Cost and payment challenges have always been with us, but unique to our times is the impending impact of significant staffing shortages just when the baby boomers will need more care than ever. Thus, more than ever before, it is important to utilize resources, specifically highly paid, highly skilled staff, efficiently and effectively.

Certainly there are also societal and political reasons that contribute to our healthcare cost increases and those reasons are beyond the scope of this book. However, there are also many process reasons. Improving operational efficiency, helping make key decisions that impact healthcare processes, and taking a systems view of an organization are the specialties and purview of the industrial engineer, often called a *management engineer* (ME) or *operations analyst* in healthcare. And despite the challenges mentioned earlier and those we read about in our daily newspapers and journals, both as a young engineer starting out and now after twenty-five years in the industry, I cannot think of another industry that is as rewarding to engineers or as appreciative of the skill sets we bring to the table.

Why Do We Need This Book and Why Now?

The industrial engineer or management engineer has always possessed a wealth of tools and approaches that can be employed in addressing the challenges of the healthcare industry. In recent years, Lean and Six Sigma methodologies have been embraced within the healthcare industry. These attractively packaged and promoted methods include only some of the tools and approaches that have historically been used by IEs to improve healthcare processes, better utilize resources, and help improve operational efficiencies. (Some engineers would argue that we have always practiced these methods, we just weren't good enough marketers to sell the ideas as well as has been done by others.) Thus, the intent of this book is both to provide an overview of the practice of industrial engineering or management engineering in the healthcare industry and offer guides to some of its techniques. It is specifically focused on helping practitioners explore and get a good understanding of the different roles an IE might take on, as well as the tools and how they might be applied in the healthcare industry. Also, it is our intent that industrial engineering students, as well as those already practicing industrial engineers considering a move into healthcare, would find the book to be of benefit.

The book may also be used as a reference to explore individual topics, as each of the chapters stands on its own. However, to get a good overview of how organizations can best benefit from the efforts of industrial engineers, it is recommended that readers at least scan all the chapters. Please note that many of the authors use the terms *management engineer* and *industrial engineer* interchangeably since management engineer is the term often used for industrial engineers in healthcare.

Though the reader may not recognize many of the authors by name, they are all longtime practitioners. Not only have they witnessed the evolution of this field up close and in person, many of them were trained by those who impacted its course and in turn have been influential themselves. My approach to inviting contributors to this book was to reach out to subject matter experts to whom I would want to go to learn more about the topic. Their generosity in sharing their knowledge and experience was inspirational. Thus, you the reader will be invited to share a unique viewpoint and a candid assessment of each topic.

Overview of the Chapters

Section I includes this introductory chapter to give the reader an over of the book. Section II of the book includes six chapters that talk about *how* management engineers function. The first chapter in this section (Chapter 2), by Steve Escamilla, talks about how management engineering is not just about application of IE tools. As internal consultants, management engineers serve as change agents and facilitators of change. And as healthcare's challenges grow, this trait becomes even more important every day. Chapter 3 further elaborates on the role of the engineer as a change management specialist and is written by one of today's most experienced experts on this topic, Dutch Holland. His practical how-to steps on what to do and what not to do to be an effective influencer of organization change offers wisdom that can be valuable regardless of the number of years we have been in the industry.

The next three chapters are very valuable for those individuals charged with setting up a new management engineering (ME) department, or for someone that uses IE tools in their organization. Chapter 4 is an overview of the management engineering function written by two Mayo Clinic management systems analysts, Tarun Mohan Lal and Thomas Roh. It talks about the history of management engineering departments and how they provide value to organizations. Chapter 5, written by Rudolph Santacroce, is a case study that describes the highly effective ME department at the University of Florida and Shands Health System. This chapter provides sample forms, organization charts, and tips on how to interact with customers and how to manage the management engineering function. Chapter 6 talks about how ME departments impact budgets, costs, and operational performance throughout health systems. Section II concludes with a primer on how to start your own external ME consulting business written by longtime successful healthcare IE consultant, John L., Templin. He provides dos and don'ts, as well as a checklist of things you may want to consider if you are thinking of going out on your own.

Section III chapters discuss what management engineers do. Chapter 8, by Amanda Mewborn and Jean Ann Larson, serves a transition chapter between Sections II and III and discusses how MEs instigate change and engage teams on all projects and engagements. It bridges the roles of the ME as change agent, facilitator, and project manager. In Chapter 9, Bennetta R. Raby discusses how to employ project and program management skills to get everyone on board and to help you achieve your projects' goals and objectives. Given that much of our work as engineers is project based and our work is done through other people through our ability to influence versus formal authority, being a strong project manager is essential.

As mentioned earlier, the shortage of nurses, technicians, and other caregivers is a perennial problem. In Chapter 10, David Z. Cowan and Joyce T. Siegele discuss how engineers help organizations manage staff productivity through labor analysis and staffing studies. To provide further information on this key area of what IEs in healthcare do, Chapter 11 by Kelly Arnold discusses the issues and challenges unique to scheduling and staffing in healthcare. In addition to healthcare being a 7/24, 365-day-per-year operation, patient conditions vary widely, individually, and over time. Also, technology and scientific advances in medicine impact staffing in ways that are often difficult to predict. In Chapter 12, "Understanding Nursing Care Models," Marvina Williams, a trained and practicing nurse who works closely with IEs, brings her nonengineering view of the impact of nursing care models on scheduling and staffing and how they may affect nursing productivity and labor costs.

Chapter 13 on facilitation changes gears as Duke Rohe describes and discusses best practices in facilitating teams, whether for process improvement, process redesign, or innovation. A critical skill, regardless of the methods or problems being solved, is that of the objective and observant facilitator. It is from this role that the wisdom of the team can emerge and organizational learning can occur. Chapter 14, by Alexander Bohn and Sue Ann Te, discusses the *how-to* of process redesign and offers a case study to illustrate how it is used. Lawrence (Larry) Dux (Chapter 15) discusses Total Quality Management and the Malcolm Baldrige Award in healthcare in the next chapter. Chapters 16 and 17 by Cristina Daccarett and Karl Kraebber discuss manufacturing industry concepts that became very hot topics in healthcare management engineering—Six Sigma and Lean. Both of these generated a lot of interest in healthcare, and there are countless books and conferences that cover these topics. Many organizations have used one or both of these approaches to entice their staffs to push forward process improvements and organizational and cultural change.

Chapter 18, by Roger Grunieson, discusses the bread and butter of any industrial engineer's work—*operations analysis*, or the ability to observe, document, and then use tools or teams to improve the current state. Chapter 19, by Deborah D. Flint and Phil Troy, describes approaches to analyzing and presenting data and ways that good data, well displayed, can be used to evaluate operations, processes, and make decisions. In Chapter 20, John Hansmann discusses how benchmarking can be used to help challenge staff and help them glean ideas for improving their functions. The last chapter in Section III, written by Amanda Mewborn and Richard Herring, discusses how industrial engineering tools can be applied to facility design, making sure that new facilities are built to include streamlined processes versus being built around less than ideal processes. At a time when organizations are becoming strapped for capital, it is even more desirable to improve and streamline a process versus building a bigger facility to accommodate inefficient processes and larger waiting areas.

Section IV is the decision-support section. And though much of our work as IEs in healthcare falls into this realm, for example, data analysis and presentation, this section gives an overview of direct activities in which IEs in healthcare may be involved, or even serve as project leads in some cases. Chapter 22, "Assessing the ROI and Benefits of New Technology" by Dean Athanassiades, discusses how in addition to helping to select new technology, we are often called upon to identify and document return on investment (ROI), whether for new information technology or clinical technology. IEs are well suited to understanding the impact of technology upon processes and other systems. Chapter 23 by Mary Ellen Skeens discusses how IEs can help organizations review information and technology system solutions, evaluate them, and then assist the organization with selection. In Chapter 24, Adrienne Dickerson shows us how an IE's facilitation, problem-solving, and analytical skills can help leaders develop a request for information (RFI) for consulting and other professional services to ensure that the engagement is a good investment and meets the needs of the organization.

Section V covers several fundamental tools that are used across the board within many methodologies and in a variety of projects. Flowcharting, the topic of Chapter 25 by Ryan Wood, discusses how this venerable tool is often the first step in analyzing a process in order to improve it. She provides examples of different types of flowcharts and how they are used. "Value Stream Mapping," Chapter 26 by Bart Sellers, gives examples of a very specific way of describing and analyzing a process. In Chapter 27, Roque Perez-Velez discusses the use of statistical analysis in healthcare industrial engineering projects and some of the unique challenges faced by the healthcare IE.

In Chapter 28, Cristina Daccarett discusses human factors as applied to healthcare. And though it may seem a very specialized topic, it is included in the fundamentals section in order to highlight one of the major benefits that IEs can bring to healthcare. They help bring the perspective of people, processes, and technology to bear in projects and improvement efforts. Their training and experience makes them uniquely qualified to assess the impact of the work environment and technology on the humans within the system. Similarly, Chapter 29 by Bridget O'Hare deals with root cause analysis. Though often considered a very specialized topic that helps ensure patient safety, getting to the root of the issue is important in all projects. As Bridget's chapter illustrates, IEs have the tools and skill set to use a systematic approach to determine root causes. "Throughput and Cycle Time Reduction" by Alyn Ford and Ben Sawyer (Chapter 30) explores how this key analytical tool used can be used for healthcare improvement efforts as resources become more expensive and as providing healthcare quickly and efficiently is a key to improving healthcare quality. Finally, given that changes that produce unintended consequences can be particularly expensive in the healthcare setting, simulation, discussed in Chapter 31 by Tarun Mohan Lal and Thomas Roh, is a key modeling tool that is used for both analysis and facility design. As a modeling method demonstrating how a proposed process solution will work, or not, it provides a picture of the different versions of a process so that the entire healthcare team can visualize it and understand it.

This book has a heavy emphasis on the use of IE tools in healthcare organizations such as hospitals, clinics, and medical offices. However, Chapter 32 by Michael Washington discusses opportunities for the use of IE tools in the public health sector, allowing IEs to have influence on a much broader international scale. This chapter should be of great interest to both new and veteran MEs given that this will be an area requiring more and more analysts and engineers in the future.

In Section VI, Chapter 33, my colleague Duke Rohe and I discuss the issue of leaving a professional legacy. Regardless of where or how an IE practices within healthcare, the rewards are great. However, as was often quoted to me by my father, the more you put into something, the more benefits you will reap. Both of us having been in this field for several decades can certainly attest to this.

Hopefully, those of you considering an IE career in healthcare will find that this book gives you the impetus and encouragement to make you pursue this career in earnest. For those of you already in the field, we hope that you will gain insight or be reminded of the other ways you may bring your skills to help your organizations and clients. Also, for those healthcare leaders looking for long-term solutions to our healthcare challenges, it is my hope that having read this, you'll consider hiring IEs on your team to help you create a better future for your patients and your community.

The bad news is that this book is not a quick fix. The good news is that if these IE tools and methods are applied to healthcare, the improvements can be both flexible and remain sustained over time. It is wise to remember that our healthcare challenges did not appear overnight, so we are not going to be able to find quick and easy solutions. Though healthcare is a very complex, and currently highly regulated industry, we are going to have to use tried-and-true methods in new ways and give them time to produce their inevitable benefits. As both consumers of healthcare and members of society, we all will be the beneficiaries of these improvements.

HOW DO MANAGEMENT ENGINEERS FUNCTION?

II

HOW DO MANAGEMENT ENGINEERS FUNCTION?

Chapter 2

It's *Not* about the Tools: The Management Engineer's Role in Achieving Significant, Sustainable Change

Steven R. Escamilla

Contents

Management engineering and performance improvement professionals, both inside and outside of the healthcare industry, are trained with a multitude of skills to improve organizational performance. Armed with expertise that includes team facilitation, data analysis, project management, decision analysis, and organizational behavior—and many other skills—management engineers (MEs) typically have a portfolio of tools at their disposal to address most barriers to designing and implementing improvement. Recently these tools have been summarized and taught under catch-all terms such as *Lean* and *Six Sigma*, and previously as *Total Quality Management* (TQM) and *Continuous Quality Improvement* (CQI).

Tools of this sort can be perceived to be the backbone of the management engineering profession. This focus on tools asks the question, "Tools: How important are they, *really?*"

I hope to provide some answers, or at least some perspective, on that question. More specifically, we will explore how important tools are in the context of *large-scale, significant, and sustainable change.*

The RME® Story: An Example of Large-Scale, Significant, Sustained Success

To begin to illustrate the role of management engineering tools, let's examine a story of large-scale, significant, and sustainable change. The story comes from CEP America, a large emergency physician group based in Emeryville, California, which operates 79 emergency departments across the US. This physician group was originally established in the early 1970s as California Emergency Physicians; then in 2005 changed its name to CEP America to reflect its national growth stemming from its operational success.

While CEP America was always a successful group of physicians, most of its affiliated emergency departments (EDs) struggled with patient flow—like most every ED in the country. Across its 46 affiliated EDs in 2002, its overall average door-to-provider time (the time from a patient's arrival at the ED until the time they see a physician, physician assistant, or nurse practitioner) was 49 minutes. While this was better than many EDs, it was still far from the generally accepted industry goal of 30 minutes or less.

Unsatisfied with typical patient waiting times, a renegade CEP America medical director at an emergency department in Brawley, California, took it upon himself to experiment with a new model of seeing patients in the ED. In the typical ED patient flow model, a patient will arrive, see a triage nurse, wait (sometimes hours) for a bed to become available, wait in the bed for a nursing evaluation, and only then will see a physician. In the renegade medical director's experimental model, an arriving patient would see a physician very early in the process, immediately upon arrival, where the physician would be physically located together with the triage nurse. With this process, some low-acuity patients could be discharged literally within minutes of arriving, while higher-acuity patients would have their diagnostics and treatment initiated much sooner than in the traditional model.

The change seemed subtle, yet dramatically improved door-to-provider times at the renegade medical director's emergency department, and in turn greatly improved overall service times. As a result, patients at the ED in Brawley were cared for more expeditiously, both patient and staff satisfaction increased, and as turnaround time decreased, ED capacity increased, and patient volume and revenue climbed. The change was far from simple though, both operationally and culturally. The change not only required significant operational changes to staffing and all other aspects of ED patient flow; more importantly, the change went against a long-standing culture of how patients should flow in an emergency.

Observing the success of this nontraditional patient flow model, an innovative regional medical director mandated that each of the 9 emergency departments in his region try to replicate the success. Working very diligently to address challenges to implementation, the regional medical director, in partnership with an assigned practice management consultant (a management

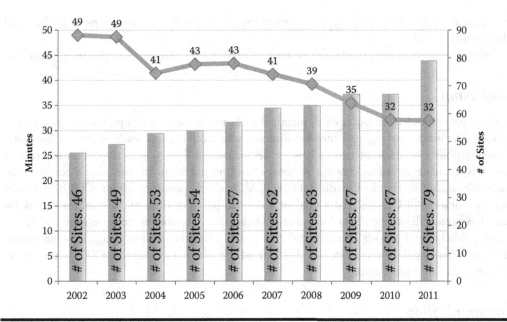

Figure 2.1 CEP America time to provider.

engineer by background, but with a different title), facilitated change at each of the 9 emergency departments, one by one. Most of these EDs recognized dramatic success (though some did not) and the Rapid Medical Evaluation (RME) process was born.

The practice management consultant (PMC) team went to work to examine the keys to successful RME implementation, and the reasons why some implementations did not work. The PMC team at the time consisted of a management engineer, two MBAs with process improvement consulting backgrounds, and an administrative assistant. Together, this team "packaged" a process for successful RME implementation, including tools for project planning, staffing analysis, current- and future-state process planning, change motivation, and return on investment (ROI) calculation.

As a result, the renegade medical director's countercultural patient flow process spread across virtually every emergency department within CEP America. New practice management consultant staff were able to work with newly affiliated CEP America EDs, and successfully achieve dramatic improvements in patient flow similar to the renegade medical director's ED and the innovative regional medical director's 9 EDs. The results were phenomenal. As of 2011, CEP America had grown from 46 EDs in 2002 to 79 EDs in 2011, and overall average door-to-provider time *dropped* from 49 minutes in 2002 to 32 minutes in 2011—*including* newly affiliated EDs who were still in the process of implementing RME (see Figure 2.1). This was truly one of emergency medicine's epic stories of long-term, significant, sustainable change.

Where Were the Tools?

How was it that such widespread success was achievable by a medical group? They found something that worked, and structured a large organization for successful dissemination of the innovation, among multiple different emergency departments, each with their own unique operations, management styles, and cultures. What made the successful RME process reproducible, and where were the tools?

Several elements of successful dissemination of innovation contributed to this story of success.

Leadership

Without proper leadership, successful, sustainable change is difficult (though not impossible) to achieve. The innovative regional medical director, who declared that each of the 9 EDs under his responsibility would implement a new model for patient flow, was an important key to success. His mandate served to create a necessary burning platform. Further, the medical group leadership, including the chief medical officer (CMO), chief operations officer (COO), and chief executive officer (CEO), declared a goal of a door-to-provider time of 30 minutes or less for every emergency department. As individual EDs achieved significant improvement, the COO would publicly grant awards to successful emergency departments at organizationwide events. This not only recognized successes, but also spurred competition among those EDs that were yet to achieve the 30-minute goal.

Communication

The advantages of successful RME implementation were diligently communicated, frequently, to all levels of the affiliated organizations. With successful reduction in door-to-provider times, physicians achieved improved productivity, satisfaction, and revenue. Nurses saw improved staffing and greater satisfaction. ED directors achieved the accolades of being recognized innovators. Hospital CEOs saw increased market share, revenue, and patient satisfaction.

Each of these advantages was identified for each audience, and turned into standardized yet customizable presentations. Understanding the advantages of the change helped most individuals ("targets of change") break through reluctance to change based on previously existing cultural barriers.

Site Visits

For many, merely *hearing* about the advantages of a change is not enough to motivate action. For them, it is necessary to *see* the advantages. Frequently, before attempting a local implementation of RME, ED teams would engage in onsite visits to see successful EDs. (For the emergency department in Roseburg, Oregon, the site visits required chartering a small jet for the ED team to visit EDs in neighboring, yet distant, Northern California. Ultimately well worth the expense!)

Site visits enabled peer-to-peer interactions that more effectively fostered understanding of the advantages of change. Skeptical physicians could speak with other physicians; skeptical nurses could speak with other nurses. Experienced, successful individuals served as advocates of change, based on their personal successes.

RME Manual (the Tools)

The tools that were required for successful RME implementation were captured and summarized in the *RME Manual*—essentially, a handbook used to jump-start implementation and begin addressing barriers to change. The manual contained tools such as standard (customizable) project plans, presentations, staffing calculators, examples of patient communication brochures, and ROI examples. Other available tools included sample treatment protocols, sample flowcharts (though no two EDs' flows were ever identical), and sample patient satisfaction scripting.

Coaching

An important part of successful RME implementation was the role of the change coach, in this case the practice management consultant. PMCs were involved to skillfully apply the multiple tools and resources available to support the change. While the general concepts behind patient flow changes were similar at all EDs, the path toward success was never the same twice. The coaching role of the PMC greatly impacted an individual ED's probability of success by customizing implementation to the site's needs.

Tools were certainly critical to the successful implementation of RME across more than 70 emergency departments. However, glaringly absent in this story is the presence of traditional tools of Lean or Six Sigma—they were virtually nonexistent! How can it be that such dramatic improvements in patient flow and overall ED performance can be achieved broadly across such a large number of organizations, in this day and age, without Lean or Six Sigma?

The Make-or-Break Role of the Management Engineer as Coach

As with the emergency departments implementing RME, each organization, each facility, and each department ultimately has a unique blend of leadership, vision, culture, and personalities. As it turns out, as important as a management engineer's tools are, *the most critical variable affecting sustainable change is the role of the coach.*

Predicting Successful Change

David H. Gustafson, industrial engineer and health systems engineering professor and researcher from the University of Wisconsin in Madison, has conducted multiple studies on change. In the article, "Developing and Testing a Model to Predict Outcomes of Organizational Change,"[1] Gustafson et al. determined 18 factors that predicted the likelihood of successful change:

■ Mandate
■ Leader support
■ Supporters and opponents
■ Middle manager support
■ Tension for change
■ Staff needs assessment
■ Exploration of problems and customer needs
■ Change agent prestige and commitment
■ Source of ideas
■ Funding
■ Relative advantage
■ Radicalness of design
■ Flexibility of design
■ Evidence of effectiveness
■ Complexity of implementation plan
■ Work environment

- Staff changes required
- Monitoring and feedback

The degree to which each of these factors is present affects the likelihood of successful change. If one change factor is lacking, strength in other factors must make up for it.

A successful ME not only has a strong grasp of tools, but also is able to coach the navigation of the multiple factors that will impact whether an organization, process, or individual will change. In addition to using the appropriate tool to define, develop, and measure an organizational change, the ME will simultaneously monitor the organizational wherewithal to implement change, and will adjust the approach to design and implementation to appropriately account for organizational challenges. This ability is far more important than the tools themselves, and reflects the capabilities of a change agent to facilitate the change.

Active Ingredient of Improvement

Dr. Gustafson's research team also studied various quality improvement approaches to determine the QI approach that yields the most significant and *sustainable* improvement.[2] Conducting improvements across many addiction treatment centers in many different states, Gustafson et al. studied whether *learning sessions*, *coaching*, *interest circle calls*, or a combination of all three had the greatest and most sustainable impact.

The results of the Gustafson study are intriguing. In this study, no significant benefit was associated with interest circle calls, where change staff received telephonic advice from peers and a coach. Coaching alone, however, was less expensive and more effective than learning sessions where change staff learned from experts in a face-to-face, multiday conference setting. A combination of learning sessions, interest circles, and coaching added cost without improving outcomes. The study showed that *coaching dominated the other methods in terms of results, sustainability, and cost.* Coaching consisted of personalized site visits, in addition to telephonic and e-mail communication with change staff and leadership.

Intuitively, the Gustafson study's results make sense. As with every organization, each of the addiction treatment centers involved in the study had a different combination of leadership, vision, culture, and personalities—not to mention different processes and systems. Merely knowing potential solutions does not ensure that a solution can be implemented. Implementation requires the modification of a solution to fit a given organization's processes and systems. And, most importantly, implementation requires a skillful adaptation to the leadership styles, the cultural uniqueness, and the personality differences present in an organization, in light of an organization's vision.

Successful Coach and Tools

It is sometimes said, "Tools add value to a *process*." While that is true in general terms, the *process* is rarely the *product*—the process itself is not what the customer views as *value*.

While tools are critical, they are only one, arguably small, aspect of what leads to significant change. Tools can be a means of managing all other aspects of change, and a means for a management engineer to serve as a coach. Together with tools, adaptable coaching of a skilled management engineer will enable success in virtually any situation. It is this role of coach that is more critical than the tool itself.

Management engineers must always keep a clear perspective on their role. As new performance improvement or Lean departments are developed, this perspective is especially important:

Tools are never the end goal; they are an enabler! The improvement coaching ability of the management engineer, and the application of appropriate tools, ultimately is the most important factor impacting the significance and sustainability of change.

Some organizations may fall into the trap of determining, for example, that implementing Lean or implementing Six Sigma is the goal. To be clear, Lean or Six Sigma should never be an end goal, even from a management engineer's or performance improvement department's perspective. The end goal should always focus on the customer, elimination of waste, and perfect care.

Ultimately, management engineers must serve as improvement coach and manage all factors affecting significant, sustainable change. Tools are an enabler for doing so, but should be kept in perspective. The bottom line on tools can be expressed in the words of the band .38 Special:

> Just hold on loosely
> But don't let go
> If you cling too tightly
> You're gonna lose control.

Endnotes

1. D. H. Gustafson, F. Sainfort, and E.M. Adams, "Developing and Testing a Model to Predict Outcomes of Organizational Change," *Health Serv Res* 38 (2003):751–776.
2. A. Quanbeck, D. H. Gustafson, J. H. Ford II, A. Pulvermacher, M. T. French, K. Y. McConnell, and D. McCarty, "Disseminating Quality Improvement: Study Protocol for a Large Cluster-Randomized Trial," *Implementation Science* 2011 6 (2011):44.

Chapter 3

What IEs Need to Know about Change Management

Dutch Holland

Contents

Introduction

Over the years I have attended many executive team meetings that were convened to select employees for a special team or task force that would focus on an important organizational problem or opportunity. A typical conversation to select an industrial engineer (IE) for such a task force might go something like this:

"Here is the IE department roster of available IEs. Let's go through the list:

- Charlie: Is he a player or not a player? *Not* a player.
- Karen: Player or not. *Not* a player.
- Warren: Player or not. Player.
- Chester: *Not* a player.
- Marybeth: Player."

The obvious question is, "Why were Warren and Marybeth labeled as players when the rest were not?" Are Warren and Marybeth the IEs who are best at formulas, constructs, calculations, speed, or reliability? No. Players are those who are known to management as professionals who have a track record of serving the organization in which they work, not just focusing on supporting the profession in which they were educated.

This chapter, written by a nonengineer, is designed to give a nonengineer's view of how industrial engineering and IEs fit into the world of work. IEs who choose to read this chapter get a gold star in my book. Those who do not immediately slam shut the book when they see the word *nonengineer* get another gold star. And finally, those who read the entire chapter with an open mind and a learning attitude get the grand prize for patience, persistence, and their willingness to look at their profession through the eyes of an unwashed outsider.

I have divided the chapter into eighteen key points; the points have been organized somewhat from *big picture* down to *details*. Regardless of the order, each point might be considered with the following questions in mind:

- Does this point apply to me?
- If it applies, how well am I doing?
- If I am not doing as well as I would like, what one thing must I do immediately to address the point?

Good reading and good luck!

1. Engineering and Business Go Together, Always

The words *science, engineering,* and *business* sometimes get all mixed up. How can they be sorted out? Consider the following assertions:

- Science mixed with business is *not* science.
- Engineering *not* mixed with business is *not* engineering.

The idea is that science should not be subjected to the pressures and constraints of business lest the scientific body of knowledge be compromised. On the other hand, engineering is about using a body of knowledge to achieve useful outcomes for a business, an organization, and for individuals. Engineering that is not mixed with business does not accomplish meaningful results; engineering disconnected from the business is just a curiosity.

■ Industrial engineers ply their trade to produce concrete, valuable, and useful outcomes for a business, an organization, and for individuals.

2. Industrial Engineering Is Done Inside a Complex System, That Is, an Organization

Industrial engineering is not done in a vacuum, but in the confines of organized entities pursuing a mission. The IE's place will always be to serve that mission. While it may be rare for an IE project to work directly on a visible mission element, all IE projects must produce deliverables that can be directly linked, through any number of organizational linkages, to one or more mission elements.

■ IEs know and serve their organization's mission.

3. Every Organization Is a Profit-Pursuing Entity (Whether Private, Not-for-Profit, or Government)

Every organization relentlessly pursues a "profit." The term *profit* has different definitions in different kinds of organizations: Profit-making organizations, like those in the Fortune 1000, generate profits and send them to investors; not-for-profit organizations use the term *margin* to describe their income after expenses have been deducted from revenue. Margin cannot be returned to investors, but it can be used to perpetuate, grow, and cushion a not-for-profit as well as to pay direct incentive compensation to employees.

■ IEs are profit-minded, profit-seeking, and profit-generating professionals.

4. Three Most Important Goals for an Industrial Engineer Are Business Value, Business Value, and Business Value

The title says it all. Business value is determined by the strength of mission accomplishment. Business value can be measured by the degree of mission accomplishment, by profit or by margin, or by increasing the value of the organization's assets.

Business value should always be a criterion in industrial engineering solutions and decision making. Business value can be directly calculated for a profit-making organization and estimated for a not-for-profit organization. Not-for-profit value can be estimated by calculating what it would take for a profit-making organization to replicate the services and impact of the not-for-profit.

■ IEs pursue business value through mission accomplishment that produces profit or margin.

5. Two Kinds of Work Are Always Going On in a Successful Business

The two kinds of work are (1) running the business for a profit this month and (2) changing the business to enable a profit next year. Healthy organizations must always be doing two things at once. Industries change over time, sometimes in an evolutionary way and sometimes in a revolutionary way. An IE may be called on to ply his trade in either run-the-business or change-the-business efforts. An IE can be called on to *refine*, *smooth*, and *optimize* today's assembly line by using Lean techniques to remove waste. An IE can be assigned to *define*, *develop*, and *deploy* tomorrow's assembly line.

■ IEs *refine* and solve run-the-business problems, and *define* and solve change-the-business problems.

6. Industrial Engineering Is Always Done in an Intense, Competitive Environment, Both Inside and Outside the Host Organization

All organizations exist in a competitive world. They face competition for customers, investors, resources, employees, and knowledge. Competition is always stiff and potentially deadly. Organizations that lead the competition *thrive* and those that fall behind the competition *die*. IEs are an important part of the organizational competence needed to compete successfully.

IEs face stiff and potentially deadly competition within their host organization. Who does top management look to for solutions when the chips are down: IEs, production engineers, market researchers, or organizational development (OD) specialists? Failure to be called on for the big-deal problems or opportunities spells real trouble for IEs and the IE function.

■ IEs work to (1) build their organization's competitive advantage and (2) develop their own competitive edge in solving their company's problems.

7. Industrial Engineers Will Always Live and Work in a Political Environment

Politics may be an unpleasant or dirty word, but life-or-death politics is present in every organization. Organizational politics can be defined as employees pursuing self-interest to the detriment of the organization's interest. *Playing politics* can dilute the strength of the organization by enhancing individual interests at the expense of the organization. Playing politics is very serious business that can negatively impact employee jobs and careers. IEs cannot escape politics, but they can weaken their impact.

■ IEs weaken wasteful politics by ensuring that their own work is (1) transparent, (2) methodologically sound, and (3) based on fact.

8. Industrial Engineers Will Always Work in Organizations That Have Layers of Employees and Managers

Regardless of contemporary organizational designs (i.e., flat organizations or network structures), organizations have pyramid shapes at their core. (When an organization is in really big trouble, the subpoenas and indictments will flow from the top of the pyramid down.)

IEs must know and understand their organization's pyramid with its levels of management from the top down. IEs cannot be like the freeway driver who is comfortable tailgating a huge truck that blocks his vision; the wary driver and the prudent IE must be able to maneuver to see the traffic ahead and to see beyond multiple levels of management.

- IEs must be able to *see through* and *play through* organizational layers. IEs know the goals of their boss, their boss's boss, and their boss's boss's boss.

9. Successful IE Assignment Must Make a Contribution to the Organization's Competitive Advantage

Imagine an IE who has the opportunity to present his completed project with all its clever and elegant details to the executive team. He smiles as he completes his summary slide, and turns to face what is sure to be an appreciative audience to hear what seems like a lifetime of absolute silence, interrupted by his CEO's question, "So what?"

An IE project is not complete or valuable without a contribution to the organization's competitive advantage. An IE project's deliverable must connect to an organizational artery rather than to fat cells.

- IEs ensure that every project contributes to competitive advantage. An IEs deliverables must be more than just a *brick* but a *load-bearing brick* in the wall of a cathedral.

10. By Definition, a Healthy Organization Is a System

A healthy organizational system is a set of unalike parts that are most productive when they work together as a single entity that is more than the sum of its part. Each part has its place in the system, and when changed, causes pressure for the other parts to adjust as well. Imagine the director of a play who makes changes in the script without going further to alter roles, redesign sets and costumes, recontract with actors, and complete rehearsals. An IE's deliverable for an assembly-line optimization problem is not complete until there is a system solution: the work process solution is detailed, the required modification of tools and systems is specified, alterations of job description and employee training are outlined, and an implementation plan is at least sketched.

- An IE always presents a system solution to an IE problem.

11. No Amount of Engineering Talent and Skill Can Make Up for a Lack of Knowledge about the Business

A successful business operating in a competitive environment has a way of operating that works to create success. That way of operating may be written down (unlikely) or it may reside in the heads of employees who have the knowledge and feel of business processes in their bones. Industrial engineering, on the other hand, is anchored in the IE body of knowledge. To function in an organization, however, IEs can only be effective by combining their mastery of (1) the IE body of knowledge and (2) the facts, details, and nuances of the work processes in their organization, as learned from the employees who have the business in their bones. An elegant engineering solution based on a wrong organization assumption or an inaccurate "business truth" will only be useful as a case study in an undergraduate IE course.

■ IEs know the work processes of the business of their organization like the backs of their hands.

12. Change Management Is a Formula Made Up of the Required Elements of an Organization as a System

Industrial engineers use change management to ensure that their technical solutions are fully implemented for business value. But what is change management? Change management is more like baking an elegant cake than about concocting a delicious spaghetti sauce. Trained chefs know how to do both, but they also know that the cooking processes for the two dishes are very different. Chefs know that spaghetti sauce is a mixture of ingredients. They know that you can add (or subtract) different kinds of ingredients and still have a tasty spaghetti sauce. They also know that a cake is a *formula* that requires a complete set of needed ingredients. They know that if you fail to add eggs, you cannot make up for the omission by adding extra flour.

Change management is a formula made up of communicating vision, altering processes and tools, and altering performance systems (i.e., roles, goals, training, and rewards). For example, failure to alter work processes cannot be overcome with snazzy multimedia messages. Failure to alter roles and provide training cannot be overcome with more modifications to tools or software.

■ IEs use the change management formula to ensure that their technical solutions are fully implemented.

13. Introduction of "New" Always Has Two Parts

The two parts are (1) preparing the "new" for the organization and (2) preparing the organization for the "new." When an IE solves a technical problem, the solution is likely to be seen as *new* (or as an innovation) to the organization (even though it may not be new to the whole planet).

For example, solving a technical problem with methods that remove waste from a production operation should be translated as altering the work processes in a production system. In other words, the IE may have worked long and hard to identify and remove the waste, but he is only half done with his assignment. He may have readied his technical waste-removal solution for his organization, but he has not as yet prepared his organization to use the solution.

■ IEs know that all problems come in even numbers: getting solutions ready for an organization and getting the organizations ready to use the solutions.

14. Industrial Engineering Will Always Have a Teamwork Dimension as a Critical Factor of Success

Imagine two situations: (1) three IEs have been assigned to resolve a technical problem in a segment of workflow, and (2) a single IE has been assigned to resolve a technical problem in a different segment of the same workflow. In which situation is there an important team dimension that must be taken into account?

That's right—both situations have a critical team dimension. Obviously, the three engineers could use teamwork, but that teamwork pales in comparison to the IE and stakeholder teamwork that will always be required for a successful project. The IE must aggressively work to facilitate a stakeholder team solution. When completed, the IE solution will not be delivered into a vacuum, but into an organization that is working "all out" to produce today's products and services. If the IE has not actively worked the stakeholders' needs and requirements into her solution, the delivered solution is likely to become dead weight on a dusty shelf.

■ Every IE problem or assignment always has an important team dimension that absolutely must be considered and worked.

15. Industrial Engineers Must Speak the Language of Operations, not the Other Way Around

Many an IE career has lost traction (or been terminated) because of the IE's use of technical IE language rather than the language of her organizational customer. Translating an IE solution into the customer's language is a vital step in completing any deliverable. Technical razzle-dazzle and the latest buzz words do not increase credibility; they reduce it, frequently to a point that will disqualify an IE for any presentations to management. If the customer's language is not used, the likely assumption is that the IE does not know enough about the business to be taken seriously.

■ IEs speak the language of their customers.

16. No Way of Doing Business Lasts Forever

IEs live and work where change is the rule. For today's organizations, change is no longer the exception but the rule. Change is here to stay, and organizations (and technical professionals) had better become very good at it. Today's statistics say that 70% of organizational changes fail to meet management's intentions and expectations. IEs work to ensure their organizations are in the 30% of the companies that succeed in making organizational changes; on target, on time, and on budget.

■ IEs lead and support organizational change, not undermine it.

17. Competent Organizational Decision Makers Should Always Process Input from the Bottom up and Then Lead from the Top Down

What we know about leadership and management today is that the best decisions for organizations are based on top management's consideration of input *from the bottom of the organization up* and implementation of the decision *from the top down*. Following that contemporary best practice requires the effective IE to perform well on two important organizational responsibilities.

The first responsibility is to provide thoughtful, competent input *up the organization* through his boss, by volunteering to be on a task team, by speaking up at employee meetings, or by posting to the company's intranet or bulletin board. Competent input should be tailored to fit the IE's business competence (i.e., providing input about *how* the organization could implement a strategic option, not about what that strategic option should be).

The second responsibility is to go "all in" to support the management decision that comes from the top down. No regrets, no Monday morning quarterbacking, no whining or grumbling; just a full-faith effort to support that decision.

■ IEs volunteer competent *how* input from the bottom up, and then focus their efforts on supporting and enabling a top-down management decision.

18. *Industrial Engineers Are Not in the Industrial Engineering Business*

Borrowing from a past experience, consider this. While speaking to an audience of some 200 CIOs, I posed the following question: "How many of you are in the information technology (IT) business?" Almost all of the audience raised their hands.

I called attention to one CIO sitting in the front row and said, "Sir, I noticed that you did not raise your hand. Would you kindly stand up and introduce yourself." He stood and faced the audience, "Hello, my name is Antonio Costa, and I am the CIO of Pirelli Tires. I am in the tire business." As the audience began to stir in their seats, I once again asked the question. This time only a few IT vendors raised their hands.

■ An industrial engineer who works in the healthcare business is in the healthcare business, not the industrial engineering business. What business are you in?

Such is the input from a nonengineer who has fought in the organizational trenches for a few decades. I sincerely hope that my views have value to you in your journey to pursue and master your profession. It is an honor as a nonengineer to be asked to write a chapter in an engineering book. Will wonders never cease?

Chapter 4

An Overview of Management Engineering and Best Practices for Management Engineering Departments

Tarun Mohan Lal and Thomas Roh

Contents

Introduction

Management engineering integrates multiple disciplines (e.g., operations research, industrial/production engineering, human factors engineering, financial engineering, quality management, computer science, general engineering disciplines, social and behavioral sciences) to study and solve complex problems from a global or systems approach. Healthcare has been slower than other industries to integrate management engineering into its business model. However, the report *Building a Better Delivery System: A New Engineering/Health-Care Partnership* (2005), sponsored by the Institute of Medicine (IOM) and the National Academy of Engineers (NAE), suggested the integration and growth of management engineering to achieve the six quality of care factors: safe, effective, timely, patient-centered, efficient, and equitable. This garnered attention in the industry and sparked the development of departments with management engineering capabilities.

Traditionally, industrial/management engineers' roles were preconceived to reside in manufacturing, but management engineers have been part of healthcare systems since the mid-1900s. The earliest management engineering work dates back to the 1800s, when Florence Nightingale championed quality improvement through the use of data capture and statistics. Early beginnings, unfortunately, did not lead to early adoption of management science in healthcare. The manufacturing and the transportation industries developed and applied these new principles much more rapidly, but new pressures similar to the ones that manufacturing and transportation faced have pushed management science to the forefront.

The complexity of healthcare provider organizations due to care transitions between primary care clinics, specialty clinics, and hospitals, and the rising healthcare costs over the past few years along with revamping of the current pay structure has made management science integral to healthcare over the past few years. In order for the healthcare provider organizations to deliver care that is reliable, high quality, low cost, and customer satisfying, management engineering departments need to grow to enable integration and coordination of professional, support, and administrative staffs; sophisticated clinical and information technology; critical processes and inventories; and facility resources.

In this chapter, we outline the role of management engineering departments, the scope of their work, and the infrastructure required to set up sustainable management engineering departments that provide value to the organization. This chapter was developed through a series of interviews with leadership of management engineering departments within several large healthcare systems, whose size ranged from 5 to 120 employees. Based on the information gathered, we also summarize some best practices for management engineering departments to adopt.

Role of Management Engineering Departments

Management engineering departments in most organizations work and serve as the internal business consulting unit for the institution and serve a wide range of roles on projects including business process reengineering, business development, project management, statistical analysis, process improvement, quality improvement, and change management. These departments are called upon to bring the objective perspective to the projects that help resolve issues that are interwoven with multiple interdependencies and interdigitating relationships. The major determining factors of the types of projects undertaken by the management engineering departments are dependent on their reporting structure within the organization. More and more management engineering departments are starting to realize the need to be closely linked to the executive level of the organization and support the overall strategic direction of the organization. Some departments therefore report directly to the chief operating officer (COO) or chief executive officer (CEO) of the organization. In this instance, resource scarcity becomes one of the greatest challenges. Hence, prioritization of efforts undertaken is the key to their success. However, it is important to recognize that supporting strategic initiatives alone is not the solution. Strategic initiatives must be balanced with the optimization of day-to-day operations of the organization. Some of the value-adding propositions/roles of management engineering departments in healthcare can be summarized as follows:

- ■ Improve the patient care experience and cost of care by utilizing systems engineering/operations research and process improvement tools/methodologies.

- Partner closely with clinical practice and leadership of the organization in order to demonstrate and facilitate the diffusion of the best practices into practice and align with the strategic needs of the organization.
- Apply project management principles and practices to achieve project schedules and budgets, and rectify problems relating to process, facility, and program.
- Provide integrating information technology (IT) support by helping to define and interpret user requirements for workflow, data, ergonomic issues, staffing, and equipment.
- Educate clinicians on systems thinking, quality improvement tools, and processes/procedures related to change management.
- Facilitate change management within the organization for successful implementation.

Effective Organizational Structure

Management engineering departments have unique qualities that allow them to thrive within an organization. A critical factor in the success of management engineering departments is proper alignment of the group within the organization. Management engineers can help organizations to achieve their goals only if they are placed high enough in the organization to access planners, decision makers, and critical operating information. Preferably, a management engineering department should not be housed within another department. The engineers need to be able to make impartial judgments while working on projects. This also helps prevent the *silo effect* that decentralization and practice specialization have had on healthcare. Management engineers need to look at the system as a whole and communicate successes throughout the institution. The majority of such departments have leadership-level staff that interacts with the senior leadership and decision-making bodies of the institution. This serves two purposes: resources are allocated to projects that have the greatest need and the largest effect upon the institution, and senior leadership is instrumental in receiving buy-in from the providers and administrators with whom a department works.

In larger organizations, the management engineering function may be distributed across the organization to ensure better resource allocation. For example, some organizations have one team supporting the hospital operations while another team supports the outpatient clinics. In some organizations there are management engineers supporting individual departments; however, such efforts have proved to be ineffective and most organizations are undergoing major restructuring changes to integrate such disjointed efforts.

Thus successful management engineering departments need to have full visibility throughout all functions of the organization with the authority to work with any level of the organization. It is highly recommended that the department has a direct reporting structure to the executive team of the organization to ensure alignment with the vision and mission of the organization's immediate needs.

Management engineering departments are often mistaken to be a part of other departments, such as information technology, quality and safety, finance, and sometimes human resources, which is not true. However, the management engineers need to work in close collaboration with these groups to support their projects. For example, most projects require data analysis, and IT departments are heavily involved in providing the required data from the existing data capture systems, such as the electronic medical records. Management engineers also work on IT projects by creating the methodology behind IT tools and facilitating implementation. Quality and safety projects are supported by management engineering departments; however, the organizations can have quality and safety departments for reporting the metrics and data to external and government agencies. Finance and human resources departments use the support of management engineers on projects ranging from staffing, culture of safety, reporting, and process improvement, and provide data to measure the success of projects on initiatives such as managing reimbursements.

Staffing a Management Engineering Department

Management engineering professionals bring the advantages of an extensive variety of work experience and educational credentials that provide them with the training and toolsets to aid hospitals and healthcare organizations in navigating this challenging operational landscape. Their role is to address the design, installation, and improvement of integrated systems of people, material, facilities, information, equipment, and energy. Management engineering professionals draw from many disciplines including management, business administration, and organization development disciplines, which have grown from the Total Quality Management, known twenty years ago, to today's Six Sigma, Lean, and other performance improvement practices, providing unique perspectives and skill sets to improvement initiatives and professional knowledge.

Management engineering departments typically hire individuals with a degree in industrial engineering or business administration. The education level varies from bachelor's to doctorate levels; however, there seems to be a preference to hire individuals with master's degrees. With an increasing demand for applying advanced analytical tools, organizations are increasing the number of graduate-level industrial engineers hired because they typically have enough knowledge of advanced statistics and operations research methodologies to be able to facilitate strategic and operational excellence in clinical practice, education, research, and administration.

Management engineers typically believe in hiring generalists instead of specialists and expect their staff to possess the basic analytical aptitude and people skills. There is also emphasis on the importance of the soft skills needed for management engineers to be successful within the organization. Given the role of these engineers, it is important for them to be able to interact with the senior leadership of the organization, apply systems thinking to problem solving, and possess a large amount of emotional intelligence. Successful management engineers are the ones who can build strong relationships and trust with clinical and administrative staff or frontline service providers of the organization to smooth the implementation of proposed solutions.

Some management engineering departments also collaborate with universities and academia to facilitate the use of the latest advanced tools and methodologies, provide education to internal staff, and to serve as a pipeline for future recruitment.

Institutional Adversity

Management engineering departments continue to face several challenges. Some of the most critical challenges stated by most organizations are as follows:

■ Leadership has started to recognize the importance of these departments, causing increased demand for services but limited bandwidth to support all the requests. The key to success is robust prioritization of efforts.

- Management engineering departments struggle with measuring their success, as most of the projects they support are very dependent on successful adoption of the recommendations that they provide.
- Finding and keeping talent for such departments continues to be challenging. The good news is that management engineering departments often provide the pipeline of potential leaders in the organization as they develop a good understanding of the organization and develop key relationships with the organization's leaders. However, this may result in a high turnover rate of engineers.
- Integration and adoption of management engineering principles require major change management efforts, and this requires a mindset change at all levels of the organization.

Keys to Success

Management engineering departments suffer when they do not have a presence throughout the entire institution. Projects need to be prioritized and disseminated on a systemwide basis. Optimizing a part of the system can negatively affect the integrated system. Projects should be focused on the greatest needs of the organization and in line with the senior leadership's vision for the organization. Effective communication of projects and their successes helps to inform departments within the organization of possible solutions to their own problems, helps them to better understand how their work and other's work is affected as a whole system, and shows the management engineering department's value to the institution. Once organizations are successful in convincing the administration of the need for management engineers, it's very important to prove the value right away. The most common approach taken by multiple organizations is to work on projects that are in the sight of the COO or other high-level administration. Being able to successfully optimize a system as a whole requires in-depth and broad organizational knowledge with the focus being on patient satisfaction.

Chapter 5

A Case Study of a High Functioning Management Engineering Department

Rudolph (Rudy) Santacroce

Contents

Do more with less. As industrial and management engineers, we are professionals who hear this phrase often and constantly strive to improve processes, streamline operations, demonstrate the value-added impact of change, and ultimately increase our hospital's quality of patient care. With the pace of modern healthcare changing at a remarkable rate, healthcare institutions are allocated fewer resources to provide more service with greater expectations for an increasing patient population. This is the challenge for management engineers as the value of the internal healthcare engineering consultant grows as hospital administrators face the challenges of modern healthcare including resource allocation, productivity, operational performance, and clinical quality. This chapter is written from the perspective of an internal management engineer whose department serves a large academic and Trauma-1 health system. The author's department is one of the oldest in the nation, having been founded in 1968. There have been many changes in department structure, leadership, and operation to support the challenges faced over the decades, but key elements that provided positive results for clients and patients throughout the years remain constant; these elements will be detailed in this chapter.

Department Structure

Internal management engineering (IME) teams add significant value to the organization(s) they serve as they provide an ongoing cycle of strategic vision, operational and technical knowledge, project management techniques, and follow-up project evaluation services. The IME professional knows the administration and key leaders and is able to align project initiatives with the goals of the organization. As opposed to an external consulting group, the IME enjoys a long-standing relationship with the organization. Since it is also outside of line operations, and typically outside of line leadership, IME departments should been seen as a completely unbiased resource. Typical IME departments are structured as a traditional team (pure industrial engineering—IEs) or a hybrid team (IEs mixed with process improvement—PI experts and/or quality experts). The classification of each professional is based on their educational background; IEs are trained through a nationally accredited five-year engineering program, PI experts receive training and certification as a green or black belt through various Lean or Six Sigma training programs, and quality experts have a strong nursing/medical provider background. Each professional brings significant value and a different perspective to the organization and the decision to keep IME departments siloed or partnered with quality generally depends on the reporting structure and the department's focus. From the author's experiences, IME departments reporting to the chief quality officer (CQO) or vice president (VP) responsible for quality will be imbedded within the quality department while IME departments with a strong operational or financial focus reporting to the chief operating officer (COO) or chief financial officer (CFO) will stand on its own. As an IME, it is important to recognize that any project dealing with extensive medical processes or patient outcomes and metrics should be performed in close partnership with quality team members, since financial, service, and quality outcomes are interdependent. An example structure of a typical mid-sized traditional IME department is shown in Figure 5.1.

Note that this structure also details typical time-in-grade requirements and a recommended staff advancement and replacement process.

Types of Services Offered

Management engineers bring many versatile tools in their tool kit that can be applied to solve complex problems based on time and data available. Many of these tools stem from traditional industrial engineering methodologies applied to the stochastic environment of healthcare, rather than low-variability manufacturing processes from which the industrial engineering profession originated. A list of these services typically includes, but is not limited to, the following:

■ Process flow mapping (Lean and Six Sigma)
■ Strategic and operational planning
■ Functional facility planning and design
■ Schedule modeling and development
■ Computer simulation and queuing analysis
■ Staffing and productivity
■ Developing management reports and databases
■ Project management and implementation
■ Financial and value-added analysis

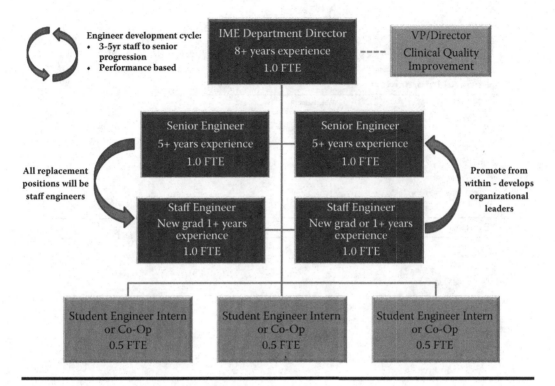

Figure 5.1   IME department structure model.

- Statistical and engineering analytics
- Benchmarking

IME departments are sometimes also asked to perform sentinel event root cause analysis, although this is typically performed as part of a clinical team where the IME brings the systematic investigation process along with data analytics as part of the desired skill set for the team.

IME Department Management Tools and Techniques

Management of an IME department's project request list is a delicate balance between the project's reflection of the organization's strategic and operational priorities, financial value-added impact, and available project resources. It is critical for the IME to constantly engage hospital administrators and market their services as a means of accomplishing key initiatives or meeting annual organizational goals, much as the leader of an external consulting practice might. Maintaining ongoing advisory relationships with past customers is another key technique that enables the IME to have a direct and ongoing pipeline for new projects from trusting customers. As projects and initiatives arise within the organization, many departments find it very helpful to post an online project request form that lists important criteria and aids the IME manager in making the right decisions regarding the timing of taking on new projects. An example Project Request Form is shown in Figure 5.2.

Once deemed appropriate and prioritized, the project must be assigned to a staff member or team. In most cases, this project allocation can be attributed to three main factors: staff

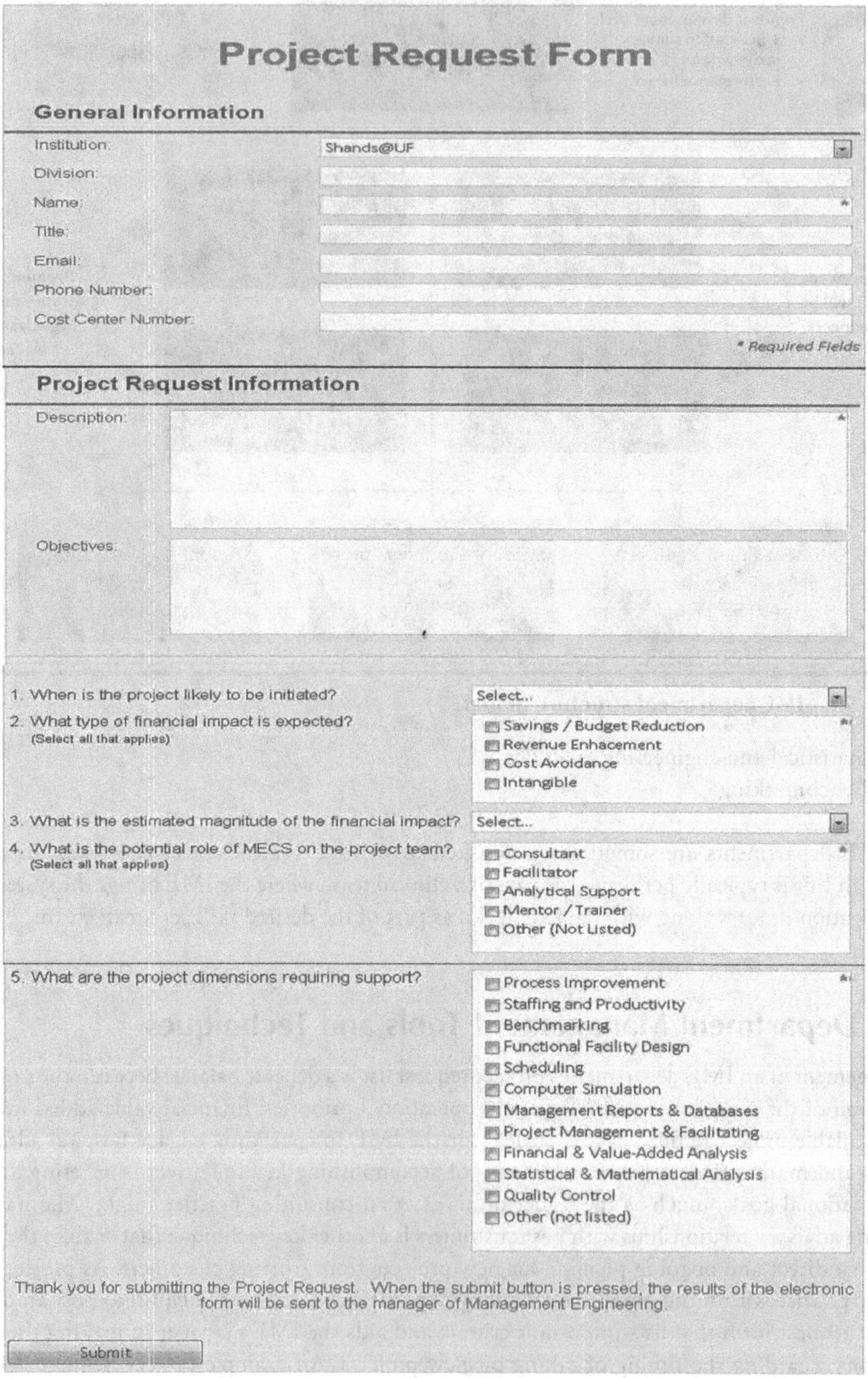

Project Request Form

General Information

Institution: Shands@UF

Division:

Name: *

Title:

Email:

Phone Number:

Cost Center Number:

Required Fields

Project Request Information

Description: *

Objectives:

1. When is the project likely to be initiated?   Select...

2. What type of financial impact is expected?
(Select all that applies)
 - ☐ Savings / Budget Reduction
 - ☐ Revenue Enhancement
 - ☐ Cost Avoidance
 - ☐ Intangible

3. What is the estimated magnitude of the financial impact?   Select...

4. What is the potential role of MECS on the project team?
(Select all that applies)
 - ☐ Consultant
 - ☐ Facilitator
 - ☐ Analytical Support
 - ☐ Mentor / Trainer
 - ☐ Other (Not Listed)

5. What are the project dimensions requiring support?
 - ☐ Process Improvement
 - ☐ Staffing and Productivity
 - ☐ Benchmarking
 - ☐ Functional Facility Design
 - ☐ Scheduling
 - ☐ Computer Simulation
 - ☐ Management Reports & Databases
 - ☐ Project Management & Facilitating
 - ☐ Financial & Value-Added Analysis
 - ☐ Statistical & Mathematical Analysis
 - ☐ Quality Control
 - ☐ Other (not listed)

Thank you for submitting the Project Request. When the submit button is pressed, the results of the electronic form will be sent to the manager of Management Engineering.

Submit

Figure 5.2   Project Request Form.

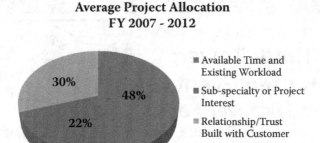

Average Project Allocation
FY 2007 - 2012

30%

48%

22%

■ Available Time and
  Existing Workload

■ Sub-specialty or Project
  Interest

■ Relationship/Trust
  Built with Customer

Figure 5.3   Average project allocation chart.

availability, staff specialization or interest, and the relationship the IME staff has with the requesting customer. The graph in Figure 5.3 displays the author's average allocation of projects to department staff over the past five fiscal years.

In order to clearly define project scope, resources, expectations, and timeframe, a Charter, Project Primer, or Project Initiation Form is typically developed at the start of a project. After the initial meeting with the client, the IME develops the Project Initiation Form and shares the draft with the customer to gain consensus. The Project Initiation Form should accomplish the following:

- Specify project goals and objectives
- List the project charter and problem statement
- Specify the project team and other resource requirements
- State initial expected project outcomes
- Detail project timeframe/phases
- Provide an initial look at value-added financial impact
- Raise initial outstanding issues

It is important to consider the Project Initiation Form as a conduit to communicate the key aspects of the project to stakeholders outside the project team. An example of a Project Initiation Form used in a recent Lean initiative for the author's organization is shown in Figure 5.4.

From this author's experience, as the project turnaround time requirement is reduced and the number of project requests increase, a department project repository and tracking mechanism becomes critical. A project database can be developed in Microsoft Access or similar software to keep track of the project status and serve as a project library once the project is complete. Features may be added that enable the IME to upload project files and key deliverables so staff and customers alike have a one-stop-resource for all projects completed in the IME's department. Detailed in a project database is information on current project status, project team composition, next steps, project background information, project type, and financial value-added information. Reporting is extremely easy and may be used by IMEs to search for similar projects performed in the past and a management tool for project status updates during staff meetings. Key reporting items include the number of projects that each IME is currently working on, the duration of each project, the next project step, any obstacles the IME may have encountered, and value-added financial information. An example of a project database input screen is shown in Figure 5.5.

LEAN Health Care Focus

SUF North Tower:
OR Kaizen Event
Room Turnover Focus
Project Primer

Project Charter:
Successfully complete a Kaizen event for the OR with a focus on improving OR Room Turnover in the North Tower, specifically ENT and TCV surgical services. Identify a focused core team consisting of representatives from each team involved in room turnover to work off-site for two consecutive days in order to determine current state processes, identify value added and non-value added steps, develop a smoother future state process flow, and determine a sustainable implementation plan for execution.

Outstanding Items and Questions:
- Determine the Kaizen team:
  - **Suggested Team (~ 11 total)**: 2 Surgeons (ENT/TCV), 1 Anesthesiologist, 1 Nurse Anesthetist, 2 Techs (ENT/TCV), 2 PST (ENT/TCV), 1 Nurse Lead, 2 Management Engineering Facilitators
- Determine location:
  - One of two South campus locations: South Tower Meeting Room or PRC Meeting Room
- Determine estimated costs:
  - Food: Breakfast ($75 per day), Lunch ($100 per day) - Total $350 (est.)
- Determine start date:
  - Kick-off Meeting end of June; Kaizen Event early July (after holiday)

Next Steps:

Stage **1**	Kick-Off Meeting (1-2 hours) *Occurs 1-2 weeks before the event in order to calibrate team and get everyone up to speed on agenda. Opportunity for questions and allows enough time for research if needed. Can invite other people outside of core team for informational meeting (i.e. administrative, mid-management).*
Stage **2**	Kaizen Event (2 days at off-site location) *Day 1 (Thursday) – Kaizen Concepts Review, Current State Process Flow, Identify Muda (waste) Steps Day 2 (Friday) –Brainstorming, Future State Process Flow, Finalize Implementation and Sustainability Plan Day 3 (Monday) – Roll out new process with team in place*
Stage **3**	Implementation and Long Term Plan *Support new process for 1 week post kaizen event through observations and call-in's to managers. Follow up with team one month post event with 1 hour meeting to discuss operational issues and sustainability.*

Figure 5.4   SUF: North Tower: Or Kaizen Event—Project Initiation Form Example.

MECS Project Database   Friday, December 03, 2010

Project Number: 01019.000
Title: South Tower Implementation: RFID AeroScout Solution, Post-Implementation
Institution: Shands UF
Department: Information Services
Division: Information Services
Primary Customer: Brad Kowal
Start Date: 8/16/2010
Estimated End Date: 9/3/2010
End Date: 9/14/2010
Primary Engineer: Anne Myers, Joanne Untalan
Secondary Engineer(s):
Supervising Engineer: Rudy Santacroce
Description: Follow-up anaylsis from project 00988.000 to assist with RFID pilot study & implementation. Collect post-implementation data at 60 day mark for the pilot phase.

Est. Financial Impact:
Recom. Revenue Enhance.: $0
Recom. Cost Reduction: $0
Recom. Cost Avoidance: $33,182
Recom. Financial Impact: $33,182

Project Update Information
Next Step: Followup postponed to week of 8/16 per Brad Kowal

Revised Estimated End Date:
Reason for Delay: Need to wait 60 days after RFID implementation to record results of new technology.

PROJECT STATUS
Completed
In Progress
On Hold (indefinitely)

Satisfaction Survey: Y
Hard Copy File: X
Electronic File: Y

☐ Student
☐ Educational

Cost Center:
Cum Hrs:

☒ Budget Finance   ☐ Process/System Design   ☐ Scheduling   ☐ Structured Estimating
☐ Database Analysis   ☐ Project Mgmt/Facilitating ☐ Simulation   ☐ Time Study
☐ Facility Design   ☐ Productivity Modeling   ☐ Skill Mix Analysis ☐ Work Sampling
☐ Facility Layout   ☐ Quality/Productivity Control ☐ Staffing   ☐ Work Distribution
☐ Flow Charting   ☐ Queuing   ☒ Standard Development ☐ Workload Analysis
☐ Patient/Work Flow Analysis ☐ Room/Equipment Utilization ☐ Statistical/Math Analysis

Figure 5.5   Project database example.

The Road Ahead

Hospital process efficiency and effectiveness are growing needs for all healthcare organizations today. A major driving force for process improvement is the internal management engineer as a trusted, unbiased resource. This chapter explored the background, tools, management techniques, and collaboration opportunities of typical internal management engineering consulting teams and used examples taken from the author's own experiences of leading an IME department. Key ideas for internal engineering consulting teams are to remain flexible, always, and quickly adapt to the needs of the organization you serve. Understand the strategic and operational goals of your institution and focus project efforts on achieving those goals. Always track projects and demonstrate the financial value-added impact of your projects. Where possible, partner with local or regional academic institutions to develop an undergraduate intern or co-op program. Finally, keep an open mind and be able to see the road ahead, and anticipate the challenges and the solutions you can provide to your organization.

Chapter 6

Budget, Cost, and Performance Improvement Approaches Used by a Highly Effective ME Department

Rudolph (Rudy) Santacroce

Contents

Introduction

Healthcare management engineers (HMEs) are constantly challenged to demonstrate financial value-added benefits to the organizations they serve. Most projects do provide value, be it tangible (hard cost savings) or intangible (unquantifiable) benefits. The ability for HMEs to quantify project value is always a challenge, if not a requirement.

This chapter is written from the perspective of an internal management engineer whose department serves a large academic and Trauma-1 health system. Annually, the author's department provides greater than 450% return on investment (ROI) to the hospital system through tangible, management-approved value-added recommendations, a result typical of a well-focused management engineering (ME) department. Tangible value-added savings, as defined by the author, are comprised of the following: labor savings, nonlabor savings, cost avoidance, and revenue enhancement. Labor and nonlabor savings fall under the category of cost reduction, which often results in the direct reduction of a department's operating budget. Cost avoidance savings are measured by the reduction to the unit cost of a service by increasing the quantity of the service without increasing costs. The revenue enhancement category contains those recommendations that result in increased net revenues for a particular department; essentially doing more, work and volume, etc., without an increase of net resources. Revenue enhancements tend to be the most difficult form of value-added benefit to accurately quantify, since future patient volumes cannot be estimated precisely.

This guidebook was originally developed to aid management engineers in finding added value in projects. It was originally published in 2001 as part of a management engineering guidebook under the Healthcare Information Management Systems Society (HIMSS) Guidebook Series.* This chapter assumes the reader has a basic understanding of fundamental industrial engineering concepts; the goal is to apply these concepts to drive cost improvement approaches for healthcare organizations.

How to Use This Chapter

This chapter is designed as a cross-reference document comprised of two significant components: budget and cost improvement opportunities and an overview of common industrial engineer (IE) and ME tools that provides a brief synopsis of commonly used techniques.

Budget and cost improvement opportunities (Figure 6.1) are divided into two columns: Project Outcomes and IE/ME Techniques. Project outcomes are divided into the four major areas of value-added savings: Labor Savings, Nonlabor Savings, Cost Avoidance, and Revenue Enhancement. Each of these categories is subdivided into specific project objectives that will commonly yield value-added benefits. Intersections of Outcomes and Techniques, highlighted by a bullet, indicate that the technique is useful in generating that outcome.

---

* Rudy Santacroce, *Value-Added Guide: A Summary of Cost Improvement Approaches for Healthcare Management Engineers*, Trans. Array Management Engineering, Jean Ann Larson (Chicago, IL: Healthcare Information Management Systems Society, 2001), 33–45.

BUDGET AND COST IMPROVEMENT OPPORTUNITIES
Using IE / ME Tools and Techniques to Generate Value-Added Project Outcomes

PROJECT OUTCOMES	Work Measurement	Staffing, Productivity	Work Re-Design	Process Flow Mapping / Lean Methods	Scheduling	Quality Control	Facility Planning and Design
Labor Savings							
Improved efficiency by:							
A Productivity monitoring with performance feedback	●	●	●			●	
B Time management techniques		●	●	●	●	●	
C Incentive programs	●	●				●	
D Short interval scheduling	●	●			●		
E Increased employee motivation, moral, and training		●	●			●	●
Reduced workload due to:							
F Work simplification: eliminate, combine, sequence, simplify	●	●	●	●			●
G Process improvement	●	●	●	●		●	●
H Improved standards	●	●	●			●	
I Improved workstation/workplace layout		●	●	●			●
J **Reduced labor costs by changing skill mix**		●	●			●	
Improved labor utilization by:							
K Reduced staff overtime	●	●	●	●	●	●	
L Reduced shift differential and on-call		●	●	●	●	●	
M Reduced fixed activities: meetings, conferences, etc.	●	●	●		●	●	
N Scheduled staff to accommodate workload peaks and valleys	●	●		●	●	●	
O Ergonomic improvements: reduce/eliminate worker injuries			●				●
Non-Labor Savings							
Evaluated materials and supplies for reduction thru:							
P Reduced rate of usage per procedure			●			●	
Q Reduced purchase price: replacing brand-name with generic products			●			●	
R Reducing costs by using reusable items vs. disposable			●				
S Reduced inventory levels: opportunity costs on capital			●		●	●	
T Reduce obsolescence, breakage and pilferage of items					●	●	●
U Reduce waste due to contamination			●				
V Reuse of supplies for same or other purposes			●				
W Resale/recycle of used supplies			●				
Reduced contract/consultant costs by:							
X Negotiations							●
Y Bidding						●	
Z Bonus/penalty clauses						●	
Cost Avoidance							
AA **Used in-house consultants vs. outside contracted services**		●	●				●
AB **Reduced unit cost: Increased ratio of output with the same input**	●	●	●	●	●	●	
Revenue Enhancement							
AC **Used existing equipment and/or staff levels to perform more procedures**	●	●	●	●	●		●
AD **Updated existing equipment/technology**		●	●	●	●		

Figure 6.1   Budget and cost improvement opportunities.

The IE/ME Technique column shows seven major traditional industrial/management engineering practice areas, or tools. For each tool column, there is a dot that corresponds to a value-added category under project outcomes. For example, using work measurement techniques, engineers should look for value-added savings through the use of incentive programs, short-interval scheduling, work simplification, and so on. Conversely, if an engineer knew that a particular project objective was to reduce labor costs by changing skill mix (row J), the engineer could use staffing/productivity, work redesign, and quality control tools to meet that particular objective.

The second part of this chapter is an overview and a reference for the seven traditional IE/ME techniques outlined under Budget and Cost Improvement Opportunities (Figure 6.1). Each section contains one particular IE technique. A brief overview of each component is given, followed by a cross-reference to the matching project outcomes shown under Budget and Cost Opportunities. This section is not designed to teach the technique per se, but to serve as a reminder of the various parameters that must be considered when using that particular tool. For a more in-depth explanation of each technique, readers are encouraged to reference the other chapters in this guidebook that specifically address a specific traditional IE/ME tool or technique.

Work Measurement

From the very start of the Industrial Revolution, work measurement was considered the basic tool for monitoring and improving the productivity of workers. Table 6.1 outlines the cost improvement outcomes for work measurement. This has always been a manual endeavor, but with the coming of the computer age, many of the repetitive manual activities associated with a work measurement study have been replaced with automated tools and systems. The basic principles, however, remain the same. Three of the most commonly used work measurement tools are summarized below.

Time Study

By definition, a time study establishes an allowed time standard for performing a specific task, based on measurement of the work content, with due allowance for personal and other unavoidable delays. The objective is to increase the utilization of both labor and equipment as measured

Table 6.1 Cost Improvement Outcomes for Work Measurement

Improved efficiency by:	Improved labor utilization by:
Productivity monitoring with performance feedback	Reduced staff overtime
Incentive programs	Reduced fixed activities: meetings, conferences, etc.
Short interval scheduling	Scheduled staff to accommodate workload peaks/valleys
Reduced workload due to:	**Reduced unit cost: Increased ratio of output to input**
Work simplification: eliminate, combine, sequence, simplify	*Used existing resources to perform more procedures*
Process improvement	
Improved standards	

against reliable time standards. A typical by-product of time standard development is the identification of obstacles to improvement or inefficiencies in the process. The only equipment required for a time study is a stopwatch and a well-designed data collection form.

Work Sampling

Work sampling is a very useful tool for the analysis of nonrepetitive or irregularly occurring activities where no complete methods or frequency descriptions exist. In order to obtain accurate results with enough data points, work sampling studies usually extend over a period of weeks (2 to 4 weeks in most cases). The formula for determining the number of observations required for a given confidence level can be found below in Equation (6.1).

Equation 6.1: Work Sampling Equation[*]

$$N = p(1 - p)(Z_{\alpha/2})^2/e^2 \qquad (6.1)$$

where

N = number of observations required

p = percentage of occurrence of element being sought, expressed as a decimal

e = precision (accuracy desired)

$Z_{\alpha/2}$ = constant associated with the normal distribution

Structured Estimating

Structured estimating is another technique used for evaluating fixed and variable activities. It is most often used when it is simply not economically feasible (due to project time constraints, activities with long duration or high variability, etc.) to conduct a comprehensive work sampling study. Structured estimating performs a weighted average on activities based on minimum, normal, and maximum time estimates. For example, upon interviewing a staff nurse, the interviewer finds the time to in-process a new patient, which is distributed as follows:

[MIN(12 min)(20%) + NORMAL(20 min)(60%) + MAX(40 min)(20%)] = *22.4 min estimated*

Productivity and Staffing

Table 6.2 outlines cost improvement outcomes for staffing and productivity.

In most cases, staffing and productivity studies are accomplished by first measuring, to varying degree levels, worker productivity. Productivity itself is an index that has no dimension. It is described mathematically in Equation (6.2).

---

[*] Aura Matias, "Work Measurement: Principles and Techniques," *Handbook of Industrial Engineering*, ed. Gavriel Salvendy, 3rd ed. (New York: John Wiley & Sons, 2001), 1452.

Table 6.2 Cost Improvement Outcomes for Staffing and Productivity

Improved efficiency by:	Improved labor utilization by:
Productivity monitoring with performance feedback	Reduced staff overtime
Time management techniques	Reduced shift differential and on-call
Incentive programs	Reduced fixed activities: meetings, conferences, etc.
Short interval scheduling	Scheduled staff to accommodate workload peaks and valleys
Increased employee motivation, moral, and training	**Used in-house consultants vs. outside contracted services**
Reduced workload due to:	**Reduced unit cost: Increased ratio of output to input**
Work simplification: eliminate, combine, sequence, simplify	**Used existing resources to perform more procedures**
Process improvement	**Updated existing equipment/technology**
Improved standards	
Improved workstation/workplace layout	
Reduced labor costs by changing skill mix	

Equation 6.2: Basic Productivity Equation[*]

$$\frac{AOMP / RIMP}{AOBP / RIBP} \tag{6.2}$$

where

   AOMP = Aggregated outputs, measured period
   RIMP = Resource inputs, measured period
   AOBP = Aggregated outputs, base period
   RIBP = Resource inputs, base period

Work Distribution/Allocation

Once it is determined that a staffing and/or productivity study will be conducted, the first step is to develop an activity or task list for the staff being studied. Once this information is prepared, it is consolidated as part of a work distribution chart. This chart represents all activities of the function and all personnel responsible for performing the specified activities. Analysis of this chart enables the HME to ask questions and solve problems relating to the following topics:

- What activities take the most time?
- Are skills used properly?
- Is there misdirected effort?
- Is anyone performing an unrelated task?
- Is the work distributed evenly?

---

[*] Marvin Mundel, "Productivity Measurement and Improvement," *Handbook of Industrial Engineering*, ed. Gavriel Salvendy (New York: John Wiley & Sons, 1982), 1.5.1.

Analysis first concentrates on the most time-consuming activities. Eliminating unnecessary work is the next step, followed by determining the proper level of work. Workload is then reallocated if necessary and staffing is adjusted to match demand. It should be noted that leveling workload to meet demand is a key element in any work distribution effort.

Incentive Program Design

Incentive programs are used most effectively when employees are performing repetitive tasks with little or no variation. Incentive programs can increase worker productivity while keeping staffing levels constant. It is important to decide on a standardized unit of measure (i.e., number of units produced, number of physician dictations transcribed, etc.) before specifying the incentive parameters. One must also think very carefully about the metric on which the incentive is based so that unintended consequences, such as high productivity levels of poor-quality work, do not result.

Work Redesign

Table 6.3 outlines cost improvement outcomes for work redesign. Work redesign has a relatively wide range of applications. On a micro level, one example could be the improvement of the process by which an AP clerk processes a patient's bill. On a larger scale, however, a related example would be the complete reinvention by which an entire process takes place from the moment the patient presents at the hospital to the moment the charges are coded and a bill is developed. Also referred to as work simplification or method improvement, and Lean methods, work redesign can be broken down into a set of steps or guidelines:

Table 6.3   Cost Improvement Outcomes for Work Redesign

Improved efficiency by:	Evaluated materials and supplies for reduction through:
Productivity monitoring with performance feedback	Reduced rate of usage per procedure
Time management techniques	Reduced purchase price using generics
Increased employee motivation, moral, and training	Reducing costs by using reusable items vs. disposable
Reduced workload due to: Work simplification: eliminate, combine, sequence, simplify	Reduced inventory levels: opportunity costs on capital
Process improvement	Reduce waste due to contamination
Improved standards	Reuse of supplies for same or other purposes
Improved workstation/workplace layout	Resale/recycle of used supplies
Reduced labor costs by changing skill mix	**Reduced unit cost: Increased ratio of output to input**
	Used existing resources to perform more procedures
	Updated existing equipment/technology

- **Determine the purpose of the work.** If the reason for the method cannot be defined, then the method is not needed, and therefore does not have to be designed.
- **Conceptualize ideal processes.** It is important to include the workers or the people affected by the process to gain insight on the ideal state.
- **Identify constraints and regularity.** Consider the necessity of each constraint. Define the regularity, which is defined as the conditions of each element that represents a large proportion of occurrences for which the method is designed.
- **Outline practical process.** Further develop ideas by applying the following principles to each: its purpose, lowest-cost input, lowest-cost output, least complicated sequence, maximum utilization of human skills, and maximum utilization of equipment capacity.
- **Select the best process.** Evaluate the best process using the following criteria: lowest hazard, economic feasibility, ability to control, psychological factors, and organizational impact.
- **Formulate details of the newly selected process.** This phase is the physical manifestation of the new method. It may include flowcharts, specifications, techniques, principles, checklists, and so on.

Process Flow Mapping/Lean Methods

Table 6.4 outlines cost improvement outcomes for process flow mapping and lean methods. In many cases, a quantitative process system flow chart helps HMEs and their customers determine problems, bottlenecks, and inefficiencies. On a basic level, a flow diagram outlines the current process and steps involved in completing that process. Typically, a proposed flow is then developed that addresses the problems with the current flow. When testing is needed, a computer-based simulation can yield very detailed and extensive feedback.

Flow Diagram

A flow diagram represents the location of activities and staff and the flow of materials between activities. Symbols in the flowchart identify certain steps in the process such as input/output, decision, terminate/interrupt, and so on.

Table 6.4 Cost Improvement Outcomes for Process Flow Mapping/Lean Methods

Improved efficiency by: Time management techniques **Reduced workload due to:** Work simplification: eliminate, combine, sequence, simplify Process improvement Improved workstation/workplace layout **Improved labor utilization by:** • Reduced staff overtime • Reduced shift differential and on-call • Scheduled staff to accommodate workload peaks/valleys	**Used in-house consultants vs. outside contracted services** **Reduced unit cost: Increased ratio of output to input** **Used existing resources to perform more procedures** **Updated existing equipment/technology**

Queuing and Simulation

Computerized simulation takes the flow diagram to a new level by modeling the process being studied. Engineers and customers alike can immediately gain insight into the process by seeing the interaction of all the different elements in the system, in real time. Bottlenecks can be immediately spotted and changes to the system can be instantaneously evaluated. Many simulation packages currently on the market provide a wide range of usefulness to the ME. As of this printing, two commonly used object-oriented simulation packages include ARENA®, and ProModel®/ MedModel®. Both provide a detailed analysis of the simulated system, as well as lists of statistics on arrival times, process lengths, departure times, wait times, and so on. The major difference between these packages is the ease of programmability and the detail of display graphics. A key benefit is that once the model is developed and validated, engineers and customers can conduct what-if analysis to see how the system changes as resources change.

Scheduling

Table 6.5 outlines cost improvement outcomes for scheduling. MEs typically assist in the development of schedules for department staff, patient arrivals, key equipment, and other resources. Unfortunately, there is no generalized scheduling methodology as healthcare remains highly stochastic. There are, however, some basic guidelines to follow:

■ **Shortest processing time rule.** All jobs/processes with the shortest duration typically should be done first. By following this guideline, expected results should include:
  - A minimized average procedure flow time
  - A minimized average procedure wait time
  - A minimized average procedure downtime or turnover (the difference between completion time and the start of the next procedure)

This method works best in environments with a high standard deviation of procedure times.

■ **Due date rule.** Sequence the procedures according to the earliest required completion time. While this rule will not minimize the average wait time, it will minimize the *maximum* wait time.

Table 6.5 Cost Improvement Outcomes for Scheduling

Improved efficiency by:	Reduced contract/consultant costs by:
Time management techniques	Bidding
Short interval scheduling	Bonus/penalty clauses
Improved labor utilization by:	**Reduced unit cost: Increased ratio of output to input**
• Reduced staff overtime	
• Reduced shift differential and on-call	**Used existing resources to perform more procedures**
• Reduced fixed activities: meetings, conferences, etc.	**Updated existing equipment/technology**
• Scheduled staff to accommodate workload peaks/valleys	

Table 6.6 Cost Improvement Outcomes for Quality Control

Improved efficiency by:	Reduced labor costs by changing skill mix
Productivity monitoring with performance feedback	**Evaluated materials and supplies for reduction through:**
Time management techniques	Reduced rate of usage per procedure
Incentive programs	Reduced purchase price using generics
Increased employee motivation, moral, and training	Reduced inventory levels: opportunity costs on capital
Reduced workload due to:	Reduce obsolescence, breakage and pilferage of items
Process improvement	
Improved standards	**Reduced unit cost: Increased ratio of output to input**

- **Slack rule.** Sequence procedures based on the shortest downtime (turnover time) before the start of the next procedure. This rule will minimize procedure downtime. This rule is most useful when scheduling multiple machines in order to have a high utilization percentage.

Quality Control

Table 6.6 outlines cost improvement outcomes for quality control. Determination of quality specifications is the basis of quality assurance in a production environment. MEs will find quality control techniques very useful for internal benchmarking, setting acceptable limits and standards, or giving department managers feedback on a wide variety of department benchmarks. Two of the most commonly used quality control tools are discussed below.

*Control Charts**

Control charts give a graphic representation of the status of a process with a clear definition of the acceptable high and low limits of that process. The process may be anything, such as operating room turnover time or pharmacy order preparation time. The process for setting up a control chart is as follows:

- Twenty or more samples are selected (identified) and sequentially numbered.
- The range of the values obtained for each sample is determined (the largest minus the smallest).
- The average range (**R***avg*) is then calculated using Equations (6.3a) and (6.3b).
- The upper control limit (UCL) and lower control limit (LCL) define the acceptable range of the process and are calculated using the following formula:

$$R_{avg} = \frac{\Sigma R}{n}$$

(6.3a)

* Christian Gudnason, "The Quality Assurance System," *Handbook of Industrial Engineering*, ed. Gavriel Salvendy (New York: John Wiley & Sons, 1982), 8.2.9–8.2.10.

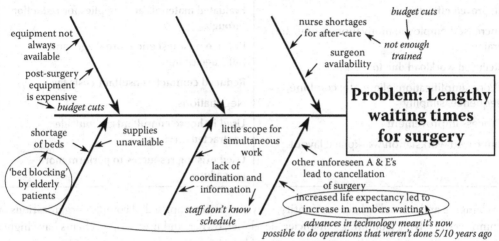

Figure 6.2 Sample Ishikawa diagram.

where
  ΣR = sum of R values
  n = number of items measured

$$UCL = D_4R \qquad\qquad (6.3b)$$
$$LCL = D_3R$$

The values for D_3 and D_4 are obtained from most quality control or operations manuals based on the number of samples.

Cause-Effect Diagram

The cause–effect ("fishbone" or Ishikawa) diagram is a basic tool used to evaluate problems inherent in almost any process and is best used as part of a process improvement team comprised of staff or users with expertise in the particular problem area being addressed. The cause–effect diagram consists of defining an occurrence (effect) and reducing it to its contributing factors (causes). The relationships among these factors are illustrated in a fishbone pattern stemming from the effect. The principle factors are broken into four categories: staff, equipment, methods, and materials. These primary four categories are then reduced to subcauses until all are listed and then are critically analyzed (see Figure 6.2).

Facility Planning and Design

Table 6.7 outlines cost improvement outcomes for facility planning and design. Modern healthcare brings new challenges to the professions of architecture and engineering. Clients themselves

Table 6.7   Cost Improvement Outcomes for Facility Planning and Design

Improved efficiency by:	Evaluated materials and supplies for reduction through:
Increased employee motivation, moral, and training	Reduce obsolescence, breakage, and pilferage of items
Reduced workload due to:	**Reduced contract/consultant costs by:**
Work simplification: eliminate, combine, sequence, simplify	Negotiations
Process improvement	**Used in-house consultants vs. outside contracted services**
Improved workstation/workplace layout	**Used existing resources to perform more procedures**

are changing and instead of being one entity, they are often comprised of complex organizations or committees involving a building's financier, developer, owner, and users. These clients have higher expectations for architectural services in terms of breadth and quality.

Traditionally, industrial engineers possess skills and analytical tools for determining site selection, space requirements, flow and activity analysis, and space–function relationship programming. These skills form the cornerstone of a function known as systematic layout planning (SLP). By using the SLP process in conjunction with the architectural design process, the engineer brings overall value by assisting in operations planning, concept design, and layout evaluation. This ultimately leads to a better design by reducing the amount of design rework, enhancing the design team's understanding of processes that will operate within the new facility, and evaluating the initial design from a functional standpoint. The components of SLP are:

- **Relationship diagram:** The relationship diagram or REL chart lists the major departments the building will have in a table form on a horizontal and vertical axis. Each area is then compared to the other by moving along an axis to the juncture of another area. At the juncture of two departments, a value of 1–4 along with a reason code is recorded. A value of "1" specifies a critical relationship between the two areas while a value of "4" represents an undesirable relationship.
- **Space relationship diagram:** The space relationship diagram takes the REL diagram one step further by quantifying the square foot requirements for each department. The relationships between the departments are represented by the number of lines connecting them. Four lines is a critical relationship while no lines or a dotted line represents an undesirable relationship.
- **Block Plan:** Final step in the SLP process. The block plan positions all the departments together considering the adjacency requirements determined by the space relationship diagram. This gives a good indication of the facility's floor plan. The block plan only considers the building's gross area, that is, hallways and doors are not represented. If the architectural floor plan is developed from the block plan, the facility will be "optimized" with regard to the locations of key departments and functions.
- **Other Services:** In addition to the SLP process, MEs add value to the design process through planning and coordinating with clients throughout the design phases. By representing the client, MEs act as the liaison between the client and the architect, ensuring the needs of the client are met. MEs may also assist the architect prior to the design process by developing a

functional space program and conducting room utilization studies. This may help in reducing the number of rooms planned in a new facility and therefore a reduction in the required square footage of a new building.

Conclusion

The goal of providing tangible, value-added recommendations to our respective healthcare organizations is an ongoing challenge for management engineers. In our business, we are often asked to help maximize resources and optimize outcomes as the cost of healthcare delivery increases along with the sheer number of patients we serve; much of the "low-hanging fruit" has already been picked by our predecessors and our goals are becoming increasingly hard to attain. It is the author's hope that this chapter serves management engineers at all levels of leadership as a cross-reference repository for aligning the common tools of the IE/ME trade with value-added project outcomes.

Chapter 7

Founding a Management Engineering Consulting Firm

John L. Templin, Jr.

Contents

Introduction

Unless you are a newly minted master of business administration (MBA), you most likely started work with a hospital or a company. As your career progressed and you gained both knowledge and experience, you may have begun to entertain thoughts of becoming a consultant and running your own firm. This may be especially true if your organization has engaged an outside consulting firm and you have been working with their consultants. You may believe you are as qualified and perhaps more qualified than some of the consultants. Perhaps your position or department has been eliminated in a downsizing or you have recently retired. In this chapter, we will discuss founding a management engineering consulting firm and several of the questions you will have to answer in order to determine if this is the right step for you, at least at this time.

Solo or Group?

That is the initial question. If your department has been eliminated or if you and some of your associates have been let go, you might consider starting a small group. More likely, you will be starting on your own. Either way, the next questions are: What skill set am I offering? Have I developed a unique set of skills that can be marketed and for which there is a demand? If I have the skill set, do I have the ability to market my skills? Do I have adequate personal financing or a second income until I both sell my services and actually get paid for the consulting? If the answer to these questions is no, you are not ready to start a consulting firm. If all the answers are yes, finish reading this chapter.

Is your skill set unique to a product such as one software package, or one department? Twenty years ago the author was one of very few nationally who fully understood the College of American Pathologists (CAP) workload recording method. He was easily able to obtain contracts to evaluate staffing levels for hospital laboratories. With very short notice, the CAP decided to abandon support of the method due to potential liability from instrument manufacturers. It was necessary to transfer that knowledge to other departments or to have additional skills in order to continue consulting.

A person may be fortunate and have an initial contract in place when their "regular" or "real" job ends. Usually this is not the situation. It could take a few months to establish the firm or your identity as a consultant and to obtain the first contract. If you know well in advance that you are transitioning to consulting, you can plan and hit the starting line at full speed. Initial questions include the following:

- What will be the legal format—sole proprietorship, LLP, C, or S Corporation?
- What name will you use?
- How do you set your consulting rate and how do you charge for various expenses?
- Where do you market and want to consult?
- How will you market your services?
- How do you price out and invoice for the services rendered?

What Will Be the Legal Format?

A sole proprietorship is the simplest for an individual and is the easiest and least expensive to establish. As a solo enterprise, expenses and income from the business are included on your personal tax return. If more than one person establishes a firm, it could be a partnership and the business will be owned and operated by several individuals. If you are certain you are in consulting for the long run, you likely want to consider establishing a corporation. It will be an independent entity from the owners and it will require compliance with more regulations and tax requirements. However, your personal assets will not be at risk. In making the legal format decision, you should seek the advice of a tax professional and a lawyer.

What Name Will You Use?

Do you simply use your name, for example, John or Jane Smith, or Smith Consulting Services? Have you developed name recognition in your field or will very few decision makers even know of you? What key words, if any, do you want to incorporate in your business name? Will it be Smith Management Associates, or perhaps Smith Healthcare Management Associates? You need to be aware of legal restrictions and copyright infringement. For example, you probably would not be allowed to use Smith Microsoft Consulting Associates. If you are going to incorporate, the lawyer you use should be able to assist in avoiding potential problems. For example, you do not want to print marketing materials or prepare a website and then find out you cannot use it.

How Do You Set Your Consulting Rate?

Too many consultants initially charge too little per hour or per day on the assumption that they will invoice close to 40 hours per week. After a few months, they find that not to be the case and their income is not adequate to cover expenses and draw a salary. Years ago, the author developed an Excel spreadsheet with which one can enter varying assumptions on salary, expenses, and billable hours. An example is provided at the end of this chapter (see Figure 7.1). In your current position, you enjoy paid time off including vacations, holidays, sick time, and professional development. You also spend several hours a day or a week in staff meetings and other meetings not directly related to your work. As a consultant, you will still want paid time off. Instead of meetings, you will spend time developing marketing materials, doing marketing, and getting your name in front of others. After allowing this time, you will likely only have 1,200 or so hours left during which to actually consult and bill. In order to meet your financial goals, it is likely your hourly billing rate will need to be 3–4 times your current hourly salary rate. If you are making $50 per hour, you will need to invoice at perhaps $175 per hour to be financially successful.

Where Do You Market and Want to Consult?

Is your plan to market and consult locally, regionally, or nationally? If you are in a major metropolitan market, there might be enough business within a one- or two-hour commute. If you live elsewhere, you at least need to consider offering your services regionally. The author defines a region as anywhere you can get to in about 4 hours or less. This could include taking a one-hour or so plane ride. A 4-hour drive provides a range of about 200 miles. You need to remember that some of your trips will be for marketing, so the longer the trip and the greater the number of trips, less time will be available to actually bill for services.

In addition to the travel factor, and really more important, is your personal situation. Are you a single parent of school age or younger children? Who will provide the child care or be able to pick up a sick child from school? Are there any personal or family healthcare issues that require attention on short notice? Are you heavily involved in local organizations such that you have commitments one or more evenings per week? If any of these situations are yours, can you and will you make the arrangements or reduce your commitments so you can be away from home overnight or until later in the evening? You will have to consider this if returning from an assignment that is 3 hours away with the last meeting ending at 9 p.m.

How Do You Market?

This depends on whether you plan to be *the* consultant or a subcontractor on a larger project. As a subcontractor, you will have to accept a lower hourly billing rate, but it is likely you will be able to bill more hours per week since you have little or no marketing time. In order to be a subcontractor, the primary contractor must have enough confidence in your ability that his or her reputation is not at risk. More commonly, you will be the consultant. The ideal situation is to be aware of a need that you can satisfy. If your skill set is tied to a software system, you may be able to find out which organizations have purchased but not installed the system, or which organizations have installed the

Development of Annual Consulting Hours & Gross Profit - 2012

COST COMPONENT		Costs based on desired salary level			Med, cost / billed hour
		Low	Medium	High	
Annual salary		$83,200	$114,400	$145,600	$105.93
Base hourly rate of pay @ desired hours per week	40.0	$40.00	$55.00	$70.00	
FICA @6.2% of first $110,100/year (6.2% employer portion only)		5,158	6,826	6,826	6.32
Medicare @ 1.45% for employer without cap		1,206	1,659	2,111	1.54
Other insurances (WC, Dis, FUTA, etc.) estimated percent	4.00%	3,328	4,576	5,824	4.24
Pension plans at maximum contribution of:	15.00%	12,480	17,160	21,840	15.89
Total salary-related costs		$105,373	$144,621	$182,201	$133.91
Total salary-related cost / annual salary ratio		1.27	1.26	1.25	
Annual worked hours @ desired weeks per year	45.0	1,800	1,800	1,800	
Billed hours per year at this percent billed	60.00%	1,080	1,080	1,080	
Billed days per month at this percent billed	60.00%	11.25	11.25	11.25	
Total salary-related cost per billed hour		$97.57	$133.91	$168.71	
Ratio of: total salary-related cost/billed hours / base hourly rate		2.44	2.43	2.41	
What are our other basic costs?		Low	Medium	High	
Health insurance and reimbursed health costs		$6,000	$12,000	$15,000	$11.11
Clerical and office support		$0	$14,400	$30,000	13.33
Office rent		0	4,200	7,200	3.89
Computer and internet costs including website		900	1,500	3,000	1.39
Telephone - regular, fax, and cell phone		1,200	1,800	2,400	1.67
Automobile, including insurance (net of charged miles)		1,200	3,000	6,000	2.78
Office equipment and supplies - not capitalized		520	2,080	3,120	1.93
Repairs and maintenance contracts		260	520	780	0.48
Postage and express mail		120	260	520	0.24
Marketing expense		500	2,000	4,000	1.85
Entertainment		120	260	520	0.24
Travel, lodging and meals - not reimbursed		1,300	2,600	5,200	2.41
Professional dues and subscriptions		1,000	2,000	3,000	1.85
Professional society meetings expense		1,000	2,000	3,000	1.85
Accounting and legal fees		2,000	3,000	4,000	2.78
Director's Fees (return on equity)		0	1,000	3,000	0.93
Subcontractor consulting expense @ 80%		0	8,000	16,000	7.41
Subcontractor consulting income		0	(10,000)	(20,000)	(9.26)
Minimum State taxes and fees		400	600	800	0.56
Interest Income (checkbook, etc.)		0	(100)	(300)	(0.09)
Interest and bank account expense		100	180	300	0.17
Miscellaneous expenses		260	520	1,040	0.48
Subtotal expenses		$16,880	$51,820	$88,580	$47.98
Total salary and non-salary related costs		$122,253	$196,441	$270,781	$181.89
Expense cost per billed hour		$15.63	$47.98	$82.02	
Total salary-related cost per billed hour		97.57	133.91	168.71	
Total cost per billed hour		113.20	181.89	250.72	
Profit at percent of total cost	10.00%	11.32	18.19	25.07	
Gross consulting rate @ billed hour percentage of:	60.00%	$124.52	$200.08	$275.80	
Ratio of: total cost per billed hours / base hourly rate		3.11	3.64	3.94	
Billed hours per year at alternative percentage of:	75.00%	1,350.00	1,350.00	1,350.00	
Billed days per month at this percent billed	75.00%	14.06	14.06	14.06	
Gross consulting rate @ billed hour percentage of:	75.00%	$99.61	$160.06	$220.64	

Figure 7.1 Development of annual consulting hours and gross profit.

software but are having implementation issues. The issues could involve medical staff or employee dissatisfaction, lost charges, other billing issues, or the recent departure of in-house expertise.

In the more usual situation, you are starting out, so you have to make your presence known to the decision makers. Traditional marketing methods include announcements, magazine ads, and letters of introduction, perhaps with an enclosed brochure. These methods rarely work and are almost never cost justified. A good way to get your name in front of others is to become active in professional organizations by serving on committees, attending local meetings, and national conferences. Your marketing should include a website, and you need a domain name. Do you want it to end with dot-com, dot-net, dot-org, or something else? Your website should look professional and it should be refreshed frequently. Information on the site should include your skill set, any client endorsements, and examples of the value you would bring to the next client.

Getting the word out through your professional organization and colleagues is a good way to start. Let them know you are now a consultant and what you can offer to their organization or to others in their networks. Introduce yourself and your new role at local chapter meetings. If you have some unique knowledge, you might present a free webinar or offer to speak at local meetings. You might want to join the local Chamber of Commerce as many chambers have forums for introducing yourself and your service. In addition, many offer discounted services including healthcare insurance, website hosting or listing, other types of insurance, discount phone service, and the like.

You will have to make some cold calls. Do not be surprised when you encounter difficulty in getting past the gatekeepers (the administrative assistants) to the decision makers. Be persistent and courteous as it may take several tries. If you can obtain the email address of the decision maker, you can try sending an email. Again, the gatekeeper will likely monitor the emails. Try sending the emails at times when the assistant might not be available, and do the same with phone calls. Many executives work late while their assistants may leave at 5 p.m. If you call at 5:15 p.m., you might get through. Keep your calls short and to the point. Do your homework before even making the call. Go to the organization's website and read the recent articles including any that specifically mention the person you intend to call. Google the organization and the individual so you will have talking points when you call them. It is likely you will have to make multiple contacts before you are successful in speaking with the decision maker. Remember, even if you are not successful this time, you want to imprint your name in their minds so the next time consulting assistance is needed, you will be on the short list.

How Do You Price the Services Rendered?

The first step of identifying your hourly or daily consulting rate has been made. You have met with the prospective client and have obtained a project scope and timetable. Both parts are necessary in order to set a consulting fee. If it is a small project, for example, less than 10 or 15 days, you do not have to worry too much about the timetable. It will take a little time for the client to get ready for the service and it will usually take some time to obtain any data you need. Then you will analyze the data, develop your recommendations, and prepare your report. The problem is more prevalent with larger projects where you have limited time for additional clients or for marketing. An axiom in consulting is that you should market when you are busy so that you are never without work. A related issue is that it can take almost as much time to market a small project as a large or long-term project. If the project scope and timeline are clear, you can confidently provide a specific quote. For example, this will be a 10-day project at a rate of $1,600 per day for a total consulting fee of $16,000, plus expenses not to exceed $2,000. You might include language such as: "The project will include one site visit of 3 days for data collection and a return visit to present findings and recommendations. Additional visits will be invoiced at the rate of $200 per hour, plus expenses."

For a longer project or one where the consultant cannot control the timeframe, it will likely be necessary to quote a project fee range. An example could be: "Based on the project scope and timeline contained in this proposal, the estimated consulting time is 36–40 days at a rate of $1,600 per day. The consulting fee of $57,600–$64,000 will not be exceeded without prior written authorization. The estimated expenses are based on a maximum of 8 site visits and are estimated to be no more than $7,500."

In addition to setting the fees, it is necessary to define client responsibilities so that you do not spend more consulting time than projected. Client responsibilities could include scheduling all meetings and interviews, assuring that client staff are available as scheduled, providing the requested data in a usable format, and providing the necessary data in a specific format. For example, you want an Excel file with the volume data, or patient-related data rather than a PDF file or hard copy.

Getting that next engagement is just as important as getting the first engagement. If you are doing one-time projects for multiple clients, you will have to spend a considerable amount of time prospecting and marketing your services. If you can provide a range of consulting services or if the service you provide can be used in multiple cost centers, the ideal situation is to establish an ongoing relationship with a limited number of clients. Implementation assistance is almost always a good situation for both the client and the consultant. You need references for your next client. You do not need a great project to be implemented incorrectly or not at all.

How Do You Invoice for Services Rendered?

For a short-duration project, you could simply submit an invoice along with or following presentation of the report. If the nature of the project does not require a report and there is a clear ending, the invoice can be sent at that time. For longer-duration projects you have two main alternative invoicing methods: periodic or phase. Periodic invoicing usually is performed monthly for time and services in the month just ended. Depending on the expected expenses, you might even have an initial invoice to provide some cash flow. Phase invoicing can be used when there are discrete project phases and the duration of each phase is not much more than one month. You do not want to wait several months before submitting your first invoice. For a fixed-fee project, you can break the invoice into one more increment than the project length. For example, if the project is expected to take four months, you can invoice 20% at the start, 20% per month for three months, and the final 20% upon project completion.

The check is in the mail. Or, when will you receive payment for services rendered? This depends on the financial situation of the client and perhaps on terms written into the consulting agreement. A typical payment cycle is 45–60 days after the invoice is submitted. In the current environment, the monthly invoices can be sent electronically to avoid mail delays. Most hospitals will still send a paper check rather than making an electronic transfer of funds. With this payment cycle it is easy to understand why a new consultant needs adequate personal financing or a second income when getting started.

Do you really want to become an independent consultant? If you have answered yes to the questions posed in this chapter and you are confident in your abilities, why not? You may not become rich, but you can have a very rewarding life with more flexibility than continuing to work for others.

WHAT DO MANAGEMENT ENGINEERS DO?

Chapter 8

Instigating Change and Engaging Teams

Jean Ann Larson and Amanda Mewborn

Contents

Importance of Change Management

Industrial engineers or management engineers are change agents wherever they work and whatever their job title. Their jobs entail helping teams and organizations change by improving processes and outcomes. They do this through improving processes, redesigning layouts and workspaces, and implementing new technologies and systems—just to name a few examples. This chapter discusses the need for industrial engineers to fully understand this key aspect of their role. It is often the least studied and the least understood, yet it can have a large impact on the success of the engineer's endeavors.

Industrial engineers in healthcare, often known as management engineers, need to be even more aware of their role as change management professionals. Their projects put them firmly at the intersection of processes, people, and technology. One of the major advantages that they bring to their projects is that their training and expertise uniquely qualifies them to ensure that the project recommendations and outcomes factor in all aspects leading to a solution that optimizes people, processes, and technology. The management engineer is the one responsible for making sure that a systems approach is taken.

The industrial engineer's role in managing change in healthcare may be more important than the engineer's technical skills. In healthcare, many decisions are not based on data or facts, and instead are based on politics or power. It is crucially important to have people onboard and supportive of changes, as most change cannot be forced upon people in healthcare. For example, analyses may suggest that an emergency department needs two trauma rooms, but the trauma physicians may insist that they want four trauma rooms. Often, in situations like these, the hospital will choose to build four trauma rooms, despite analyses indicating that only two trauma rooms are necessary. Change management can be the key to the industrial engineer's success in healthcare, where decisions are not based solely on objective data and analyses.

Why Is Team Engagement So Important for Effective Change Management?

Though the management engineer's ability to instigate and drive change is critical to the success of the project, he or she cannot do this alone. The most successful engineer works with the project sponsor or team leader to make sure that all the stakeholders and team members are on board with the team's purpose and the project initiative. And though it seems like taking these steps to engage the team members up front is slowing the project when senior leaders are pressing for urgency, in the long run, going slow in the initial phases will not only speed completion of the project or initiative, it will ensure success and may even be the difference between success and failure. Similar to the Plan-Do-Study-Act (PDSA) cycle, the better the quality of planning and the more thought that is put into the project up front, the more successful the outcome of the project.

When Do You Engage Teams around Change?

In the healthcare industry, it is rare for an engineer to work completely alone. Granted, he or she may spend time in the office doing extensive analysis or even documentation. However, even those seemingly solitary activities require significant input and review by team members who are close to the process—whether that process is a business process or a care delivery process. It is important for the engineer, regardless of role on the project (e.g., operations analyst, facilitator, project manager, or lean expert), to quickly get to know the members of the project team, from the senior executive to the person who only occasionally is part of the process but who has a part to play. The sooner the engineer can begin to establish a good reputation for trust, objectivity, and his or her competence, the better. A few examples of ways to build trust and establish competence include:

- Inviting a team member to lunch, so that each person can gain an understanding of the other's background, skills, and training, as well as learn a little about each other's personal lives. This information helps to understand each other's value system, and identify what is probably important to the other person. When one knows what's important to each member of a team, facilitation of the team becomes much easier.
- Request an opportunity to observe operations in areas that are unfamiliar. This will provide the industrial engineer with information on the culture and flow of work in the area.

Additionally, the engineer will be able to engage staff members in conversation, understanding what is working and what could be improved at the front line. This also gives the engineer an advantage when the group may be discussing the details of how work is done in a given area, as the engineer will have experienced it firsthand.

■ Seek out opportunities to get to know people personally. Perhaps your child plays the same sport and the two of you can sit together during a game and develop a personal rapport. Or perhaps the two of you share a hobby that you can enjoy together—such as movies, plays, hiking, or sports teams. Any personal connection that can be developed with others can carry the engineer a great distance in regards to change management.

How Do You Engage Teams?

In order to engage the team, the engineer starts by getting to know team members one individual at a time. He or she meets with the senior executive or project sponsor to get a clear understanding of the project purpose and the importance to the organization of that purpose. Ideally, the project is important to accomplishing one of the organization's key strategies. Sometimes listening to the sponsor talk about the project also helps the sponsor and engineer clarify project scope, boundaries, and even the real or more fundamental reasons for undertaking the project. This is critical and can help the engineer be invaluable to the project sponsor and the team in that he or she can keep an eye on making sure the project meets the stated expectations, as well as those that are not stated outright.

In addition to time spent with the project sponsor, the engineer may want to spend some time up front getting to know key players and some of the key challenges of the processes and systems that impact the project. Even before the initial kickoff meeting, he or she can begin building trust and confidence in the team and in their ability to work together to accomplish significant goals.

During the initial kickoff meeting, it is important that the senior executive, project sponsor, team leader, as well as the informal leaders, make sure that everyone on the team understands the purpose of the project, why it is important, and why each team member was selected to be on the team. Team members also need to understand the expectations of the team (i.e., what leadership wants the team to do), and the expectations of each individual. The engineer should take this opportunity to clarify his or her role with the team and make it clear whether he is the facilitator, analyst, or project manager—depending on the specific role—and how he or she will help or support the team. It is also important that the team understands what his role is *not*. He is not there to do all the work and solve all the problems. Although the engineer has unique perspectives, skills, and competencies, the project and its success or failure belong to the team.

How Do You Help Teams through Change?

The first thing to keep in mind about helping teams get through change and use it to their advantage is that a team is made up of unique individuals, each with his or her perspectives, concerns, and biases. The purpose of the project must first appeal to each and every member of the team. The initiative should be one that they individually and as a team want to be a part of. The initial kick off meeting should be part motivation, encouragement, and pep talk, making sure that team members understand the importance of the project initiative and how important each of them are both individually and collectively to the success of the project. The engineer serving as the facilitator or project manager should make sure that the team has the skills, tools, and time required to work together and individually outside of team meetings to get the work done. The project sponsor and team leader, along with the engineer, manage the group process and morale. Team meetings need to be productive and engaging so that team members look forward to the meetings and feel that they are accomplishing something that will truly better serve the customer—which could be other department colleagues, physicians, patients, or even the community—making it worth the effort and hard work that they will put into the project.

Good facilitation and group process skills are critical. In this book there is an excellent chapter on facilitation that is recommended for those engineers who take on the role of facilitator. There are also excellent references cited at the end of that chapter for those who want to learn more or further develop their skills. A classic book that has served many facilitators well is *The Team Handbook* (Scholtes, Joiner, & Streibel, 2003).

Another key skill to help manage the change and move the project and team along is project management. Again, there is an excellent chapter in this book that gives a great overview of project management regardless of the engineer's role on the project.

Barriers

Due to the fact that we are writing this chapter and as witnessed by the more than 70% of change initiatives that fail (Blanchard, 2010; Kotter, 1995; Senge et al., 1999), there are many barriers and obstacles to success. The best advice is to be aware of them, learn from other's successes and failures, and make sure to employ the best facilitation, project management, process, and systems-thinking skills. We have listed a few of the more common barriers or obstacles to watch out for.

- Lack of awareness (or lack of a business case) for why the project must be successful. Just announcing a change initiative and telling people what is going to happen, generally backfires. People need information both about the impact on the organization and how it might affect them personally. With a top-down announcement or mandate, trust is lowered and resentment sinks in. All team members must be part of the process and part of developing the solutions and the future state.
- Overemphasis on the technology or the new system. Certainly, implementing new technology or an organizationwide information system can seem daunting. But it will be the people working with that new system or technology that will make it work or doom it to failure. Do not underemphasize the importance of the team and the individuals to making the project a success.
- Focusing on the clock or calendar (time) versus the compass (where you want to go.) Though team meetings need to have tight agendas and need to keep moving, a good facilitator recognizes a breakthrough or a need for more discussion and keeps an eye more on the goal than on the clock.
- Ineffective team meetings that seem to last forever and go on and on with no apparent agenda, process, or valuable outcomes, can be a slow death to the project. People want to feel that they are part of something that will make a difference and that their time is well spent.
- A perceived solution that the team leaders or executive sponsor is using the team to implement. If a management decision is made, don't manipulate the team into buying it. Make clear what the team's purpose is and what their true role is. Do not charter a team to justify a good or bad management decision. It will lead to cynicism and cripple future team efforts.

Enablers

Despite the many barriers that can prevent successful change efforts, many enablers can ensure desired outcomes. Some of the most common enablers of change management success can be understood through the ADKAR model. For more information on the ADKAR model, check out Jeffrey M. Hiatt's (2006) book *ADKAR: A Model for Change in Business, Government and our Community*. According to Hiatt, the acronym ADKAR is derived from the following components, which must be achieved by the project team in this sequence:

- *Awareness* of the need for change—establishing a clear rationale and compelling reason to change. Examples may include gathering information from the customer as well as communication from management.
- *Desire* to participate and support the change—each team member must have a reason to engage in the team and make a change. The reasons may be as simple as respect for the leaders involved or hope for a better future.
- *Knowledge* on how to change—change management does not come naturally to most people. For most, the mantra is, "Change is good, as long as it's not affecting me!" To ensure success, the entire team must be trained on change and have the requisite education to lead others through change.
- *Ability* to implement required skills and behaviors—having knowledge is not enough if we are unable to apply that knowledge to achieve the desired results. As with anything new that is learned, application is when the learning becomes real. In this stage, the important elements for success include coaching and mentoring to encourage people to continue along the path and stick with the plan.
- *Reinforcement* to sustain the change—after the change is implemented, the hard work of sustainment takes over. There are many enablers to ensure sustained success. Recognition and providing incentives are two ways to reinforce the change and maintain the new way of doing business.

There are many enablers of change management success, and awareness of the enablers can ensure that change is managed to include the enablers and ensure success.

Roles and Responsibilities

As with any project, establishing clear roles and responsibilities is key to success, and each role is described in the following with regard to the responsibilities of the role in change management.

- Project Sponsor—The project sponsor is usually a very senior executive who oversees operations or finance across the enterprise. For example, a chief operating officer or chief financial officer may serve in this role. The project sponsor is responsible for setting the vision and purpose of the project, and establishing a sense of importance and urgency for addressing the project or issue.
- Project Champion—The project champion is a senior leader who is responsible for the area or department where the change will be taking place. The project champion is closer to the operations and more aware of the details and dynamics of the project area. As an example, the director of nursing may be the project champion for a project focusing on improvement

of nursing workflow. The key roles of the project champion for change management are communication with other leaders and staff and removing barriers that the team encounters.

■ Project Manager—The project manager is responsible for identifying all tasks and sequencing of the tasks to accomplish the project, along with coordinating various resources and following up to ensure tasks are completed on time and correctly. The key roles of the project manager in a change initiative include coordinating and ensuring all tasks are completed at the right time by the right party, and communicating any barriers to the project champion.

■ Project Team—The project team includes the people assigned to work on the project. These are the folks who actually do the work. The key roles of the project team related to change management are communicating with peers about the project and reasons for change, and completing assigned tasks in a thorough and timely manner.

The role of the industrial engineer in change management varies depending on his role on the project. The industrial engineer may be asked to serve the team as the project sponsor, project champion, or project manager; in these cases, the engineer would fill the roles previously described. However, if the industrial engineer is asked to be part of the project team, the engineer's role would include that described previously along with other support, such as:

■ Conducting analyses, such as time studies, process maps, spaghetti diagrams, or simulation, to demonstrate compelling, objective reasons for change and to identify potential better ways of conducting business.
■ Studying workflow and identifying waste and methods to reduce waste.
■ Identifying the "what's in it for me" for each group of people, and developing tools to communicate the information and engage people to support the change initiative.
■ Facilitating the group process used throughout the project.

The industrial engineer is uniquely positioned to support the team and organization through change management initiatives.

Conclusion

The topic of change management is complicated and often overlooked. However, change management is the key to success of any project. The industrial engineer is uniquely positioned to ensure that the solutions implemented are ones that optimize people, processes, and technology, at a system or enterprise level. Change management in healthcare is very important as decisions are often based on politics and power instead of data and objective facts. Establishing personal relationships and rapport with team members is a key element to successful change management, as these relationships help to establish trust, objectivity, and a mutual understanding of skill sets and competence. When engaging teams, it is important to clearly establish project purpose, scope, and the roles of each team member. Beyond understanding roles, team members need to know why they were selected for the team, and what skills they must bring to the group. Without the right skills, tools, and time, no project can be successful. After managing the change throughout the project, it is important to ensure the outcomes of the project are sustained. If the change and the associated results cannot be realized and sustained over time, what is the purpose of any project? An industrial engineer has many skills and tools that can assist with both the technical and the human factors associated with change management. It is critical for the industrial engineer to make sure that the two types of skills are well balanced when working in a healthcare environment.

References

Blanchard, K. (2010). "Mastering the Art of Change." *The Training Journal,* http://www.kenblanchard.com/img/pub/Blanchard_Mastering_the_Art_of_Change.pdf.

Hiatt, J. M. (2006). *ADKAR: A Model for Change in Business, Government and Our Community.* Loveland, Colorado: Prosci.

Kotter, J. (1995). "Leading Change: Why Transformation Efforts Fail." *Harvard Business Review* (March–April).

Scholtes, P. R., Joiner, B. L., AND Streibel, B. J. (2003). *The Team Handbook,* 3rd ed. Madison, WI: Oriel Incorporated.

Senge, P., Kleiner, A., Roberts, C., Ross, R. B., Roth, G., and Smith, B. J. (1999). *The Dance of Change: The Challenges to Sustaining Momentum in Learning Organizations.* New York: Doubleday/Currency.

Chapter 9

Raising Your Project Management IQ

Bennetta R. Raby

Contents

Introduction

Everyone at one point or another in their career, community, or personal life performs the act of managing a project. A project can be as apparent as implementing a new system, a new process, or setting a plan in place for remodeling your home. For most situations, the nature and dynamics of a project are much more complicated. The for-profit and not-for-profit landscapes alike are mired with an arsenal of initiatives geared at quickly fixing the next new problem, budgetary constraint, or providing the appearance that we are making progress. The problem is that most of these initiatives end up never seeing the light of day because a key component is missing. The basic understanding of what a project is and how it flows from start to end is not clearly understood at all levels.

What Is a Project?

First, do you really have a project? Let's dive into how a project is defined. The word *project* originates from the Latin word *projectum*, which translates to "cast something forward." The word itself originally meant "one thing that comes before another happens." When the word was accepted into the English vocabulary, it referred to the *arrangement* of something, not the physical act of carrying out the plan. By definition, a *project* is a special endeavor that has a specific goal, utilizes resources, and has a distinct start and end. That said, you might think that just about anything can fit into that mold. However, it is important to recognize that this "special" endeavor is being executed to solve a particular problem or address an issue that would not ordinarily be addressed if it weren't for the creation of the project. In the many years that project management has been practiced, the very best way to digest it is at its most basic, commonsense level.

A project only happens one time. Performing monthly security risk assessments on network computers is *not* a project. It's not a project because it is the performance of an ongoing set of routine tasks, *routine* being the operative word. Conversely, detecting that the network has significant risks, and there is a need to determine a plan for reviewing, arranging, and carrying out the assessment for the first time *is* a project.

A project contains three distinct restrictions, which are also known as *project constraints*. *Time*, *cost*, and *quality* are defined as constraints because the engagement is naturally limited by these three related factors that must be considered. We cannot change one constraint without affecting at least one of the other two. For example, if the specifications require more work to complete the project, then the costs will most likely increase. Good project management is getting the job done on time, within budget, and according to specifications. Furthermore, a predetermined budget for your project, a rigid deadline, and limited availability of a process owner or a resource with a specific skill are common constraints. In other words, constraints are any factors that can limit your options in how you complete the project and achieve the project goals. These constraints must be documented, their risks examined, and then the project manager must plan how to meet the project objectives within the identified constraints.

Roles and Responsibilities within a Project

As leaders or the visionaries of a project, the engagement will need the very special attention of several people—a sponsor, a project manager, and a team. How the resources are solicited and secured is just as important as the identification of the initiative. Within the project setting, a clear definition of the roles and responsibilities that individuals play will be critical to the success of the project. In addition, a person may play more than one role simultaneously. Individuals must clearly understand the documented roles they play to know what responsibilities they have in making assessments, carrying out tasks, reporting progress, and reviewing the work that has been performed. Clearly defining the roles raises the probability of the project being judged a success by: (a) bringing clarity to the project environment, (b) predetermining how each task will be completed, (c) identifying who has decision-making responsibilities and authority, and (d) reducing confusion.

A simple document outlining the role definitions and showing *who does what* should be created once resources have been identified and cleared by their designated manager. Each one of the roles listed in this chapter is necessary for a successful project. The *project sponsor*, also called the *internal customer*, ties the project to organizational business goals or strategic plans. The sponsor typically should know the *what*, *why*, and *who* of the project. He or she has the final authority on the project, helps the team to secure resources, and resolves project issues. The *project manager* is responsible for managing the project using the strategies covered in the remainder of this chapter. Project managers are required to organize and direct their assigned projects. This may include organization and direction of tasks from the start to the end of the project by coordinating the project team and managing the budgetary resources to ensure the project runs smoothly and is done on time. The *project team* represents the combined group of individuals who are responsible for performing or managing the performance for each of the functional areas of work. Examples of functional areas may include information technology, nursing, finance, management engineering, or process improvement. Team members must be clear on the fact that if they don't agree with something, don't understand an assignment or task, or have a concern, it is critical that they speak up as soon as possible so that early issues don't become bigger problems toward the end of the project.

Project Management Critical Success Factors

As introduced in the first part of this chapter, there are a few critical success factors that can make all the difference in ensuring that a project will achieve its final goals at the project's conclusion. Being aware of these factors and bringing them to bear can save the leadership of the project a lot of headaches down the road and can keep them out of "fire-fighting mode." Strong sponsorship is arguably the most important success factor for a project because not only does the sponsor hold the key to the vision of what needs to be accomplished, but due to their commitment to seeing the engagement through, they will validate for those that have a vested interest why the project is critical to the future success of the organization.

Following the full life-cycle phases of a project ensures the timely and effective completion of the project and is the foundation of the initiative. Based on international standards, the specific phases of the project life cycle are: *initiation*, *planning*, *execution*, *control*, and *close*. An easy to remember acronym is IPECC. The phases are defined and described as follows:

(a) **Initiation:** The initial idea for a project is carefully examined to determine whether or not it benefits the organization and supports or enables the organization's strategic plan.

(b) **Planning:** A project plan and project charter containing the scope (body of work) outlines the work to be performed and desired outcomes. During this phase, the team should be developed and recruited, the budget and schedule created, and a kickoff meeting coordinated.

(c) **Execution:** The project resources work efforts are carried out, and deliverables and milestones are met.

(d) **Control:** The project managers will compare what was planned and the actual progress to plan, as resources perform the scheduled work. During this phase, the project manager makes the necessary approved adjustments to keep the project healthy and on track.

(e) **Close:** Upon the completion of all projects, final client acceptance/approval and evaluation of the outcomes are performed to highlight the project success and learn from the project experience and history.

Starting a phase before the prior one is complete is acceptable, but it does carry some risk that must be managed by the project manager.

Attributes of a Successful Project

Project management must be accepted as a *norm* within the culture of an organization. If the discipline is treated as a one time tool that has been infused to provide a quick fix to long-standing problems, it will always fail. Instead, the discipline of project management is just that. It is a *discipline*, and it provides a structured approach to identifying and addressing organizational goals and issues. Of course, no organization wants to get lost in the abyss of processes, details, and schedules, but envisioning and executing projects is serious business.

The Project Management Institute (PMI) is the most credible and internationally recognized professional organization for PM professionals, and the road to certification can take several years. Most practitioners of project management start out in a very organic role as a team lead, supervisor, or as an executive who has been asked to manage an important initiative. Not everyone demonstrates the desire to become a career project manager or project management office (PMO) director. However, those who aspire to function in that role usually seek to further their studies via a formal certification as a Project Management Professional (PMP), graduate studies, or professional training. Many organizations still seek individuals who possess either a PMP and/or a master's in project management.

A common mistake that organizations make with these highly sought-after, highly compensated individuals, is that the organization puts out an all points bulletin to find them and recruit them. Upon arrival in the organization, the new project managers are then strapped down with 10–15 projects that have no link to what's vital or strategic. While there, they work on less important projects, and the organization's executives begin to ask why the organization employs these high-priced individuals. If key stakeholders in the organization initially buy into the fact that project management is a mainstay and basic foundation to the accomplishment of every strategic initiative, then the project managers' help and guidance can be ensured. Furthermore, it enables leaders to find the courage to motivate others to remain focused on ever-present problems such as resource utilization and budget management.

Every project requires a vision that is identified, defined, and linked to the existence of the business. If a project is not tied to a business driver, it will perish. It is during the initiation phase that the overall objective is identified, and this is where the real essence and value of the project becomes clear and manifest, not the execution. Keep in mind that successful implementations are 80% people, processes, and culture, and 20% software, hardware, and technology. Early on in the initiation phase, the sponsor and the project manager should sit down and obtain a clear understanding of the what, how, and when of the project. It doesn't have to be a perfect 15-page document of details; it just needs to be concise enough to tell the story. This will keep the charter and the scope at a commonsense level where everyone from the grassroots up to senior management can understand the purpose of the project and why the organization is investing resources to complete the project.

Project Killers

Though it is an unpleasant topic, it is good to be aware of what can kill a project. Every leader or project sponsor believes that his or her idea is the winning key to success for taking the company to the next level. However, a common fault is to think that a half-baked idea is a truly viable project. This is where the damage starts because a project must be vetted through the initiation and planning phases discussed earlier in order to validate that it is a reasonable endeavor. Other potential "gotchas" include:

a) Not taking the time to identify and get the project sponsor fully onboard and behind the project.

b) Mismatching novice- and expert-level project management resources to low or highly complex projects.
c) Setting impractical goals and timelines that push the limits beyond what is reasonable.
d) Allowing a project to span a longer timeframe without including smaller, manageable phases.
e) Not establishing project performance metrics that will provide a pulse check throughout the project life cycle to track whether the project is still on course.
f) Projects involve some uncertainty, but the timeline and deliverables should not be changed every time a challenge is presented.

If we fail to define the key project parameters, the chance of project failure increases. Whether it's a meeting, brief chat in the hallway, phone call, or via email, it is critical for the project manager to work with project participants to uncover this information.

What Is a Program?

The main characteristics of a *program* are: (a) the outcomes of the program are driven by strategic targets or significant changes to the organization, (b) there are significant risks but also great gains at stake, and (c) the overall payback is achieved over a lengthier duration. Program management is the compilation of initiatives and projects that together are designed to accomplish a key strategic business objective. As mentioned earlier, it is imperative to know what the major business drivers are for the work being done. Projects can carry a hefty price tag in terms of both money and physical and human resources, but there is a much higher cost incurred due to the length and scope being quite complex. Programs in the governmental realm cost taxpayers millions of dollars and generally span several years, which heightens the stakes and increases the risk of failure.

Within all organizations there is a need to focus on handling very complex initiatives. These initiatives may combine system releases, product and service delivery, business process reengineering, a new partnership, and so on, and can result in wholesale, systematic changes to the organization. Program management is intended to go beyond the system in scope. It includes the project's business purpose, the operational processes that will be affected, many departments, and a multitude of participants. A program is a collection of many individual projects.

All Good Programs Must Come to an End

Although the systems and processes within a program must be operable by quality and reliability standards, a program may never be deemed as complete. This means that programs include continuous process improvement and ideally improve from year to year. However, as with project management principles, the ultimate question is, "Have the overall results of the program accomplished the main objectives?" Overall program efforts and their large resource pools typically develop greater momentum than standalone projects. This drive and forward motion helps programs accomplish serious outcomes and deliverables, but this very momentum can make programs resistant to change or closure. Lack of vision, changes in vision, and poor direction can lead a program to consume enormous amounts of money in relatively short time periods without providing real additional value or useful results.

Fortunately, applying sound techniques and practices specific to program management can enhance an effort's chances of success and reduce risk. For enterprise-scale work efforts, these practices can enable an organization to pursue its business strategy and remain competitive. One of the keys to successfully managing and completing any program is the development of a comprehensive plan of action or plan of record with milestones. Once the final milestone is met, the overall program should be deemed complete. If another generation of the program should morph, then an entirely new program should be started. The most important thing to remember is if a plan is devised for program closure directly in the beginning, then closing down the program is more of a possibility. A few key tips for ensuring that a project will close correctly are: (a) make certain that all program deliverables and milestone documentation have been completed and delivered, (b) create a closure report that summarizes what steps were taken to close the program and how the program will be supported in a normal production environment, and (c) obtain formal sign-off from executive sponsors or the project steering committee. The best forum for keeping the fire burning until everything is fully baked is to hold a lessons-learned or closeout celebration. All good programs and projects must come to an end, but that does not mean that the process isn't allowed to provide some fun and camaraderie for the participants.

Project solutions to common issues are a combination of people, processes, and knowledge. There is no "magic button" for getting more projects done. However, it takes forethought, time, and basic know-how to plan, set goals, and tie them to strategies prior to embarking on projects. Project managers must be bold enough to contribute and give feedback when executives' expectations are unrealistic. Leaders must be bold enough to learn what project management is and how it can change their future. Team members must get on board once projects have begun and task assignments have been communicated. It is everyone's responsibility to raise their project management IQ.

Chapter 10

Workforce Management

David Z. Cowan and Joyce T. Siegele

Contents

Workforce management is one of the most important functions of healthcare management. It includes productivity management, which is traditionally in the purview of the management engineer. But the role of the management engineer logically expanded to a broader scope as the healthcare workforce has grown in number and complexity. Labor is the largest and the most variable of an organization's expense. Therefore, it is often the first and most important target of expense management. It is a ripe application field for the management engineer applying modeling, optimization, process design, and statistical control techniques. This chapter presents the workforce management concept, the ways it can be impacted, and the tools of the management engineer.

Workforce management does not stand alone and should be addressed in the context of many other initiatives and organizational changes. In other chapters you will have considered the impact of information technology, facilities design, quality management, and customer satisfaction. In each of these, labor planning has a significant and often a primary role. In every new information system installation, staffing must be adjusted to take advantage of the new capabilities—a new work process might be required: staff trained in a new skill, a different number of staff, and staff scheduled differently. The same is true with a new facility. How the pods are designed in the emergency department (ED) depends on the staffing patterns of the nurses and the doctors. In one project, it was determined that nursing in the ED had a assignment of one nurse to 8 patients and a physician has a 1–16 assignment. Therefore, pods were designed with 8 exam rooms with 2 pods connected linearly. Work design and staffing are integral to almost any major change in an organization. Finally, good customer service is impossible without staff positioned and trained in the appropriate places.

Understanding Workforce Management

Workforce management reflects a continuum of management from design to control including design, deploy, adjust, plan, and control. Each phase has a unique set of decisions and can employ a variety of engineering tools.

Design: How is work organized? This can be from the micro level of the definition of each job to the macro level of structuring the organization of workers into departments and divisions to achieve the organization's mission. Work design is the process of matching the work to the skills and capability of the workforce. At the individual job level, work descriptions and performance metrics can be developed. The work can be organized into teams and shifts, and these into departments. Working with a laboratory or environmental services department, it is important to understand the volume and flow of work. This will guide the organization of work units— teams of varied skilled workers best suited to produce the needed service or tasks. Consider the work of phlebotomy (collecting patient blood samples for diagnostic laboratory testing). Is there enough consistent work to justify a dedicated staff (as in a large hospital), or should the work be distributed among a larger group? This workforce analysis compares the increased speed and quality expected from a single group of experts to the flexibility of having a larger group of multiskilled workers who can provide the service. A challenge in environmental services is often found in turning over rooms after a patient discharge. If a housekeeper is assigned to a unit that has 2–3 simultaneous discharges, the last room might not be ready for several hours. But if the turnover team was a housewide service, then 3 housekeepers could be deployed to the unit and all rooms would be available in 30 minutes. All of this is a part of job design and the organization of work units.

Design at a macro level considers how departments and divisions are structured, and how patients flow through the departments and divisions, paying particular attention to hand-offs. Traditionally, hospitals were organized by functional department, for example: radiology, med-surg nursing unit, and housekeeping. A trend toward a customer-focused organization has been used in many larger organizations. A women's center, or a cancer center can have many of the services (such as imaging, environmental service, and registration) in their management purview. A matrix organization is used in many mid-sized organizations. This means that the departments are usually organized around function, but there is a separate leadership that is organized around service lines. Functional organization may achieve the greater levels of efficiency, but service line organizations can often provide better patient-centered care. Each method has its own benefits and challenges. The management engineer should help in the design of new structures or in the consideration of reorganizing existing structure.

Deploy: Select the right staff, train them, and place them to accomplish the work. The work of the healthcare organization is varied, variable, and sometimes difficult to predict. Matching the staff to the work involves determining how many staff are needed, with which skills, and then scheduling to the predicted workload. Staffing studies are conducted to define the workload and set staffing targets. Scheduling staff in a 24/7 operation can be quite complicated. Whether the organization uses a manual or a computerized scheduling system, management engineers best understand the theories of these scheduling systems and can provide support and coaching to use them to effectively deploy staff.

Adjust: Because of the variance in workload and inherent challenges in labor (vacation, illness, etc.), THERE can be a need to make changes monthly, daily, and in some cases even hourly. To hit staffing targets, managers cannot routinely staff to the highest possible workload. The management engineer and the scheduling systems will help the manager find the right staffing level that allows the manager to dynamically flex staffing up or down on a weekly, daily, or hourly basis. The management engineer can help establish the appropriate size and use of staffing pools, agency nurses, and overtime. Managing the daily staff assignments and adjusting the number of staff on the nursing unit is particularly important. The work requirements of a patient are quite dynamic, and change on an hourly basis. Unique tools are developed to help a nursing manager adjust the total number of staff needed on a shift-by-shift basis and to make assignments of patients to nurses to balance the workload more evenly. A simple table reflecting the census level and the staffing requirements (the staffing matrix) is a common tool to support these staffing adjustments. The staffing matrix will be discussed later in this chapter. Patient classification systems used widely 20 years ago are returning to more common use. The work requirements of a patient are predicted by 5–20 indicators on a shift-by-shift basis to estimate the number of hours of care needed and to assign a patient care level (classification). The manager uses this patient classification to assign the correct number of patients to each nurse so the totaled care hours of the assigned patients can be accomplished within the nurse's shift. If there is more workload than nurses, based on the classification system, the nurse manager can request additional staffing.

Plan: Because labor is the largest expense of a healthcare organization, it is also usually the centerpiece of the annual budgeting process. The management engineer can help forecast work volumes, update staffing standards, and readjust targets to help the organization balance the revenues and the expenses. The budget process is rarely easy. When expenses exceed revenues, staffing budgets are the first targets for adjustment. Sitting in on these negotiations while understanding the details and the big picture, allows the management engineer to offer valuable advice in this planning process.

Control: Labor is not only the single largest expense of a healthcare organization, it is also the most manageable. In efforts to balance expenses with revenues, labor must be watched carefully on a monthly and sometimes a daily basis. Statistical process control is the basis of labor productivity monitoring, the centerpiece of the workforce management system that supports managers in controlling their labor expense. Organizations usually use industry benchmarking systems to keep in step with industry trends, not only in staffing, but in other aspects of expense and quality.

Potential Impact

Labor is approximately half of a healthcare organization's expense. Many things affect the labor costs, and all of them can be managed:

■ **Number of staff:** The most basic productivity systems match hours worked to the volume of output (for the inpatient unit it is hours/patient day, the clinic it is sometime expressed as the reciprocal) for patients seen per provider shift. If the number of patients is increased, the number of staff will need to be increased as well. The number of staff should be considered, not just the number of hours. The balance of full-time and part-time staff impacts staff effectiveness, scheduling flexibility, and labor cost. Full-time staff typically functions at a higher level of efficiency and teamwork due to their familiarity with the workplace. Part-time staff provide staffing flexibility—easily adjusting hours up and down to meet workload changes without incurring overtime. Managing productivity by only addressing the staff hours can help an organization reduce cost as much as 5% in a focused effort. Reduction in force beyond that can bring immediate expense relief but may severely impact the quality of care or the production results, which may harm an organization.

■ **Salary cost:** The hourly cost is greatly affected by the kind of staff or the skill mix of the work team. The hourly rate can range from $7/hour to over $100/hour. Matching the skill mix with the workload has a significant impact on total cost, but also on staffing flexibility and the quality of results. Trends have swung in both directions—from highly skilled all-RN staffing of nursing units to very task-oriented Licensed Practical Nurse (LPN) and aide teams led by an Registered Nurse (RN). It is usually found that the most cost-effective approach is a balanced skill mix and a careful analysis of the labor cost per unit of service.

■ **Benefit cost:** Included in the labor cost is more than the hourly rate but also paid leave (vacation, holiday, and sick pay—often 10% of the labor cost) and full-time employee benefits (insurance, retirement, etc., often represent another 15% of labor cost).

  – **Paid leave:** This is often referred to as *benefit time* and represents the difference between *paid* and *worked* hours. Benefit cost is variable and how the organization replaces it is variable. It is a manageable expense. Unique programs have been set up to drive vacations to expected low workload periods of the year to avoid overstaffing; for example, hiring several of the respiratory therapy staff to work a "teachers year" (full time September through May, with the entire summer off) allows the department to have full-time skilled staff in the winter months when the workload is highest and to staff down in the summer when the work is lowest.

  – **Paid benefits:** These are usually provided to full-time employees, but not part-time employees. This is another factor in determining the value of a part-time workforce.

■ **Premium pay:** Overtime, shift differentials, and agency costs are a big part of labor cost. Because these staff are so easy to add, many organizations have to periodically address the creeping growth of these expenses. If an organization has not addressed this type of staff in several years, there is often significant savings to be achieved. But the opportunity to engage this staff can also benefit an organization. The short-term staffing flexibility allows an organization to add and delete staffing more quickly than any other method. Those organizations that implement rules of "no overtime" or "no agency" often find that their baseline staffing is higher or that staff turnover grows. When organizations don't use staffing flexibility methods, they often establish higher baseline staffing to accommodate the workload fluctuations. These organizations will usually have higher average hours of nursing staff to patient day.

The number of staff is often the beginning of the cost management process, but each of the other factors has a significant impact on cost. Each parameter of staffing must be balanced with the work requirements, the flexibility of staffing decisions, and the timeliness of work.

Many in the organization are concerned with workforce management and can engage the management engineer to help in workforce planning, staffing, and scheduling improvement, and to build productivity monitoring and control systems. The chief operating officer (COO) is most interested in specific departmental studies as he works with managers or doctors concerned about new or significantly changed services. The COO will also usually review the monthly reports to identify opportunities for improvement. The chief financial officer (CFO) will engage the management engineer in the budgeting process. Forecasting workload and reviewing the fixed and variable portions of the budget plan are common. The VP of Patient Care Services is more focused on deploying staff by making daily adjustments to match staff with a changing workload. The VP of Human Resources will want to analyze staff turnover, benefits, and premium pay costs. He will also be concerned with long-range planning for skilled staff. Increasing turnover makes the design of orientation and training programs more important.

Management Engineering Role

The management engineer's role can take many forms. In some organizations, the management engineering function is centralized. There may be a single department dedicated to productivity management. The engineer may be a consultant either on the organization staff or with a firm on a contracted assignment. In general, the engineer is engaged in one of several distinct roles as the workforce management issues are addressed.

Management Engineering Department: This centralized department will maintain and manage the productivity monitoring system, develop standards, and work with managers to establish productivity targets. Often they maintain and utilize an industry benchmarking system to support the development of these targets. The department will typically take on a strong support role each year in the development of budgets at both the departmental as well as the organizational levels. They will often be called on to do more detailed studies to identify, improve, and help to better manage the workforce.

Departmental Staff: Some organizations use management engineers throughout the organization. Departments will employ individual management engineers to manage specific aspects of labor management. For example, Patient Care Services might have an engineer developing and maintaining the staffing matrix for nursing units, and implementing and managing a computerized staff scheduling system. Financial Services will use a management engineer to implement and manage support systems, which often include benchmarking and budgeting modules. Also a management engineer may be in Human Resources building job descriptions, incentive pay plans, and managing the position control system.

Consultant: Whether internal or contracted, consultants are often used in organizations, even those with internal management engineering departments. Labor studies are often affected by bias and using a third party may improve results. Complex departments, such as Imaging and Surgery, may have greater confidence in consultants who have extensive experience in those specialties. Small and medium-sized organizations use consultants periodically to set up and update productivity and benchmarking systems. Large-scale, one-time reorganization and productivity studies are often best left to external consultants.

Workforce Management Methods and Toolbox

The tools used by the management engineer include both basic tools, such as categorization and statistical process control, as well as more sophisticated tools involved in staffing and scheduling algorithms. The management engineer needs to be adept in data mining because the labor and volume statistics are not always obvious, clear, or complete. Team skills and tools and negotiation methods are also needed.

Productivity monitoring: This is *good ole engineering*, the most basic tool of the management engineer. It is simply periodically reporting a department's productivity—the average number of paid hours used to produce a single output. For example, hours per patient day, hours per admission, hours per pound of laundry cleaned, and so on. Context is provided by comparing actual productivity to established targets, to budgets, to industry benchmarks, and to historical trends. Data is typically collected automatically from the organization's accounting systems, specifically the payroll (for hours and labor cost) and revenue (for output volumes) systems. Establishing and maintaining the system can consume the resources of a small department for a large organization, but without it, effectively managing the workforce is impossible. For the management engineer, the system is only a tool to use in identifying opportunities for improvement, as baseline data for more detailed staffing studies, and for an illustration in mentoring and coaching managers. Productivity monitoring systems are almost always built into accounting systems, but because the information is buried and lacks graphic representation, standalone systems are almost always preferred. Productivity systems report on a monthly or biweekly schedule. The definition of outputs, the development of targets, and the analysis of the reports for opportunities should all be included in the role of the management engineer.

Data mining: This is an excellent source for developing productivity standards because it enables the management engineer to have access to several data points without having to gathering them personally. Information systems that are in place today allow us to mine the data available to develop productivity standards much more easily than before. An example of this would be radiology. Within the radiology system, one can obtain tens of thousands of records within a short timeframe to determine the amount of time to perform different radiology procedures. The radiology information system can report the type of the exam or procedure, modality (e.g., computerized tomography [CT], magnetic resonance imaging [MRI], ultrasound, etc.), start time with the technologist, end time with the technologist, and patient identifier. Calculations can be made to determine the length of time required by exam/procedure or by modality. Depending on the level of detail desired, productivity standards could then be developed for the department as a whole with procedure mix based on the point in time that the data was pulled. Another data-rich department is surgery. Surgical information systems can report the provider, procedure, patient identifier, time entered in the operating room (OR), start time for the surgeon (cut time), stop time for the surgeon (close time), and time exited OR. Productivity standards could be developed or a weighted average determination of a standard can be applied to a case minute.

Staffing studies: Detailed analysis is often required when a department confronts significant changes. The work of a healthcare department is often complex and dynamic. The representation of productivity by a simple ratio of hours per unit volume rarely represents the broad range of tasks and services or the roles of varied skilled workers. The management engineers will need to immerse themselves in the department to understand the work—what is done, when it needs to be done, how it is done, and so on. This often involves many other tools described in this book such as process improvement, quality management, and Lean/Six Sigma. But the end result needs to recommend a new department organization, staffing budget, and staff schedule to reflect the new demands of the department. Almost always, the request comes from the department manager with an expectation of increasing staffing levels and ends up with a redesign of work and budget-neutral staff reorganization.

BUILDING BUY-IN

The hospital's pharmacy department expenses were growing beyond the budget because new regulatory requirements added a number of new steps to each process; many tasks were taking twice as much time to complete as before. The management engineers, working alongside the pharmacists and techs, observed the new procedures. The regulations certainly increased the workload and new productivity standards were developed to reflect these changes. The management engineer and the pharmacy director searched for any opportunity to find new labor efficiencies in other areas of the department's function to limit the request of additional budgeted staff and expense. Together they reported back to the COO with the staffing budget request and the revised productivity targets.

Staff scheduling: Scheduling staff in a 24/7 operation can be quite complicated. Most department managers will build schedules manually, but there are many automated scheduling systems in use, particularly to support the staffing of inpatient nursing units. Staffing algorithms that drive the automated systems can also be used to support manual scheduling. These staffing matrices (described in a following section of this chapter) simplify the determination of how many staff are needed on each shift based on the predicted workload. A scheduling process can be developed to help managers set up the schedule to avoid the need for overtime, the use of work stretches (consecutive days of work) that are too short or too long, to fairly allocate unpopular weekend and night shifts, and to assure that the right mix of skills and leadership are available on each shift. Managers without a computerized system can spend many hours preparing biweekly or monthly staff schedules. But an engineer can help a manager establish a methodology to more quickly build a schedule with the needed coverage and the best fit to employee expectations.

Staffing matrix: One tool that is helpful for managers as well as frontline supervisors on inpatient nursing units is a staffing matrix. This is a simple table relating the unit census to the shift-by-shift staffing needs. This is based on an average acuity level for each patient. In a previous section of this chapter, a discussion of a method of classifying patients based on their clinical acuity and care needs is another level of refinement of this staffing matrix. In order to develop a staffing matrix, one must start with the productivity standard. A typical unit of measure for inpatient nursing units are hours per patient day (HPPD). There are several different methodologies to develop HPPD productivity standards (e.g., nurse staffing ratios, acuity-based standards, etc.). The HPPD standard is the variable component of the standard for the inpatient nursing unit. There is also usually a fixed component of the productivity standard relating to leadership and clerical support as well as other activities that are needed to support the unit overall. Both the variable and fixed components are utilized in developing the staffing matrix.

To develop a staffing matrix, one typically starts with the census levels that apply to the inpatient nursing unit. Most matrices start at a census of 1 and stop at the total number of beds physically available on the unit. Another methodology centers around the census levels that are most common on the particular inpatient nursing unit. One then does the mathematical calculations at each census level with both the variable and fixed components to develop the number of hours available to staff at that census level. A management engineer can develop a first pass of the appropriate staffing at each census level. However, it is usually best to have nursing leadership involved as well, especially regarding appropriate skill mix.

If, for example, a unit has a nurse-to-patient ratio of 1:5 and a tech-to-patient ratio of 1:10, one would want to use that as the basis for developing the staffing level at each census. Certainly, the census levels that are in between the whole number dividers make it challenging to determine the appropriate skill mix and staffing levels. This is when it is helpful to involve nursing leadership. Once the staffing matrix has been developed and agreed upon, it is a beneficial guide to frontline supervisors in determining the number of staff needed at each census level. Critical thinking and clinical judgment are also factors in determining the number of staff, especially if the census is right at the point where an additional staff member may be needed. Frontline supervisors appreciate having a tool such as this in which to base their day-to-day and shift-to-shift staffing decisions.

Managing premium pay: One of the challenges of building staffing flexibility is the reliance on nurse staffing agencies and overtime. Nurse staffing agencies have a pool of nurse employees that are dispatched to area hospitals on short notice. These nurses typically work for higher wages without benefits. Hospitals pay the agencies 1.5–2 times typical wages to use these nurses. Hospitals with "holes" in their staff schedules find it convenient to just call the agency to fill the gaps. In most healthcare organizations, the use of these agency nurses might grow over time to be very significant and the extra cost (premium pay) of staffing with these nurses over routine staff becomes a "budget buster." Hospitals can rein in these costs with better staff scheduling, but to maintain the staffing flexibility, the hospital can build their own temporary staffing pools. These pools can be of *PRN* (as needed) staff. These are part-time staff that are willing to be considered for scheduling at the need of the organization. There is a need for a fairly large pool of PRNs, and scheduling coordinators may need to call many of these staff before filling all the "holes." Another interesting approach used by many hospitals and aided by web-based applications is shift bidding. After a staff schedule is developed, the unfilled slots are offered to the PRN staff to indicate which shifts they are willing to fill. Those slots that are difficult to fill may be incentivized with a premium pay (usually much less than an agency would cost). Overtime is also a key to staffing flexibility. Casual overtime is an issue of management and process improvement efforts and should be made to eliminate it. But many times, overtime is the most economical decision to meet workload requirements. It is almost always more desirable than overstaffing and agency staffing. The management engineer can help develop rules for appropriate overtime use. In most acute care organizations, overtime in nursing units of 2–3% and in the emergency department and surgical suite of 3–5% is usually appropriate and represents good staff management (if the other indicators show that the total hours per patient is at or below industry averages). Addressing premium pay, building optimization models, and providing managers with effective staffing decision support tools will almost always result in cost savings and improved staffing levels.

Chapter 11

Staffing and Scheduling

Kelly Arnold

Contents

Introduction

Many industries and organizations understand that the most valuable resource they apply to their efforts are human resources—people. This concept is true as well in any healthcare organization, particularly hospitals. Healthcare has been and is projected to continue being one of several industries that will contribute heavily to economic recovery and job growth in the United States. At the same time, there will be mounting pressure on healthcare providers to reduce the cost of care. These two facts make a complete and thorough understanding of staffing and scheduling in hospitals essential. This chapter will give the reader a better insight into the complexities of utilizing human resources in a productive and efficient manner in a healthcare setting.

Staffing Defined

Staffing in a healthcare organization essentially refers to the same thing that it does in any other industry or organization. *Staff* refers to the persons that it takes to effectively deliver the service that is sought and paid for by the consumer (typically referred to as the patient). The complexity, variability, and life-or-death (in some instances) nature of service provided makes hospital staffing uniquely challenging and more complex than any other service industry.

Scheduling Defined

Scheduling is simply defined as how you assign the staff in any area across service type, hour of the day, or day of the week. Again, the complexity and variability of patients requiring service or care makes the task of scheduling more difficult than in most other industries. An additional consideration for effective scheduling in a hospital is that service or care is provided in two different types of settings. These settings are inpatient and outpatient areas.

Types of Staffing

Whether staffing is for an inpatient, outpatient, or support department setting, there are two types of staffing patterns—fixed and variable. Generally, fixed departments will have the same numbers of staff regardless of the numbers of patients receiving care in the hospital. Variable departments will vary staffing up and down as the volume of patients increases or decreases. Support departments are those that support the areas that provide care to the patients. There are many support departments in a typical hospital today. Examples of support departments include finance, environmental services, nutritional services, information technology, materials management, building services, and education services, just to name a few. Most of these areas will have fixed staffing, but there has been movement recently to move some of these areas to variable staffing patterns whenever possible. Most clinical areas serving inpatients and outpatients are expected to staff on a variable basis, which rises and falls with patient volume. Many clinical areas that staff on a variable basis will reach a low point of volume that results in staffing minimums. Minimums will be discussed in detail later in the chapter.

Skill Mix

Hospitals, over the years, have become organizations with a large number of specialized types of workers or employees. In some hospital settings, there can be 500 or more different types of employees with different skill sets. While this number may seem surprisingly high, most clinical areas will generally have less than 6 types of direct personnel. Nursing is the largest area in any hospital in terms of labor, both numbers of staff or full-time equivalents (FTEs) and expense. An FTE is defined as the total hours worked in a specific period that is considered full-time. In a week, this is 40 hours (8 hours a day for 5 days) and for a year, 2080 hours (40 hours a week for 52 weeks a year). The specific needs for direct care personnel types in nursing areas is captured by the term *skill mix*. Skill mix in these areas will generally be divided into two categories—professional and assistive personnel. As discussed previously, it is important to schedule enough total personnel to meet the care needs of the patient. Skill mix is an additional scheduling consideration, in that the ratio of professional and assistive personnel must be appropriate for care needs. As an example, it is a poor use of RN professional time and skills to be performing tasks that an assistive person can perform. By contrast, too many assistive personnel will result in the higher level care needs of patients being unmet due to inadequate numbers of professional staff. You might wish to give examples of a few professional or clinical tasks versus that of assistive personnel. Professional staff typically perform tasks that require critical thinking and assessment skills (calculation of IV medication administration rates, for example). Assistive staff, by contrast, are primarily working with patients to assist in activities of daily living (ADL). Several examples would be bathing, feeding, and toileting.

Scheduling Patterns

Scheduling patterns are an additional contributing factor to the innate complexity of a healthcare organization. Some industries (manufacturing, for example) will operate on a 24-hour-per-day basis for periods of time. Healthcare is unique because hospitals operate 24 hours a day, 365 days per year; in other words, they never close. Having sufficient numbers of staff to meet this service/care requirement is a significant and ongoing challenge. A second challenge is how to schedule the staff across the always-open-for-business operation that hospitals have become. Support department schedules can fall into normal business hour patterns, Monday-Friday, 8 a.m. to 5 p.m., or they can also be required to provide service at all times.

The more difficult areas to establish effective scheduling patterns are primarily clinical areas. Scheduling in these areas has evolved over the last 15–20 years to allow employees to work more than the normal 8 hour days and have longer stretches of time off. The most popular scheduling pattern in many clinical areas is 12-hour shifts. This scheduling pattern allows staff to work 6 days (not consecutive) and be off 8 days in a two-week period. Outpatient areas are more likely to have 8- and 10-hour shifts than inpatient areas. The dominant 8-hour scheduling pattern has historically been 3 shifts (7:00 a.m. to 3:30 p.m., 3:00 p.m. to 11:30 p.m., and 11:00 p.m. to 7:30 a.m.) There are still significant numbers of departments in hospitals that utilize these scheduling patterns. This is true for support departments, as well as those providing care to inpatients and outpatients. As the workforce in healthcare organizations age, there is an increasing awareness that the 12-hours shifts are more difficult for staff to work. This will be discussed in detail later in this chapter.

Workweek Hour Commitment

Scheduling of available staff is impacted by the type of workweek hours commitment to which each employee has agreed t. There are primarily 3 types of commitments into which an employee could fall. The first is full-time hours, which would be 40 hours in one week. The second type would be part-time hours, which vary greatly in a week. In order for an employee to be eligible for employer-paid benefits (typically health insurance), the minimum part-time hours are 30–32 hours per week. However, many employees will be in a part-time position of less than 30 hours per week. The third category of workweek hour commitment is known as PRN. These positions are established to have an employee work *as needed* and have no benefits. There are increasing numbers of healthcare workers who elect this option as they do not need benefits and this affords more flexibility of when to work or be off. In some clinical areas the numbers of PRN staff can approach 20% of the total contract staffing.

Fluctuations in available healthcare workers have occurred over the past several decades. As a result, contract or agency employees have become an increasing part of the hospital's total workforce. These types of employees are similar to *temp* personnel that are seen in other industries. The majority of these contract employees are clinical, but other areas may also have significant numbers, primarily in finance areas. There are significant premiums paid to these employees amounting to an incremental expense of $20–$25 per hour for registered nurses. Contract employees are typically hired for a defined period of time ranging for 4–13 weeks per contract. Should the workload decline in an area that is utilizing these employees, they will be still be paid the guaranteed hours whether or not they work. Many areas that utilize these employees have concerns about the quality of care delivered by a person who is unfamiliar with the facility, patients, and physicians. One of the advantages to hiring contract employees on a short-term basis is that they are typically ready to work on day one and do not require a lengthy orientation as new hires will.

Productivity Impact on Staffing and Scheduling

As margins in healthcare organizations get tighter and payers decrease levels of reimbursement, there is increasing pressure on staffing and scheduling to be as efficient and effective as possible. Managers of all areas in hospitals understand the need to achieve productivity targets, but some are less prepared to do so than others. Managers of clinical areas are frequently promoted to their position because they have been a high performer in a previous clinical role. Many of these managers have little or no previous education or experience dealing with productivity or finance. As a result, they tend to approach staffing and scheduling from the perspective of a staff member. The end result is frequent staffing levels and schedules that result in variance from desired productivity and financial goals. Organizations attempt to address this knowledge gap by offering periodic classes to new or experienced managers. While this approach is somewhat helpful, if there is not ongoing reinforcement and support for materials taught, the manager will not retain as much as needed. Managers in hospitals are no different than those in other industries in that they have large numbers of priorities to address daily. Those in hospitals, especially clinical managers, will allow productivity and finance to be a lower priority as clinical issues are usually viewed as more urgent. A clinical manager is likely to allow staffing levels to rise above target if concerns about patient care and safety or complaints from physicians and family are more urgent. It is not uncommon for clinical managers to fall back on what they know best (patient care) and sort out issues of staffing versus productivity later.

As volumes fall to low levels in clinical areas (typically on weekends and holidays), staffing decisions are frequently made with consideration of minimum staffing numbers. A good example of application of minimum staffing would be an inpatient clinical area that has 1 to 3 patients. While a professional caregiver is capable of meeting the care needs of these patients, the possibility of rapid changes in a patient's clinical status dictates the necessity of 2 caregivers. The thinking behind this staffing model is both financial (lawsuits for bad outcome) and quality based (patient death or injury). While these types of staffing models at minimums are not common, they occur in many clinical areas across hospitals.

Regulatory Factors

Healthcare is one of the most heavily regulated industries by virtue of the heavy influence of governmental payment sources. These regulations extend to most areas of hospital operations, but are most applicable in matters of staffing and scheduling. The most well-known regulatory agency is the Joint Commission (JC; formerly known as the Joint Commission on Accreditations of Hospital Organizations, or JCAHO). While the JC does not set staff levels for hospitals or specific areas, it does expect the organization to have a well-defined and articulated staffing plan. The focus of this plan is always about providing consistent and safe care to patients.

Another example of regulatory impact on staffing and scheduling can be found in California. In 2001, the California Nurse Association was successful in having mandated nurse-to-patient ratios established as state law. In addition to mandated ratios, the law also addresses required break times and ratios for other caregivers. The law obviously makes scheduling decisions easier as they are defined by law. Implementation of these staffing levels are impacted by many of the factors discussed in this chapter. The end result is that defined staffing levels cannot be achieved. The difficulty for hospitals is most obvious in increased cost of care of the front end. The impact on total cost for a patient across a continuum is not well understood. Examples of where this cost could be lowered would be through reductions of errors, rework, and readmissions. There has been ongoing research regarding the implications of mandated ratios to mortality and morbidity in hospitals. Even 12 years after the establishment of the law, the discussion is still ongoing with arguments for and against the continuation and expansion of these ratios. It is likely that in an increasingly tight reimbursement environment, significant expansion to other states is unlikely.

Self-Scheduling

A relatively recent development in hospitals has been the advent of *self-scheduling* of employees in their areas of work. This development is based on the idea of empowering employees, resulting in happier, satisfied, and more productive employees. This scheduling model is most commonly seen in nursing areas. Self-scheduling can be approached in two different ways—committee and individual employee. Many specialized areas like the intensive care unit (ICU), labor and delivery, and emergency departments will have scheduling committees composed of staff-level employees. The committee members will create the initial schedule for a coming period (usually 4 weeks) for all staff employees. The initial schedule is then reviewed by individual staff and managers for final approval. Managers have the final approval authority and individual staff can make requests for changes for specific reasons. Areas that allow individual employees to self-schedule will post a blank schedule asking each employee to fill in their hours for the coming period. Each person must meet their hours commitment in the period based on their hours commitment (full-time, part-time, or PRN as discussed earlier). The final approval of individual hours and total schedule is made by managers.

Acuity Impact on Staffing and Scheduling

In most industries, the complexity of a product built or service delivered determines the amount of labor that is utilized. This is particularly true in healthcare with the general measure of complexity of care captured by acuity. A high-level, widely known measure of acuity in healthcare is CMI or case mix index. This measure is calculated on a facility-specific basis as determined by data submitted to Centers for Medicare and Medicaid Services (CMS). There are a number of other acuity measures that give more specific indication of complexity at an area or department level. Hospital areas that have specific acuity indicators include lab, nursing, radiology, respiratory therapy, surgery, and emergency departments to name a few.

The obvious impact on needs for staff from acuity is that a higher complexity of care requires more personnel. The approach to measuring and applying acuity impact on staffing can be either art or science or both. Again, nursing areas are the 900-pound gorilla in the room when dealing with acuity measurement. Some hospitals will apply science in measuring acuity by having computer-based systems with specific algorithms that give precise staffing recommendations on a shift or daily basis. There are many such systems on the market today. Some facilities will take this scientific approach utilizing systems developed in-house by IT or other technically savvy personnel (including management engineers [MEs]). These systems that apply mathematical precision to acuity measures are the best and most accurate approach to acuity measurement.

The art side and approach to acuity is based on the experience and intuition of the person responsible for making staffing decisions on a daily basis. The important decision driving staffing on a daily basis in many clinical areas is how many patients the professional or assistive employee can care for at one time. The data from systems above will give a more precise picture of patient assignment, but the same decision will likely be made by an artful and clinically experienced decision maker. While the exact measure of acuity associated with an individual patient is not available, the care needs contributing to complexity are known. The artful decision maker will be aware of these care needs on all patients and attempt to factor these into the final decision regarding staffing. As financial pressures increase on many hospitals, there has been a migration away from a science-based approach to acuity measure with many hospitals relying on the artful decision maker's judgment, clinical knowledge, patient care experience, and intuition.

Workforce Implications

There are a number of workforce implications that impact the staffing and scheduling functions in healthcare organizations. This discussion will focus on two that are most important—competition for employees and an aging workforce. Given the recent Great Recession of the last four years, there have been several industries that continue to be areas of job growth. Healthcare has typically been high on all lists in the media. Given the ongoing need for healthcare personnel, the demand and competition for talent has intensified. One of the allures of the healthcare profession is the relative certainty of employment and diversity of jobs and locations even for a single profession in healthcare. All of these factors contribute to high levels of healthcare employee turnover relative to other industries. The phrase "the grass is greener on the other side of the fence" captures the movement of these employees within and between hospitals. Adding to the difficulty of staffing and scheduling related to this issue is that the best employees have options elsewhere and will take them if their present setting is not meeting their personal and professional needs and goals.

Continuous long-term employment has been a feature of many people's experience in hospitals and has contributed directly to the second issue—an aging workforce. Plentiful careers and jobs in healthcare have attracted large numbers of new and younger staff. At the same time, large numbers of professional and other healthcare staff have stayed in the same job and frequently worked at the same hospital for much of their career. Many healthcare employees had periods of leave from jobs for the birth of children. Now, at a later point in their careers, these same people are taking extensive leaves to care for aging relatives or address their own illnesses related to diseases of aging and lifestyle. While these employees have a wealth of knowledge and experience, they may not have the physical stamina or emotional capacity to deal with the ongoing demands of caregiving.

Technology Impact on Staffing and Scheduling

As with the previous section, there are numerous technology factors that directly impact staffing and scheduling in hospitals. The use of computer-based systems to measure acuity was discussed previously. There has been a dramatic rise in the number of staffing solutions available on the market in recent years. While some of these systems still reside on hospital-based LANs, there has been a logical shift toward web-based systems and applications. The wide availability of these products has greatly eased the effort involved in producing schedules for a specific timeframe. These systems can also have a positive impact on the changes made to staffing on a day-to-day basis. However, these types of daily and shift changes to staffing levels still require input from managers or supervisors who rely heavily on that person's intuition and experience. Therefore, these technology-based aids to scheduling are of limited use on day-to-day staffing decisions.

Another significant area of technology impact on staffing is the relatively recent emergence of electronic medical records (EMRs) and computer-based charting. A full discussion of these topics is beyond the scope of this chapter, but they do have an impact on the levels and amount of staff needed to provide care. Many hospitals are in the early phases of bringing these systems into their organizations. Payment, privacy, and quality concerns will likely ensure that all hospitals in the near future implement these systems. Given the relative newness of these technologies and early phases of development and deployment, hard data regarding these systems is not widely available. It is certain that there are issues relating to moving from paper-based systems to computer-based, which will have negative impacts on staffing throughout hospitals. The first issue identified early on is the learning curve associated with any new systems. Hospitals are filled with examples of the latest and greatest equipment and technology. Given the relative age of many employees in hospitals, learning curves and associated times to effectively take advantage of the new technologies can be lengthy. The second associated issue is the time involved in charting and documenting in a computer-based system. A clear advantage to EMR is integration of data and rapid access to that data for all those providing care to an individual patient. This integration and access comes at a cost as the systems in use today still require more time to chart.

Many hospitals are attempting to quantify the time impact of changing from paper to computer EMRs. Some are further along than others, but financial constraints make it difficult to staff at higher levels to compensate for the extra time involved.

Healthcare Reform and Quality Implications Impacting Staffing

The exact details of healthcare reform resulting from the Affordable Care Act are still emerging and changing over time. It is clear, however, that access to high-quality, affordable care for all citizens is a key goal of the legislation. Many hospitals are in the position of making decisions regarding the relative importance of cost of care versus quality. While all hospitals understand that both are important, many are now confronted with the difficult task of providing quality care that is measured against published standards of quality. Quality need not cost more, but many hospitals have numerous systems issues that make it difficult to balance the cost and quality equation. Clinical leaders and staff will often question that the overall care being provided in a hospital is not at an acceptable level of quality. There are frequent cries over past years that staffing levels need to be raised in order to meet the demands for higher quality of care. The difficulty in hospitals versus other industries is the ability to clearly define the standard measures of quality associated with patient care. In most industries, the quality associated with different products is tangible and higher quality can be priced higher. Neither pricing or quality in healthcare are straightforward.

Management Engineer's Role in Staffing and Scheduling

Management engineers (MEs) or industrial engineers in healthcare have always had a role to play in the improvement of operations and performance in hospitals. The biggest barrier to achieving significant impact in healthcare is a lack of understanding of what an ME is and the tools and skills they can bring to bear. Engineers by training and nature are problem solvers and critical thinkers. Most, but not all clinical employees in hospitals, need these skills to perform their jobs at a high level. There should be a natural synergy between these two groups of professionals. In the areas of staffing and scheduling, an ME would apply their analytical skills to greatest effect. Many clinical managers are uncomfortable with analysis of data, which is not clinical in nature. The ability to transform data into information for decision making is a needed skill in many hospitals. Such an analysis of staffing and scheduling data by MEs will lead to better decisions by clinical managers than they will make in the absence of the analysis.

An additional area in which ME skills can be applied would be operational analysis with subsequent process redesign. Many hospitals are pursuing a variety of in-house and consultant-led initiatives that fall under the broad terms of Lean or Six Sigma. MEs have these skills as part of their education and often as part of their past professional experience. They are well suited to lead these initiatives. A big challenge that confronts MEs who are new to healthcare organizations is a lack of understanding or exposure to clinical operations. The ability of an ME to positively impact staffing and scheduling can be greatly enhanced by exposing themselves to clinical operations. By reaching out to partner with clinical leaders for education on the clinical world, MEs will be more effective and trusted when applying their skills to assist in the improvement of staffing and scheduling processes.

Chapter 12

Understanding Nursing Care Models: Industrial Engineering Healthcare Book

Marvina Williams

Contents

Introduction

There are many professions in healthcare, but registered nurses (RNs) are definitely the majority. Registered nurses are the backbone of the hospital and ambulatory care facilities. Their expertise is essential in the care of patients. Nursing care is carried out through various organizational methods. These methods are models of nursing care [1]. A model determines the roles of the nurse and other caregivers, and the way they all work together to provide care for the patient [2]. These models address and affect the following issues:

1. Staffing of nurses and their partners in care
2. Salaries or operating costs
3. Effectiveness and efficiency of care for the patients

Nurse staffing and the nursing care models vary depending on the following:

1. Acuity of the patient
2. Area to which the nurse is assigned
3. Duties or tasks required
4. Partnerships with the nurse
5. Culture of the facility

The nursing care model can affect the outcomes and safety of patients. Patients are grouped by age, such as pediatric and adult, and by the acuity of nursing care required. Some facilities will set the cutoff for pediatric patients at age 16, while others set this age at 18. Depending on the facility, there may not be pediatric services and the facility may transfer the patient to another facility if admission is needed.

With regard to acuity, there are acute care floors and critical care or intensive care floors. Most of patients in the hospital setting are considered acute care patients, and are separated into medical and surgical patients. The location of the patient depends on the type of service the patient requires. Some facilities will break down medical services even further into areas such as an oncology floor or pulmonary floor, and surgical services into subspecialties such as orthopedics. Smaller facilities may merge the medical and surgical patients together. The higher-acuity patients are in critical care units such as:

a. Intensive Care Unit
b. Cardiac Care Unit
c. Trauma Intensive Care Unit
d. Pediatric Intensive Care Unit
e. Neonatal Intensive Care Unit

Based on the facility type and size, there may not be all of the intensive care units previously listed. Some smaller facilities have a mix of intensive care patients in one unit, while others may not provide pediatric or neonatal intensive care.

There is another group of patients that some facilities recognize by providing care in step-down or telemetry units. These patients may be released from the intensive care settings and require less care, but still need more care than can be given on an acute care floor. Others may be admitted, and need more than just an acute care setting but not need intensive care services. Not all facilities have step-down units and may have patients stay longer in the intensive care setting. Patients remaining in the intensive care setting for extended periods of time may remain there due to physician preference for their patients. This situation is controversial with respect to inappropriate use of resources and the inability of the facility to accommodate patients that need this level of care into this setting because beds are being taken by patients who no longer need intensive care.

In nursing models, nursing management must provide safe patient care at a responsible cost [3]. It is very important that the model used in a particular setting provides safe care of the patient and the prevention of adverse outcomes. Adverse outcomes can be described as events such as patient falls, hospital-acquired infections, medication errors, or pressure sores, to name a few.

At this point, there is no proven right or wrong nursing care model. Nursing care models have developed over time. They will continue to develop along with changes in technology, society, patient care needs, and human knowledge [2].

The caregivers in a nursing care model may include certified nursing assistants (CNAs), licensed practical and vocational nurses (LPNs/LVNs), and registered nurses (RNs), and at times, clinical nurse specialists (CNSs) and clinical nurse leaders (CNLs), who have a master's or doctorate [4].

Nursing Care Models

Team/Functional Nursing Care Model

In this model, the focus is primarily on a staff and skill mix structure. It was created in response to the nursing shortage resulting from World War II. It is based on the premise of collaboration and division of responsibilities for the nursing care of patients [5]. A team is developed that includes RNs, LPNs, and CNAs. The nurses are is assigned to tasks according to skill level and qualifications. A registered nurse is assigned as a team leader and the LPN and CNA perform activities such as bathing, feeding, and other duties. They work as a team with specific job responsibilities. Each team is assigned a group of patients. In some team models, the work is divided up by function such as *medication nurse* or *treatment nurse*. The team model is a very efficient way to deliver care, but care of the patient is fragmented. One RN may be the team leader one day and a team member the next day, thus continuity of care may suffer [6]. This can create dissatisfaction among patients and nurses.

Many facilities have adopted this type of model or created a hybrid. They use senior RNs in a supervisory role on a team. They function as the leader, guide newer RNs and LPNs, coordinate with physicians, and navigate some of the paperwork needed such as in discharging patients. The new RN or LPN assumes the majority of frontline tasks with the patient, such as administering treatments and some medications, and executing the patient care plan. In one particular model, there is no CNA but there are 2 RNs or 1 RN and 1 LPN assigned to 7–10 patients. In some facilities this model has worked, while in other facilities the model has failed because the nurses feel that it has not lessened their burden.

Primary Nursing Care Model

Primary nursing refers to comprehensive, individualized care provided by the registered nurse throughout the period of care. It emphasizes continuity of care and provides a nurse to direct patient care with a small group of patients [1]. The primary nurse (PN) accepts total 24-hour responsibility for planning and overseeing care. Each time the PN works, they are assigned the primary patient for as long as the patient remains on the unit [6]. The advantages are the increased satisfaction and continuity of care for the patient. This model was seen as a way of improving quality of care and increasing job satisfaction among nurses. The disadvantage is the greater number of RNs needed and the need for RNs to spend time doing tasks that other less-expensive staff could perform. Some argue that this is neither a cost-effective nor an efficient model.

Patient-Focused Nursing Care Model

As mentioned earlier, nursing care models evolve and with this come hybrids. This model involves the use of multiskilled staff and a team approach to nursing [5]. Services are brought closer to the patient and staff skills are broadend by cross-training. This model recognizes support services in the efficient delivery of quality care. A pharmacist being involved in the distribution of medication and linen being delivered from the laundry to a patient room are examples. These support services allow nurses time to care for the patient rather than using their skills on non-nursing functions.

Medications are a major source of potential errors. Examples of such errors include medication lists lost during transfer of a patient, the patient receiving old medications rather than newly prescribed medications, or errors in recording the medication history. Medication management has usually been handled by the nurse. Many facilities are bringing in the pharmacist to complete the team. The pharmacist partners with the physicians for medication management and helps the RN on some of the medication record tasks. In critical care units, such as the intensive care unit (ICU) and the emergency department (ED), the pharmacist may actually work in those departments at satellite pharmacies and help give medications.

Offloading some of these medication responsibilities can help increase RN productivity and provide more accuracy in paperwork and medications delivery. In this type of collaboration, there can be substantial reductions in costs per case. The RN is a care manager, and LPNs and CNAs have expanded roles such as lab draws and performing certain assessment activities. With this type of model, there may be design changes in a unit such as the addition of a satellite pharmacy. Technological advancements such as improved computer systems and wireless phones play a major role in improving the nurses' effectiveness. The staff becomes multiskilled and clinical case management is incorporated into the operational process. This model has shown increased patient and staff satisfaction. More direct patient care time is available to the RN.

Future of Nursing Care Models

There are many more nursing care models, but those previously discussed are the three most common. In 1996, the Institute of Medicine reported that there were insufficient data to draw conclusions about the relationship between nurse staffing and inpatient outcomes. However, later studies have revisited this issue, allowing a review of the literature relating patient outcomes to various measures of nurse staffing levels, such as full-time equivalents (FTEs), skill mix (proportion of RN hours to total hours), or RN hours per patient day [5].

With the Affordable Care Act, payment transformation is reshaping healthcare. Nursing care models will play an important role. There are many cost-cutting campaigns being conducted throughout the country due to forecasts of a tough road ahead. Restructuring costs and operations to break even requires assessing staffing efficiency, staff consolidation, premium labor, and salaries. Many organizations are looking at how they can redesign inpatient nursing care models.

Some facilities have laid off employees and shifted to team-based nurse staffing; others have closed services and reduced inpatient beds, and still others have implemented wage freezes and reduced hiring and eliminated underperforming employees.

According to the Institute of Medicine, U.S. healthcare wasteful spending in 2009 was reported to be $1.47 billion and wasteful spending at $765 billion. The Healthcare Advisory Board states that labor costs comprise the majority (51%) of the costs. Some of their findings recommend maximizing staffing efficiency through redefining the core staffing models, changing composition of support staff, and nontraditional shifts to minimize handoffs and maximizing PRN (as needed) pool participation [7].

There are important items to keep in mind when changing staffing models. The success of any staffing model depends on how nurses are assigned to the work area and their duties, who they partner with (i.e., CNA, LPN, pharmacist, etc.), and the technology available to them. Tasks that are nonvalue-added will hinder the performance of the staff in any model. The *Journal of Nursing Administration* shows that RN nonvalue-added time represents a majority of the total cost in a hospital. It is estimated that nurses only spend 20%–30% of their time on direct patient care [8].

Nursing staff are at times assigned many tasks that are below or above their competencies. This can cause a high turnover rate in staff and can waste resources. So it is important to align roles and responsibilities within the nursing model. Trying to reduce costs but relieve unnecessary work on the RN has opened up other models of care.

Some studies show that there is evidence that leaner nurse staffing is associated with increased length of stay, hospital-acquired infections, and pressure sores [3]. Other studies show that increasing skill mix with richer nurse staffing is associated with better patient outcomes. However, no studies specifically identify the ratios or hours of care that produce the best outcomes for different groups of patients or different nursing units [3]. More studies are underway to look at the work environment of nurses, nursing interventions, and adverse events. Future research may one day establish a best practice in nursing care models.

References

1. "Models of Nursing Care Delivery," Nursing Theories, January 28, 2012, http://currentnursing.com/nursing_theory/models_of_nursing_care_delivery.html (accessed December 13, 2012).
2. Sanford, K.D. *Care Models and the Bottom Line*. Healthcare Financial Management Association, January 6, 2010.
3. Seago, J.A. "Nurse Staffing, Models of Care Delivery, and Interventions," in *Patient Safety and Quality: An Evidence-Based Handbook for Nurses*. Rockville, MD: Agency for Healthcare Research and Quality, 2008.
4. Neisner, J., and Raymond, B. *Nurse Staffing and Care Delivery Models: A Review of the Evidence*. Oakland, CA: Kaiser Permanente Institute for Health Policy, March 2002.
5. University of North Carolina at Chapel Hill School of Nursing. Leadership in Nursing Practice: Nursing Care Delivery Systems, 2005.
6. The Advisory Board Company, *Risk and Reward: Positioning Your Health System to Deliver Value in a Transforming Health Care Marketplace Report*. Atlanta, GA: Advisory Board Company, 2012.
7. Storfjel J. et al. "Non-Value-Added Time: The Million Dollar Nursing Opportunity." *Journal of Nursing Administration* 39, no. 1 (2009): 38–45.

Chapter 13

Facilitation Techniques

Duke Rohe

Contents

There are plenty of books on the market that do a great job of providing the method and technique of working with teams. One of the most popular is the spiral bound, *The Team Handbook*. This chapter attempts to provide what is not offered in most books. Consider it more of the inner game of facilitation along with alternate techniques on the process improvement, business process reengineering, and innovation. Over the course of an engineer's profession, developing the skills to facilitate is beneficial to his or her existence.

An engineer without facilitation skills is like an engine without a transmission. It has great power and potential yet little forward motion. This chapter will focus on one of the most crucial yet seldom taught skills for engineers: facilitation. Facilitation or managing group process is the transmission that powers a team meeting toward effective, decisive output that channels discussion, activity, and decisions toward action. Without good group process skills, discussion tends to fall off-target, out-of-scope, and off-meaning. Facilitation attempts to make every minute count toward meeting the project goal. To illustrate a range of facilitation applications, this chapter discusses the use of facilitation on three fronts: small process improvement teams, larger business reengineering initiatives, and innovative ideation sessions.

Process Improvement

Your greatest asset can often become your greatest weakness when it comes to facilitation. Engineers, and most healthcare professionals, are wired to solve a problem in an expedient manner. It is involuntary to their thinking. In fact, they look for a challenge to solve a problem that others think cannot be solved. In facilitation, most, if not all of this instinctive skill must be set aside in order to assure that team members are successful in solving *their* problem. It is the team's problem to solve. The facilitator's role in that meeting is to simply manage the group process, and lead the members toward achieving the project and meeting the goal. Be on guard against anything that gets in the way of pure discussion directed toward achieving the meeting's purpose and the ultimate goal of the project.

In order to accomplish this, you will have to place much of what you think you know and your hard-earned engineering skills on the back burner, while focusing solely on optimizing the discussion, decision making, and action inside the meeting itself. This requires deliberately being in the moment, observing the action and the direction of the team discussion. Anytime your mind hops off the group process and onto what you know or what you are going to say, you have just stepped out of the facilitation role and into a member role.

The trick to being in the moment. In order to be in the moment, focusing on the content, you cannot be absorbed *in* the content. This requires you to listen from a facilitator's perspective. To help remain in the moment, do something different than what you would ordinarily do. For example, put a coin in your shoe that will constantly remind you to be continually focusing on group process. Another trick is to deliberately alternate your focus on each member around the table. It helps remind them of the importance of their participation and helps you listen to your listening, which is an important developmental skill for facilitators.

Ask permission to manage the group process of the team. Explain that this permission may include interrupting and redirecting the conversation in order to keep the team on target and on time.

Setting clear team ground rules that each member will abide by is always recommended. As a facilitator, you may first offer those that you feel will be needed to help you manage the group process, then let the team add to the list. Your first responsibility is the group's effectiveness, so make sure there are rules for individuals to follow to enable that. Examples include equal air time, speak one at a time, respect each other as equals, do your assignments, show up on time, have a meeting agenda, stay on topic, and so on. As members add others or the situation deserves another, simply ask the team if they agree. Remember, these are rules you enforce to keep their discussion healthy and effective.

Work with the team lead ahead of time to set the agenda to accomplish the meeting's purpose. Time box each agenda item as a guide for how much time to spend focusing on it. A typical meeting time allotment may have a review of promised actions (10%), working on or making decisions around meeting content (70%), and a closing with assignments due at the next meeting (20%). Effective meetings have both prework and postwork. If there are no assignments at the end of the meeting, the team is losing ground. As facilitator, remind the team lead that it is their responsibility to check up on assignments between meetings. One member dropping an assignment affects the team's progress.

Talk less, manage more. A good facilitator nudges the team to conduct their own meeting, and to do what they've been instructed to do, group process–wise. During the meeting, monitor the flow and direction of the team discussion. It should always be positively moving toward a decision or an action that moves the team closer to its ultimate goal. Anything other than this should be considered a waste of the team's time.

Use questions to guide members toward the team's goal rather than offering input or instruction. Phrase your suggestion in the form of a question that steps them into considering the input you feel they need to explore. Ask questions such as: "What else is missing?" "Have you considered …?" "What is the downside of this?" "Is this topic worth the time given?" "What else is on the agenda?" Be careful to give them the responsibility of making the decision. Remember, it is their choice and their solution.

When one person dominates or speaks for all the team, redirect the focus to the intimidated members. Say to members, "Members, here is one opinion. What do you think?" Then expect a long pause. Eventually one member will chime in their thoughts. Then, others will join in. This reinforces that they are responsible for thinking and working collectively as a team. There is one exception to this. If the dominating person is a person of authority, such as a physician, he or she may not be able to recognize that they are in a director mode or be able to contribute as a member. In these cases, the facilitator may have to alter the facilitation role to simply maximize team member contribution given the dominating behavior. Depending on the effect on the team's progress, a discussion with the physician or manager outside the meeting may be in order. Politely explain to them that it is their position of authority that is inhibiting the team contribution.

Monitor when the team should move on to the next agenda item. If the team members don't feel they have solid footing around a decision, their forward progress and confidence will be at risk. Allow discussion to broaden their understanding, yet move them on if they are covering the same territory or their focus is on an area of little consequence. Remind the team of the remaining time and the material they have committed to cover and ask them if they want to delay to do more fact-finding.

Give the team a picture of what a high-performing team looks like upfront. They should come in knowing that their presence and participation are crucial and that team time is a prized commodity for action taking and decision making. It is important that they come prepared knowing what is expected of them with all conversation vectored toward both the goal of the meeting and the purpose of the project. The meeting time is where what is heard is clarified through validation, where authenticity, respect, and trust prevail, and where time is monitored and measured by the agreements, actions, and decisions recorded.

Goals of Facilitation

1. **Getting the team to think in unison.** Team members come with a variety of motives, motivations, knowledge, and capabilities. The trick to facilitation is to take this mix and maximize it to the benefit of the team's purpose. Get them to think (thus work) in unison.
2. **Getting the most out of the meeting.** Each team member should come with an expectation that the meeting will be worth his or her time and effort.
3. **Getting the greatest value possible.** Teams are there to do what individuals cannot. Facilitation manages the group process to bring the team out of the individuals.

Roles in Facilitation

1. **Coach the team to success**. To get them to do the best they can do together in a designated time is your goal. Coaching the team to manage their group process is key, not doing it yourself.
2. **Mediate differences**. Teams come with an array of backgrounds, skills, experiences. As facilitator, your role is to harness them into a common effort that eventually achieves the team's purpose. Some examples include leveraging introvert/extrovert, right brain/left brain, detail/big picture, job functions, and so on to the advantage of the team.
3. **Mature the team's focus and output**. Each meeting should grow a higher expectation of team focus (the goal of the team) and output (bias toward action). Once they know the group process guidelines, they have to employ them.
4. **Validate understanding**. A team falls out of alignment unless *all* its members are rowing in the same direction and in the same rhythm. Typically this occurs when a team member is behind in his understanding of the content of the meeting. Stop and secure validation of understanding, agreement, or input before moving on.
5. **Talk less, manage more**. A good facilitator nudges the team to conduct their own meeting, and to do what they've been instructed group process–wise. Consider the content of the meeting as the flow of river—you simply speak up when the river is getting out of its banks or not following its established course.

Actions of a Facilitator

1. **Ask the team for permission** to manage their group process: interrupt, redirect as needed to achieve effective use of meeting time. After the team grants you permission to manage their discussion and direction, you have the liberty to intervene to keep it moving forward on their behalf.
2. **Manage guidelines**. Team agreements should grow as the members learn how to operate inside their differences. Team ground rules should be established early and managed to assure each member is operating within the team guidelines.
3. **Create a bias toward action**. The facilitator should be channeling team conversation toward either a decision or an actionable item. Everything else that does not contribute to these should be considered noise to the team's output.
4. **Give the team accountability**. Team success is up to the team. Make it clear up front that the facilitator simply manages group process; the team is what generates success. Until success and failures are on their shoulders, they won't be invested in a team outcome.

Warnings to a Facilitator

1. **Be in the moment**, solely observing the group process. The minute your mind runs outside the boundaries of managing group process, you are letting them down.
2. **Listen differently**. Listen for what's missing. Listen for alignment with meeting purpose and team purpose. Listen for the contribution level. Inquire for understanding, clarity, and validation.
3. **Force decisions**. If a discussion is not gaining traction toward an action or decision (covered the same point three times) firmly suggest the team either make a decision or drop the discussion. Give every member permission to use ELMO: enough, let's move on.

4. **Beware of stepping out of your role**. If you do, you can be perceived as a member. You can take off your official facilitator hat and put on a member hat for a period, then put it back on. Or you can phrase your suggestion in the form of a question that steps them into considering the input you feel they need to explore.
5. **Run interference**. If there are needs that are outside the control of the team that must be addressed, the facilitator may have to step in and provide support. Being objective, the facilitator can approach leadership for support.

Don't Forget to Do a Hot Wash-Up

At the conclusion of each meeting, do this consensus-building exercise. This is called a *hot wash-up*.

1. Tell everyone to write on a piece of paper the word *Like*. What was one thing they liked about this meeting?
2. Give them 20 seconds to think and write.
3. Next, tell them to write the word *Better*. What is one thing that could have been done better? This is sort of a continuous improvement statement.
4. Finally, ask them what percentage of the meeting time was effective?
5. Now ask them to take turns sharing their Likes.
6. Then have them share their Betters.
7. Then go around and give their team effectiveness rating.
8. Discussion is allowed as long as it makes the team stronger and sharper next time.
9. Ask if they want to convert any of their Likes and Betters to ground rules.
10. Typically, the team uses the Betters to hone their group process dynamics in future meetings.

Business Process Reengineering (BPR)

There are basically two ways of fixing problems: renovation and reengineering. Renovation takes what exists and remodels it to be the most efficient, effective, waste-free, service-driven process possible. Reengineering on the other hand, attempts to transform what exists by designing what needs to be (without the existing problems), then wiring it back into the existing culture and organization. One way finds a problem, analyzes it, and fixes it; the other way designs a way without the problem in it, then retrofits it back into the culture and organization. Since problem solving is second nature to most engineers, this section focuses on how to facilitate a design method using reengineering. With waves of demands and change from the Healthcare Reform Act rolling out, traditional methods of problem solving, such as plan-do-study-act (PDSA), Lean, and Six Sigma may not move fast enough, be innovative enough, or be nimble enough to deliver required results in such a short timeframe.

A popular quote back in the reengineering era was, "If you think departmental change is a battle, organizational change is an all-out war!" This section proposes facilitating a design method that excels in solving messy, cross-functional, cross-organizational problems. Many stakeholders and process owners rely on the process, yet no one fully owns it. It is a method that efficiently uses facilitator and team members' time, requires little additional training, and it trusts that the answers lie within the staff affected. If this sounds like snake oil, it is because it is not a problem-solving method, it is a design method. One method solves a problem through analysis; the other dissolves it through design. It is important to remember that this approach does not replace proven problem-solving methods; it is simply an option when complexity, time, and size of a problem call for something more creative.

A design method called *Solution Session* developed and used at M.D. Anderson Cancer Center since 2001 has been used twenty times and has never failed to deliver positive results. The method has been employed at two other hospitals by other facilitators with similar success. Team leaders who have used it find it the method of choice to apply to their other messy problems. Both staff and leadership find it an extremely efficient method of making change happen. And finally for the facilitator, it best leverages the team's time in producing valuable change. Every engineer should have a version of this design method in his or her hip pocket to be used as appropriate.

Ingredients of a Solution Session combine three concepts: GE WorkOut™ (change acceleration process), Osborn–Parnes Creative Problem Solving Process, and an Accountability Maturity model. It draws on all roles and departments impacted by the problem to come together (team size ranging from12 to 60 members) to an event to identify all the messes, issues, and ideas related to the problem; then participate in subteams (silos) to design their part of the solution. As the design from the six to eight subteams' solutions mature, they are ultimately wired together into a single system of changes, and then rewired back into the culture and organizational processes.

Facilitating a Solution Session

Typically a team leader will approach the facilitator with what seems to be an impossible mess of a process they want to fix. The Solution Session method will deliver success as long as its process is followed. The facilitator builds confidence with, "Since it has worked twenty times in past projects, this project will not fail either." Talk the team leader through the steps (see Figure 13.1, the ideal schedule) and the roles to show her what it takes.

Facilitator: This person, usually the management engineer, sees to it that the team leader administers the methodology steps. The facilitator's boldness, confidence, and encouragement are what convince the team leader that her project will succeed. The facilitator runs the four-hour Solution Session idea generation event using the creative problem-solving process. The facilitator also rides shotgun on the *change* aspects of the project and coaches and warns the team leader when to communicate to keep momentum high, assure effective meetings, prompt her of next steps, and so on. In short, the facilitator sees to it that the team leader knows and is effective in her role.

Team Leader: This person is truly the key to the project's success. The facilitator remains vigilant, infusing input, confidence, and caution along the way. The team leader administers the methodology and sees to it that the sponsor, subteam leads (explained later), and members all know and perform their roles effectively. She is also responsible for all the communication, follow-up, and clerical work needed to keep the project effective. This may sound like a daunting role; however, once she makes the roles and accountabilities clear up front, the accountability is placed squarely on the members' shoulders. Then she simply follows up on the subteam leaders' progress and makes sure everyone is performing their role as appropriate. The subteam lead effectively manages meetings after the Solution Session.

Mr. Big Sponsor: The senior executive sponsor is the point of authority who goes to battle for the resources the project team needs. For best results, the sponsor should have a span of influence over a large portion of the process being redesigned. Sometimes this may require two or more VPs to be the Mr/Ms Big over the success of the project. The sponsor commits to *endeavor* to do anything in his or her power to do the blocking/tackling needed for project participation and implementation.

Possible Solution Session Planning Schedule

color (copy/paste) the percent complete

1. Prework   Wk | 1 | 2 | 3 | 4 | 5 | 6 | 7 | 8 | 9 | 10 | 11 | 12 | 13
a Secure a Team Leader champion to commit to complete process
b Valid vision/strategy completed/tested Case for change completed
c Secure a supportive, legitimate Mr. Big to champion the Session and implementation
d Develop the rules for session engagement
e Develop list of prework Fact Finding questions by function if possible
e Send out a Call for Commitment to targeted team candidates (all who influence/affected by output)
f Call one-on-one if response is slow (leverage Mr. Big if needed)

2. Sensing Session   Wk | 1 | 2 | 3 | 4 | 5 | 6 | 7 | 8 | 9 | 10 | 11 | 12 | 13
a Schedule session with key function candidates
b Meet with Mr. Big - to understand session role and follow through enforcement
c Get candidates to develop lists of questions they want answered from other areas
d Create communication plan needed to inform, create momentum, open interdepartment networking
e Encourage/attend departmental data gathering/sensing sessions with functions staff
f Fact Finding -- make sure all areas arrive at session with available facts

3. Session Planning   Wk | 1 | 2 | 3 | 4 | 5 | 6 | 7 | 8 | 9 | 10 | 11 | 12 | 13
a Scope size of session based on team ability, session complexity,
b Develop the Agenda timing of Mr. Big, CPSI Training, Probing Statements, Action Plan creation and Presentation
c Poster the Ground rules, Fact Finding turned in, Purpose, Agenda
d Prethink the session set up needs: tables, material, fun things, scribing support, post-its
e Create walkaway workbooks: tabbed with prework, tools, agenda, training slides, session output, commitments,

4. Session Running   Wk | 1 | 2 | 3 | 4 | 5 | 6 | 7 | 8 | 9 | 10 | 11 | 12 | 13
a Facilitator equipped with CPSI knowledge, Team Leader role defined participant/leader
b Mr Big establishes importance, commitment, support and challenge to have committable action plan presented in designated times
c Run the folks thru Mess/Problem/Idea Finding using both divergent/convergent thinking
d If running multiple teams - schedule collective sessions to report output findings
e If team is cohesive -- move to entire group participating in Idea
f If teams can not, then run finding sessions separate. Combine their output at the end.
g Schedule Mr Big to return to hear highlights of the ideas
h Team presents their committable action plan to Mr. Big
i Gather all pieces of data and send session summary of finding to team members

5. Implementation Follow through   Wk | 1 | 2 | 3 | 4 | 5 | 6 | 7 | 8 | 9 | 10 | 11 | 12 | 13
a Team Leader schedule necessary followup session to report on their commitments
b Sub team meet before follow-up meeting
c Follow-up meeting
d Sub team meeting before final-up meeting
e Final-up meeting
f Develop a strategy for implementation success: Start with we are successful, how did we get there? Then turn into action steps
g Followup on each member commitments, team leader runs interference where needed, Use Mr. Big leverage to push support thru
h Keep communication of progress to members to inform/ keep momentum high
i Along side each implementation step, pave way for management/culture acceptance
j Set D-Day for implementation -- allow for lead time for training, equipment acquisition
k Create an action item punch list and update weekly for team
l Update culture as the implementation progresses. Be honest with results.
m Bulldog each impediment in the way of success until it happens. People rarely fail, they just quit
n As key success factor data comes in, report it to the masses
o Personal and organizational confirmation/celebration in use

Figure 13.1 Possible Solution Session planning schedule.

Member: These individuals represent their functions and professions in the project design and decision making. Communications that affect the areas they represent are funneled through (to and from) them. They commit to take the time necessary to meet, design, and implement the solution created by the team.

Accountability principle: The fear of being the first to fail keeps it from happening. In each of these roles, it is made clear that out of the twenty projects using this method, none has experienced failure. The expectation to succeed builds an accountability line-of-sight from the sponsor down to each of the members. No one wants to be the failure point for the whole team.

Secure and interview your Mr. Big: Mr. Big Sponsor or the senior executive leader must be powerful enough to influence participation and implementation. Once a Mr. Big Sponsor is chosen, a meeting is held to (1) validate his/her interest in the importance of fixing the problem, (2) discover any preconceived or pet solutions to the problem they might have, (3) see what financial limits there are to team solutions with good business cases, and (4) establish the level of communication (content and frequency) desired.

Case for action and purpose: People have a hard time fighting for what they don't understand. To solidify why a change is needed in the mind of all, the team leader drafts a couple of compelling paragraphs describing the imperative for change. It would be wise to validate the case for action with a few who were affected by the change. The team leader also crafts a single-sentence purpose statement that captures the essence of what the change effort is trying to achieve.

Create a fact-finding question: Some team leaders consider fact-finding the most important step. It surfaces facts, perceptions, reluctances, and processes existing in the current system. Targeted fact-finding questions are crafted to draw out the facts, knowledge, and sacred cows of those attending the session. Typically there is a set of general questions to all attending the Solution Session, and a set of custom questions tailored for the major functions represented. The responses to these questions are displayed in a matrix and distributed for all to see prior to the session event.

Principle: People are reluctant to make decisions until all the facts are known.

Sensing Sessions: The purpose of the Sensing Session is to inform and legitimize the following to those coming to the Solution Session event: (1) the case for action, (2) the conditions of their participation, (3) the importance of their role and responsibility, (4) what to expect at the Solution Session event and subsequent subteam meetings, and (5) how and when the fact-finding questions are to be completed and returned.

Preparing for the Solution Session event: Ideally, it takes 5 weeks from the time the team leader and facilitator meet to the time the fact-finding questions are returned and communicated. Though the fact-finding questions will not be reviewed at the session itself, they are the prethinking exercise to bring forth all the available facts around the current system. Preparing for the session, the facilitator consults with the team leader to secure Mr. Big's availability, the room to accommodate the session, 3 × 5 Post-it™ pads (1 pad per every 2 attendees), Post-it flip chart paper, Crayola® washable maker pens (slim style), and snacks. It is also good to make a poster of the session purpose statement. To add legitimacy, make a certificate of appreciation for participation signed by the team leader and Mr. Big(s).

Solution Session (idea generating) event: The Solution Session is a rapidly paced idea generation event that uses the Osborn-Parnes Creative Problem Solving Process, which generates three times the traditional brainstorming rates. In 4 hours, as many as 60-plus members will generate literally hundreds of problems and related ideas that will be the starter fluid for developing design solutions. This is the first opportunity for members to bond as a team to collectively design the system that will rid them of the problems plaguing them. Instead of individuals whining that the system does not work, they are *all* generating ideas that will ultimately be considered in the design of the new system without the problems. As facilitator, your job in 4 hours is to push the attendees from diverse functions to generate as many ideas as possible to dissolve the critical problems that exist. This is a generative right-brain process (discussed in the Innovation section) that should have very little discussion or analysis. The more ideas generated the better. Quality is equal to quantity because there are more option from which to choose. The ideas from these 4 hours will later become the starter fluid for the subteam (workgroups) solutions designing the ideal system.

Agenda for a Typical 4-Hour Event (Full process explained in the "Innovation" section)

A typical agenda begins with a kickoff (including Mr. Big), and an explanation of the project's purpose and importance, along with the idea process, which lasts about 20 minutes. This is followed by:

- **Mess-finding:** generating all the possible messes related to purpose, then cluster by theme (25 min).
- **Problem-finding:** generating all the problems in the form of how-to statements (how to educate staff, how to enforce compliance, how to …), then cluster by theme (45 min).
- **During a break**, all the problems from the multiple teams are consolidated and the team sits down to come up with ideas to solve them.
- **Idea-finding:** each problem is called out, determined if it is a keeper or a sleeper, then ideas (practical to whimsical) are generated and attached to it (60 min).
- **Subteam sign-up:** subteam presentation to Mr. Big (20 min).

During subteam sign-up: There are usually 6 to 8 themes or clusters of problems (with ideas attached) on the wall. All members attending sign up to be on one or more themes or subteams. Each subteam converts the ideas into proposals for legitimate short- or long-term solutions. A subteam leader either volunteers or is assigned. Anyone who does not sign up for a subteam can be assigned by the team leader. Note: Member sign-up increases both knowledge and acceptance of the final solution.

At the end of the session: Mr. Big returns to hear about some of the ideas generated for each of the subteam categories. A brave volunteer from each group presents a few ideas. The team is informed that a follow-up meeting will be scheduled in three weeks for each subteam to present their preliminary proposals to Mr. Big. It is a nice touch to conclude the session with certificates of participation signed by Mr. Big and the team leader and to serve lunch (thinking is hard work).

Processing Session Output

Tape down all the problem and idea Post-it notes generated on the flipchart paper. Type up and send each subteam's output to the leads of the subteams within 3 business days. The subteams cannot meet without this processed list of messes/problems and ideas.

Subteam Meetings: Subteams meet as often as needed (suggest 60- to 90-minute meetings) to work through adding and converting the ideas into a set of solutions to address all the problems related to their theme (i.e., education, accountability, automation). There is often overlap in solutions designed between subteams, but that is to be expected when working in focused silos. Their goal is to return to the follow-up meeting with 80% baked solutions to present to Mr. Big and the rest of the team. This focused effort further bonds the members to the purpose of the Solution Session. No one wants to let their subteam down or be a failure point for the entire team. If there are difficulties with a member's participation or departments not being helpful, the team leader contacts Mr. Big to help change their minds. It is the team leader's responsibility to assure these meetings are facilitated efficiently and effectively. If the team leader is not confident that the subteam lead can manage this, she must assign a facilitator or act as facilitator herself until the team can function effectively.

Communication creates momentum: The team leader is the listening post for all the sub-teams' needs and progress. It is best to broadcast once or twice a week to all the team members each subteam's progress to keep the importance and momentum high. This keeps the effort in the forefront of everyone's mind. Encouragement, progress, and hurdles are all helpful to report. A good team leader is a master of knowing the frequency and content to communicate.

Follow-up meeting: The follow-up meeting is simply an executive summary of the proposals from each of the subteams to date. This is when Mr. Big and all the subteams get to see the beginnings of the solutions being formed. It is also quite bonding when each member realizes they are an integral and accountable part of the rest of the team. The announcement of the date of a final-up meeting for final proposals (3 to 6 weeks later) is given at this time. **Tip:** Let the subteams know that Mr. Big will attend the meeting and it is amazing how fast they work to deliver a top-notch presentation. It should be noted that the duration between the follow-up and final-up meeting could be months depending on the season and the complexity of the problems.

Final-up meeting: After the subteams have received the input and knowledge of the follow-up meeting, they return to refine and craft their final proposals so they fit into a comprehensive system. Each proposal must have a good business case and plan for implementation. All along, their meeting minutes have been channeled through the team leader who has been monitoring/communicating/coordinating the loose ends to the respective subteams. All subteams prepare to deliver their final proposal to Mr. Big and the collective team members. Both short-term (within 6 months) and long-term (beyond 6 months) proposals include everyone's input.

Implementation and conclusion: The members that created the solutions are the same ones who implement and retrofit them back into the existing organization. The old way, with all its problems, is dismantled and replaced with the new way. Some Solution Session implementations have taken years to complete due to complexity and resources; but there has yet to be a team that has quit or lost steam in making the solution a success.

Here's an appeal: We suggest that you at least try using this right-brain approach in developing and integrating change. It is fast, respectful of each member's time, engaging to the end, and built to last by those who are affected. It also leverages the facilitator's (your) value to the organization. You simply see to it that the methodology is followed and everyone remains in their role. Team leaders call the methodology *magic* for they don't know how it works; it just creates great results. If it can get an aircraft carrier of an academic state institution like ours to turn on a dime, just think what it can do for your healthcare organization.

Success Factors for Broad-Scale Change

The following are success factors in proverb form distilled by observing twenty successful broad-scale change projects using the Solution Session methodology. See if they can help out your projects.

1. **Know when to renovate or reengineer.** Renovate analyzes what exists then fixes it. Reengineer creates what needs to be, then retrofits it back into the organization.
2. **A passion to make a difference does.** A team leader's willingness to incur sacrifice for a great cause ushers the resolve to achieve it.
3. **The confidence that you *can* is the courage to try.** If you knew there was a project method at which you could not fail, would you be willing to attack the seemingly impossible?
4. **If you remain in your role, you remain effective.** The sponsor, to resource and reinforce; the team lead, to administrate and communicate; the member, to design and implement;

and the facilitator, to prompt the team lead. Any one of these not fulfilling or attempting to fulfill another's role degrades effectiveness.

5. **All affected can design a solution acceptable to all.** Exclude a representative of any and you run the risk of content or acceptance failure.

6. **The fear of being the first to fail keeps it from happening.** Place the accountability of success or failure squarely on the shoulders of each role, and they will make the right choice.

7. **People aware of their role and its importance have no excuse not to produce.** So the failure to clarify both places their participation at risk.

8. **Pressure of letting the team down keeps it from happening.** And the bigger the team the greater the pressure to do your part well.

9. **Decisions are more apt to be made when all the facts are available.** Fact-finding up front is the beginning of ignorance management, so come equipped to make decisions.

10. **The fact that you have political power keeps you from having to use it.** When others know you can call on powers of the sponsor to keep the project successful, resistance is dissolved.

11. **When the boss is waiting for great results, they are delivered on time.** Members' excuses and priorities shift once they know leadership is listening.

12. **Time is your enemy, momentum your friend.** Too much time between deliverables creates project inertia, so set time-pressured deliverables that are within reach. Momentum is communicating progress, which spurs the rest of the team to keep up.

13. **Effective meetings generate action.** The team lead has the responsibility of assuring meetings are effective.

14. **As long as people can give their input, they won't have to get their way.** Giving those affected the opportunity to provide input is the grease to gaining their acceptance toward a collective decision, even if it doesn't go their way.

15. **A good business case and timeframe keep perspective for solutions.** Team members need common parameters to evaluate and devise their solution. Money and timing help that focus.

16. **All systems degrade.** Design effective monitoring and maintenance as part of its solution.

17. **You develop faster in silos; you integrate better in glue.** Specialization maintains team focus and action, but eventually all parts must be glued together into a total system.

18. **Even your method of change must be able to change over time.** A good method must always be adaptable to improve.

19. **If it is real change, you are changed.** And the sponsor, team lead, facilitator, member, even the organization has this opportunity.

20. **People rarely fail, they just quit.** So don't!

Tips for Facilitating Large Meetings

It seems the larger the number of attendees in a meeting, the less productive it is. Facilitating large groups (more than ten attendees) is more like maintaining focus and attention in a board meeting. You are there to help them achieve their goal within each agenda item. Here are some tips to consider.

1. Before the meeting, get with the team lead or chair to clarify their view of what to watch for: Difficult people, out-of-scope issues, team leader cues, previous agreements to enforce.

2. At the start of the meeting, gain permission to facilitate. Ask if you can have permission to manage the group process and enforce the ground rules. Then you have permission to interrupt, redirect, enforce for the sake of group process.

3. Be acquainted with the ground rules. If there are none, then make up some good ones. One talking at a time, on focus, limits for discussion time, monitor in-scope and out-of-scope discussion.
4. A good facilitator deputizes all the attendees with the rules to manage the group process. They make great sentries for ground rules violations.
5. Use inquiry to guide the group: Is this in scope? Should the discussion be offloaded to a workgroup? Has there been enough discussion?
6. Manage the group process within the timeframe of each item:
    a. 10-minute item: 2 min context, 5 min discussion, 2 min decision, 1 min scribing action.
    b. Call out remaining minutes at the half mark, three-quarter mark, and 1-minute mark.
    c. Migrate discussion toward an action or decision.
    d. Treat discussion like a volleyball going across the net. After the discussion bounces from person to person three times without a conclusion, then it is time get the team to spike a decision.
7. Be in the moment. It is a deliberate, conscious act.
    a. Any time your mind wanders off group process and into the content, you're jeopardizing your role and the team's effectiveness.
    b. Continually move your eyes from person to person to gain their nonverbal cues and to keep yourself in the moment.
    c. Ride shotgun to the content of the meeting. Observe discussion within each agenda item and the progression of the meeting as a whole.
    d. Keep an eye on the team leader for prompts to move on, allow extra discussion, intercede, and so on.
    e. Manage time over value of each item discussed. Every minute the team is not moving toward a decision, action, or approval is considered waste. Informing is often a misuse of time.
    f. Monitor the detail level of the discussion. Too low a level, it gets bogged; too high a level is too broad to draw a conclusion or take action.
8. If conversation is between two, ask if the discussion should be handled outside the meeting.
9. To get folks to elaborate, use the following cues: "Tell me more ..." or "And that means ..." Then pause for an answer.
10. Manage what is in scope and out of scope of the discussion. If scope is unknown, rely on the team lead's cue.
11. Make sure there is time at the end to *review agreed-upon action items*, parking lot items, and meeting metric (% of meeting time that was perceived to have been effective).
12. Be on fun patrol. Feel free to lighten things up if you can do it without getting too deep in the content. If it is chaotic, holler "Children!" Then smile.

Your facilitation gets better the more you learn from doing it. And if you trip up, great. You probably won't do that again. Don't be surprised if it takes you five times to feel accomplished.

Innovation

Over the years, audiences of engineers and improvement specialists have been asked, "How many have ever attended a conference on creativity?" Rarely a hand goes up. It is because there was no emphasis on creativity (using the right-side of the brain) in college. Ought we not prepare ourselves to be masters of sparking innovation in others?

There are two creativity organizations that you may want to Google. The Creative Problem Solving Institute and the American Creativity Association. Both organizations have conferences that expose attendees to creativity in a variety of unusual ways. Warning: Creativity often looks crazy because it is not rational or logical. It would be wise to explore what the right brain can do.

Would you like to learn how to facilitate a creative problem-solving process that generates ideas to solve problems at three times typical brainstorming rates? It is energizing and produces ideas for solving problems at amazing speeds. This generative process is called the Osborn-Parnes Creative Problem Solving (CPS) process. Alex Osborn and Sid Parnes are the fathers of brainstorming. They studied geniuses to discover how they mentally processed information. Geniuses alternate their thinking in two modes: divergent thinking (right brain) to generate as many ideas as possible, and convergent thinking (left brain) to select the best idea, prioritize, combine, and so on. You will alternate through both these modes throughout a CPS session. I recommend that you Google Creative Education Foundation/our process/what is.

Tips

Here are some tips on how to conduct a CPS session with 60 participants, and it also works the same with 6 participants:

1. Describe the purpose statement of the problem-solving session.
2. Describe the idea generating process they are about to go through. If they go along with the process, they will generate more ideas than ever before. If they don't, they can actually hurt the final outcome of the session. The facilitator's confidence in this process helps attendees trust the process.
3. Describe the process of generating ideas. Take a Post-it pad (which is their idea collector) and a marker pen, break into groups of 6 to 8, and stand around a flip chart posted on the wall. One idea per Post-it and use at least three words to describe the idea. As team members think of an idea they call it out, write it down on a Post-it with at least three words, then slap it up on the flip chart. Sometimes they assign someone to place the Post-its™ on the flipchart. Then, as fast as they can, they create the next idea. A little context around the thought may be shared, but only enough for others to understand. Discussion must be limited; this is a generative process and the more Post-its the better the outcome. Note: The speed of idea generation and the lack of time actually propels them into use their right (creative) brain. Spontaneous is right brain; discussing and analyzing is left brain.
4. **Mess-finding**. In the divergent mode, generate as many messes of the current system/process as possible. Remember, in the divergent mode, quality of ideas = quantity of ideas. Quantity gives you more ideas to choose from. As facilitator, your role is to assure that team members are successful at generating lots of ideas, so if you do not see Post-its slapping up on the flip chart, go over and help them get started generating more and discussing less (i.e., start making up some of your own). After the divergent thinking comes the convergent thinking where they move the Post-its, finding commonalities of the messes, and cluster them into themes (affinity); then place a header over each. As a facilitator, give a countdown of the time remaining to hustle them along generating and clustering. After the energy drops or time is up, have someone from each flip chart call out their headers. It is often an eye

opener of the similarities among groups. Note: you may allow extra time in mess-finding since it is their first finding process to complete.

5. **Fact-finding.** This steps helps identify all the facts/data/requirements that are known about the system and processes relating to the purpose statement. This would be both qualitative and quantitative. (Note that in the Solution Session mentioned in the previous section, fact-finding is conducted prior to the event to save time.)

6. **Problem-finding.** Instruct them to remove the flip chart page with all the messes and place it next to the blank flip chart. The next step is the most important finding exercise, which is problem-finding. What are all the problems in the existing system or in the way of the purpose statement? Name and list all of them. Your problem statements must be written in the form of a how-to statement. How to communicate, how to reduce, how to alert, how to automate, and so on. How-to statements beg for a solution or idea. The more specific they are, the better. As facilitator, don't be surprised if you have to visit each of the groups and help them with examples of how-to statements. Give them more time in generative divergent mode for Post-it note writing and converging them into clusters (with headers).

7. **Consolidation.** Have each of the groups call out their cluster headers, then ask one or two members of each group to bring their problem-finding sheets of Post-its and help consolidate them on a single "wall" of problems. Problems under similar headings are consolidated. The left-brain organizer members love doing this. This often entails eliminating duplicate problem statements, combining/renaming similar clusters, or making new categories or clusters. If you had 5 groups, then 5 groups of problems are consolidated onto a single wall of problems. While this is going on, chairs in the room are positioned facing the wall of problem statements.

8. **Idea-finding.** This is the hardest of all finding efforts, for it requires concerted focus from the entire group for up to an hour. Imagine 60 people generating ideas for a hundred problems. That's a lot of brain power. Here's how it goes. All team members still have a Post-it pad and markers in hand. The team leader calls out a how-to problem statement to the group. She asks if the problem statement is a "keeper" (significant, specific, and clear enough to generate ideas) or a "sleeper" (duplicate, too broad, not relevant). If it is a sleeper, the Post-it is discarded. If it is a keeper, all minds in the room endeavor to generate ideas that might be used in the solution. Tip: The shortness of time actually generates more (spontaneous) ideas. If there are only 60 minutes to address 120 problems, that leaves only 30 seconds per problem to consider, call out, and write down on a Post-it all potential ideas.

9. **Writing down ideas.** As the ideas are called out, they must be written on a Post-it and run to the team leader so they can be attached to its problem. The facilitator may have to motion to the initiator to write it down on a Post-it; it is handed to the facilitator or runner, and delivered to the team leader who attaches it to the problem statement. Tip: It is best to have the person who will be processing (typing up) the Post-its of problems with related ideas assist the team leader to collect/attach/add clarification to the Post-its. If the ideas called out are vague, the facilitator asks for elaboration (tell me more) to gain specificity. Specific ideas lead to specific solutions.

10. **Solution-finding** (idea + implementation = solution). Which of these ideas have implementation implications that would make them a practical solution? They can be short range—implemented in the next 6 months, or long range—implemented in 7 to 12 months. (Note that in the Solution Session, the solutions are designed in the subteams after the event.)

11. **Action- or acceptance-finding.** Determine which actions can be taken and the acceptance that has been gained to get the solutions implemented.

The CPS process can be completed in 60 to 90 minutes. The more specific the problem statement, the more specific the solutions. My first experience with this process was how to design a better bathtub. It was amazing how creative (and fun) it was. By the way, if you are not having fun, you are not being as creative as you can be.

Forced Connections, Random Words Tool

The right brain has a lot of problem-solving potential; we're just not used to stretching it. There is another technique called Random Word, which uses forced connection between a problem statement and a random word to derive a solution. Try this with a group.

1. Write a problem statement on a flip chart.
2. Make a list of ten random words to the side (Google random word generator or create your own).
3. Ask the group to read the problem, then pick two of the random words.
4. Now have each find associations between the word (or words) and the problem, and write them down.
5. Move away from the problem and focus on the word(s). What other related words come to mind? Write down words and phrases associated with that word.
6. Try to force a connection between the problem and your words or phrases into a solution. How might random or associated words frame a solution or remedy? Talking it out with another can spur more creative possibilities as well.

Don't let logic discount this method without trying it. You'll be surprised how inventive that little mind of yours is.

Conclusion

In order to make more change happen faster with fewer difficulties, having an array of facilitation competencies is necessary. The more you try it, learn from it, and refine it, the more confident and competent you will become, and the more value you will provide those you serve.

References

Random Word technique and example, Creativity Unleashed Limited, 2006, http://www.cul.co.uk/creative/ranword.htm.

Scholtes, Peter R. The Team Handbook: How to Use Teams to Improve Quality. Joiner, 2003. Madison, WI.

Ulrich, D., Kerr, S., and Ashkenas, R. *The GE Work-Out : How to Implement GE's Revolutionary Method for Busting Bureaucracy and Attacking Organizational Problems.* New York: McGraw Hill, 2002.

Chapter 14

Process Redesign in Healthcare

Alexander Bohn and Sue Ann Te

Contents

What Is Process Redesign?

Process redesign is the application of process improvement methodologies to a current system to remove waste and increase efficiencies. It is a fundamental tenet of industrial engineering (IE), and utilizes a full spectrum of IE tools to continuously improve processes or programs in any industry. Distinct from process reengineering, which creates an entirely new process from one that is obsolete, process redesign seeks to improve aspects of the current state while keeping the foundation of the process intact. Process reengineering can be thought of like the transition from cassette tapes to compact discs, an entirely new format for playing music. Process redesign is similar to the next generation of a smart phone, the technology is simply given more features, a more efficient processor, and a new look.

How Do You Employ Process Redesign?

Defining Project Scope, Resources, and Goals

Identifying the primary process and opportunity for improvement is the first step in any process redesign project. As frontline staff is most familiar with the daily work, one way to achieve this is to ask the staff for their perceived areas of inefficiency or opportunities for improvement. Often, nurses, physicians, or other healthcare staff have a greater understanding of what needs to be improved. It's up to the process improvement (PI) team to quantify the problem and provide a structure and approach to develop a solution in conjunction with the healthcare stakeholders and the available resources. The team should maintain a list of potential process redesign options or opportunities, and then develop the feasibility and potential return on each one to help identify where to begin.

Once the targeted process has been identified, it is important to completely define the problem, areas for improvement, and expected outcomes of the future state design. Develop an abstract around the inefficiency that describes in detail why the inefficiency exists in the current state and what the redesign aims to solve. This abstract can, if necessary, be reviewed and approved by administration and frontline staff as a kickoff agreement for the project. Clearly outline the focus of the process redesign and be sure that the stakeholders understand exactly which aspects will be improved upon. This will focus the efforts and guard against scope creep. Investigate if the existing process has any metrics currently being tracked within it that can be used as quantitative benchmarks. Finally, document a list of expected outcomes for the project. Try to be as specific as possible with the outcomes (using the collected metrics, if applicable) and set high standards for the hospital or department.

Current State

Current state is the term used to describe the system or process as it exists today. It may be represented by a process map, standard operating steps, or other means. It's nearly impossible to design an improved process without first gaining a clear understanding of the current state model. The current state is generally developed in conjunction with department staff who helped identify the process to redesign in the first place. The current state should be simple and straightforward enough to be understood by any of the process owners or stakeholders including staff members or senior leadership from throughout the organization.

The first decision to make is how the current state process will be represented. If the process is straightforward with few deviations and entry or exit points, an Excel spreadsheet representing the steps might suffice. Process mapping (such as those developed in Microsoft Visio, see Figure 14.1) can be utilized for processes with many decision points, as it more effectively displays multiple points of entry and paths that a process can take. For very standardized, precise processes, consider using a systems modeling software such as Arena or STELLA, to represent and see the potential effects of process changes digitally, before implementing them.

It is imperative to obtain honest feedback while documenting the current state process to ensure that the information is representative of the actual workflow, and not simply what the hospital policies mandate. Healthcare is dictated by strict guidelines and procedures, so staff are often hesitant to admit if rules are being bent or shortcuts taken. Due to this challenge, make it a priority to meet with the frontline staff personally. Ensure that the staff and management are able to comfortably and honestly explain the details of their job, even if the *ideal world* and *reality* of the functions have some differences. You may even want to walk through parts of the process with

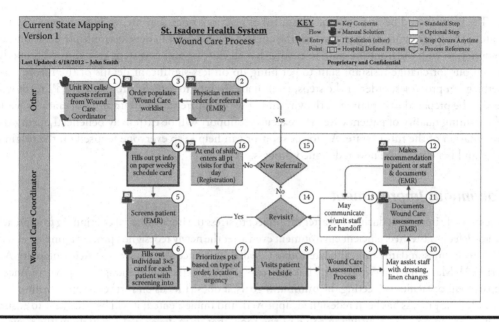

Figure 14.1   Wound care process flow example (Microsoft Visio).

frontline staff to better understand, verify, and document the process. Staff tend to speak more candidly about their work in this setting.

It will be necessary to meet with staff and management multiple times throughout the current state, developing multiple iterations. Use the current state to highlight potential areas for improvement or *key concerns* that will be the focus of the future state design. These identified points can be developed as a separate document to be used in conjunction with the current state to help justify the process redesign. The current state stage can also be used as another project sign-off to keep all stakeholders engaged.

Future State

Once the current state is fully captured, this knowledge will be used to design the future state. As noted previously, the *future state* is not a completely new process, but rather the current state with key improvements to increase efficiency and quality. Again, it's important to always keep the patient's perspective and experience in mind when designing the future state. Building the future state directly from the current state map or document will ensure that every element of the current state is accounted for and the changes can be easily noted since the two processes will resemble each other.

A very important aspect of the future state is integrating benchmarks or milestones to quantify the improvement that the process redesign achieved. Any current state metrics should be considered as this provides a clear before-and-after picture, but it is also encouraged to establish new milestones throughout the process. These targets could be a time period between events, a reduced amount of wasted resources, or a desired "defect" rate. You may even include as a target, the elimination of steps in the process for both the patients and the staff. Ensure that the milestones can be tracked and reported accurately through software, paper logs, or other technology solutions. These benchmarks, while justifying the effectiveness of the redesign, also give the staff measureable goals to meet and a sense of accomplishment once those goals are met.

The team should be prepared for a handful of reactions once they are ready to present the first draft of the future state designs. As with the current state, expect to develop multiple iterations, in conjunction with the frontline staff, to ensure that all existing and new steps are captured properly. Watch out for change-resistant staff to get hung up on less-significant details of the future state (verbiage in processes, order of the steps, etc.) in an attempt to impede progress. The PI team will need to be prepared to explain exactly why and how the future state will improve operations while maintaining quality of patient care. The executive support will be extremely beneficial during the presentation of the future state. A project sponsor can help keep everyone focused on the original goals and benefits of the new redesigned process.

Continuous Improvement

It's extremely important during and after the project to stress the importance of continuing to approach a zero-defect, waste-free, efficient environment even after the newly redesigned process is implemented. With so many standards in healthcare today (Health Insurance Portability and Accountability Act [HIPAA], Magnet, payer criteria, etc.) it is very easy to fall into the "good enough" trap where, once a department or facility is meeting the minimum goals, it doesn't focus on further improvement.

After the process has been redesigned, approved, and implemented, it will be necessary to ensure continuous improvement utilizing some of the tools that were developed throughout the project. First of all, establish a regular schedule for executive rounding or meetings with frontline staff in order to continue the forum for staff-to-management communication of inefficiencies and ideas for improvement. Also, the milestones and benchmarks that were developed during future state design can be continually monitored and adjusted as they are met to keep the entire department focused on increasing operational effectiveness.

Special Considerations and Issues

Process redesign in the realm of healthcare also encounters some unique challenges that a PI team should look out for. The quality of care given to the patient should always be the number one priority of any healthcare organization. Any redesigned process cannot compromise patient care, and in most if not all cases, should seek to improve an aspect of care. A process that saves capital, time, or resources will likely encounter strong pushback if patient care is negatively affected or even perceived to be negatively affected, and will need to go back to the drawing board. If this is not addressed, the project may even be shut down. The industrial engineer's bias may be to view the patient as a product on an assembly line, with the goal to get the patient out the door healthy and defect-free. This mentality can be very successful in healthcare process redesign, as long as the team has an in-depth understanding of the aspects of a system that ensure the patient experience is great, and improves or maintains these pieces. This is why it is imperative to partner with and have strong clinical advocates on the process improvement team. These advocates understand clinical challenges and can help lend credibility to the efficacy of the redesigned process.

The term *patient experience* is simply defined as any aspect of interaction with or care received by the patient. Patient experience encompasses everything that the patient and his or her family encounter or perceive as part of the healthcare process or event, including quality of care, bedside manner of caregivers, freshness of food, and cleanliness of facilities. Although a process redesign may not immediately appear to have an impact on the patient experience, almost every process can be tied back to this experience in some fashion. A PI team should always identify and work to improve a piece of the process that will have a positive impact on patient care.

An unfortunate reality of change management and process redesign in healthcare (as in many other industries) is resistance to the unfamiliar or becoming entrenched in the trap of a "but that is how we have always done it" mentality. One way to proactively avoid this potential road block is to gain strong support from leadership and administration at the beginning of the project. In addition, the more that frontline staff are involved in the potential solutions, the easier it will be for them to accept the necessary improvements and changes. The necessary resources will vary depending on the scope and size of the process redesign, with facilitywide processes potentially requiring the support of the C-Suite (chiefs, vice presidents, etc.) or organization leaders. Meet with these key management stakeholders to explain the full scope of the process redesign and what it aims to achieve. Ensure that all of their questions can be answered and they are clear on the vision of the project. If it becomes a hard sell to key leaders in the area of focus, then you and the team may wish to consider other processes that could be redesigned for better outcomes.

Obtaining this administrative buy-in can swing the momentum of a project completely. Management must understand the key aspects of the process redesign, otherwise they may be unable to address concerns that their department may bring up. However, if staff leadership recognizes the value of the project and what can be expected to improve, they will become a much more effective advocate for selling the future state than any outside department or resource. This approval should be considered an integral step in a process redesign project; it can not only help ensure success if obtained, but also lead to a complete project breakdown if ignored.

Frequent and regular meetings with department leadership at the beginning and throughout the process redesign project can also create a forum of communication between frontline staff and administration. Management may not be aware of certain breakdowns in processes that occur on a regular basis. Hosting meetings that are focused on identifying these issues will often allow staff to speak more candidly about the reality of their work, rather than continuing to work inefficiently to meet the expectations of the patient and their employer. The PI team member is uniquely qualified to facilitate these discussions and the involvement of this objective resource can ensure that the meetings lead to positive outcomes and understanding of critical next steps. Management may also pose different types of questions than caregivers, and these considerations need to be given to redesigned processes. An improvement in one department of a hospital may inadvertently disrupt operations elsewhere, and administration may have a better picture of the entire system. The PI professional should make sure that he or she is also keeping an eye on the bigger picture to fully appreciate the systemwide impact of potential redesign solutions.

Project Example

Let's look at a very straightforward process redesign project in a healthcare setting, and how patient care should be considered.

Background

Fairview Hospital is a 350-bed facility that has been operating over or at capacity over the past 3 months. The lack of inpatient beds has resulted in Fairview having to divert patients to competitor hospitals, a potentially significant loss of revenue. Emergency Department (ED) boarder hours (the number of hours patients are holding in the emergency department waiting for an inpatient bed) have steadily increased. Last month, ED boarder hours reached a record high of 1,500 hours. Another indicator that has significantly increased is the facility's average length of stay, from 5.4

days to 6.1 days. As the year approaches, Fairview's peak admission period, addressing their capacity has become a consistent topic of discussion at senior leadership team meetings. At last week's meeting, the chief operating officer proposed that the PI department lead an initiative to address the capacity challenge.

Defining Scope, Resources, and Goals

An initial meeting was held with key stakeholders from the ED and inpatient units since these areas are known to be experiencing the effects of the capacity challenge. Staff attending the meeting included inpatient nurses, ED physicians, ED nurses, hospitalists, and house supervisors. The PI team facilitated a discussion to gather the staff's input of potential root causes and factors contributing to the capacity challenge. The team identified several items for consideration:

- Admissions from the ED were difficult to predict, so house supervisors were unable to plan for and balance ED admissions with other admission sources (surgery, direct admits, hospital transfers, etc.).
- Nurses were unaware of hospitalist or attending physician plans to discharge a patient.
- Patients were often unaware of hospitalist or attending physician plans to discharge them.
- Once a physician discharge order was received, a nurse could spend up to 3 hours to complete all the necessary paperwork required to discharge a patient.
- Once a patient was discharged, there were delays in getting the bed cleaned.
- Nurses noted that some ED admissions seemed questionable (i.e., in their opinion, the patient did not need to be admitted).

While there were several factors contributing to the capacity challenge, the team agreed that many of the factors centered on the discharge process. The goal of the project was determined to be decreasing the time from a physician discharge order to the time the patient left the hospital. Once the target process was determined, the team identified every role that participated in the discharge process. This helped to identify the resources required for the initiative. A few of the new roles identified were case managers, unit secretaries, pharmacy, and transporters. After the meeting, the PI team worked to develop a process for gathering the current time between a physician order and the patient leaving the facility. This not only provided a baseline for current performance, but also provided a way to track and measure the impact of future improvements. It currently took an average of 6.5 hours for a patient to be discharged once a physician order was written. Fairview's goal was to decrease that average to 2 hours.

Current State

Next, the PI team led a working session with frontline staff to document the current discharge process. Because of the multiple roles involved and the various locations patients were discharged to, a process flow map was used to document the process. The staff helped to identify steps in the process that were barriers to patient discharge, and these steps were marked with a red dot. Examples of barriers included steps not being completed consistently, delays in obtaining necessary information or materials, and variability in the process based on resource.

After the working session, the PI team created an electronic version of the process documented on paper during the session. This electronic version was distributed to the staff who participated in the session for validation. As staff provided feedback, the document was revised until approval was obtained from all team members. The final current state process flow was shared with key stakeholders, including operational and senior leadership.

Future State

Once the current state was completed, the PI team led a second working session with the team to develop a proposed future state process. Since this was a process redesign effort (as opposed to a process reengineering effort), the team focused on the red dot items identified during current state. For each red dot item, the team brainstormed ideas for improvement and all ideas regardless of cost, effort, or impact were considered. For example, one of the red dot items identified during current state was that patients were unaware of the physician's plans for discharge. The team came up with several ideas for addressing this barrier:

A. Hire a team of discharge nurses who focus on communicating discharge plans to patients and preparing them for discharge.
B. Build a discharge lounge that patients could wait in for their loved ones to pick them up, freeing up their bed sooner for the next patient.
C. Incorporate discharge planning discussions into the existing daily multidisciplinary rounds on each unit. Develop a template to structure these discussions to ensure consistency across the organization.
D. Post the patient's expected discharge date on the white board in the patient's room so the patient and care team work toward a common goal.
E. Evaluate the tasks and the paperwork nurses were required to complete to discharge a patient and determine if all are truly required and if any could be completed prior to a physician discharge order.

Next, the team evaluated the effort and cost required (high or low) to implement the idea as well as the expected impact of the improvement (high or low). Ideas that required low effort or cost but were high impact were favored to be incorporated into the future state process flow. The team also noted a risk to patient satisfaction with idea B (see Figure 14.2).

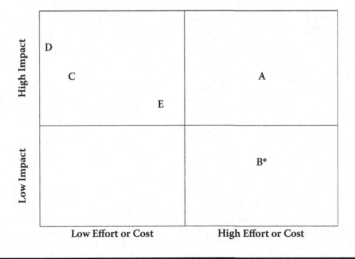

Figure 14.2   Effort versus impact grid.

In this example, ideas C, D, and E were selected to be reflected in the future state flow and recommendations. After multiple iterations, the future state was finalized and implementation plans were developed. Over the next few months, Fairview experienced a steady decrease in the performance metric they chose to track (physician discharge order written to patient out of bed) and a significant increase in patient satisfaction. This was a direct result of the decrease in the amount of time patients waited to leave the facility as well as the increased communication, giving patients a sense of involvement in their care.

Chapter 15

Total Quality Management and the Malcolm Baldrige Quality Award

Lawrence (Larry) Dux

Contents

Brief Background

The healthcare industry has long recognized that patient care quality and safety is paramount and healthcare organizations incorporate these concepts into their mission, vision, and value statements. The following sample mission and/or vision statements from two recent Malcolm Baldrige Award Winners reflect this commitment to quality and safety.

Henry Ford Health System—Detroit, Michigan

Mission Statement: To improve human life through excellence in the science and art of health care and healing.

Vision: Transforming lives and communities through health and wellness—one person at a time.

Values: We serve our patients and our community through our actions that always demonstrate: Each Patient First, Respect for People, High Performance, Learning and Continuous Improvement, and a Social Conscience.[1]

Sharp HealthCare—San Diego, California

Mission Statement: To improve the health of those we serve with a commitment to excellence in all that we do. Sharp's goal is to offer quality care and services that set community standards, exceed patients' expectations, and are provided in a caring, convenient, cost effective and accessible manner.

Vision Statement: Sharp will redefine the health care experience through a culture of caring, quality, service, innovation, and excellence. Sharp will be recognized by employees, physicians, patients, volunteers, and the community as: the best place to work, the best place to practice medicine, and the best place to receive care. Sharp will be known as an excellent community citizen embodying an organization of people working together to do the right thing every day to improve the health and well-being of those we serve. Sharp will become the best health system in the universe.

Core Values: Integrity, Caring, Innovation, Excellence."[2]

While these mission, vision, and value statements reflect the organizational commitment to the quality and safety of patient care, the Institute of Medicine's 2000 landmark report *To Err is Human: Building a Safer Health System* highlighted the fact that there are between 44,000 and 98,000 deaths annually in hospitals due to medical errors.[3] This report identified that the healthcare system itself was between the fifth and ninth leading cause of death in the United States. The conclusion from this report was that while there had been significant improvements in the technological aspects of healthcare delivery in the United States, there were still challenges in the creation of a well- coordinated healthcare system that could systematically address the problems associated with the underuse of beneficial services, overuse of procedures that are not medically necessary, and mistakes that lead to patient injury. This chapter will provide insight on how the healthcare industry has adapted the concepts and tools of Total Quality Management and the framework of the Malcolm Baldrige Award[4] to address these problems (see Figure 15.1).

Healthcare Quality from a Process and Systems Perspective

The early work of individuals such as W. Edwards Deming, Walter Shewhart, and Joseph M. Juran introduced the world to the science of quality improvement, and while their initial work focused on the manufacturing sectors, the healthcare industry has been able to learn from and adapt the methodologies and tools that were originally developed in the 1940s and 1950s in Japan and the United States. W. Edwards Deming contributed his fourteen key principles to managers for transforming business effectiveness. The points were first presented in his book *Out of the Crisis* in 1986 and revised in 1990 (see Table 15.1).[5] Although Deming does not use the term in his book, it is credited with launching the Total Quality Management movement. Walter Shewhart is best known for his work in the use of statistical process control (SPC) charts and the concepts of

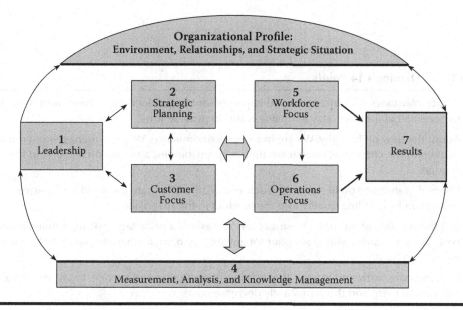

Figure 15.1 Malcolm Baldrige framework.

common cause and special cause variation. The Shewhart Cycle, which has been widely adopted in healthcare, is commonly referred to as the PDSA (Plan, Do, Study, Act) cycle. Joseph M. Juran taught us the importance of using a project-by-project, problem-solving, team method of quality improvement in which all levels of management must be involved—Total Quality Management. The Juran Trilogy[6] identifies the three processes necessary to manage quality.

Joseph M. Juran was a vocal advocate for the Malcolm Baldrige National Quality Award program. Prior to the passage of the congressional act that created the Baldrige Award in 1987, he testified in front of Congress on behalf of creating the award to help bring the focus of quality to the United States. He was also one of the original overseers of the Baldrige Award process.[7]

The approaches and tools created and used by these individuals formed the foundation for what is now referred to as Total Quality Management (TQM), where TQM is broadly defined as a management philosophy and process focused on committing organizational resources in an environment of teamwork and collaboration to meeting and/or exceeding customer expectations at a cost that represents value to the customer.

The first key point of this definition is that the senior management of the organization must provide the leadership to embrace this management philosophy, or as stated in the definition of *visionary leadership* within the Malcolm Baldrige criteria: "Your leaders should ensure the creation of strategies, systems, and methods for achieving performance excellence in health care, stimulating innovation, building knowledge and capabilities, and ensuring organizational sustainability. The defined values and strategies should help guide all of your organization's activities and decisions."[8] The second point of this definition is that TQM requires both structure and process in order to achieve the desired outcomes, or as stated in the definition of *management by fact* from the Malcolm Baldrige criteria: "An effective healthcare service and administrative management system depends on the measurement and analysis of performance. Such measurements should derive from health care service needs and strategy, and should provide critical data and information about key processes, outputs, and results."[9]

Table 15.1   Deming's 14 Points

1. Create constancy of purpose toward improvement of product and service, with the aim to become competitive, stay in business and to provide jobs.

2. Adopt the new philosophy. We are in a new economic age. Western management must awaken to the challenge, must learn their responsibilities, and take on leadership for change.

3. Cease dependence on inspection to achieve quality. Eliminate the need for massive inspection by building quality into the product in the first place.

4. End the practice of awarding business on the basis of a price tag. Instead, minimize total cost. Move towards a single supplier for any one item, on a long-term relationship of loyalty and trust.

5. Improve constantly and forever the system of production and service, to improve quality and productivity, and thus constantly decrease costs.

6. Institute training on the job.

7. Institute leadership (see Point 12 and Ch. 8 of "Out of the Crisis"). The aim of supervision should be to help people and machines and gadgets do a better job. Supervision of management is in need of overhaul, as well as supervision of production workers.

8. Drive out fear, so that everyone may work effectively for the company. (See Ch. 3 of "Out of the Crisis")

9. Break down barriers between departments. People in research, design, sales, and production must work as a team, in order to foresee problems of production and usage that may be encountered with the product or service.

10. Eliminate slogans, exhortations, and targets for the work force asking for zero defects and new levels of productivity. Such exhortations only create adversarial relationships, as the bulk of the causes of low quality and low productivity belong to the system and thus lie beyond the power of the work force.

11. a. Eliminate work standards (quotas) on the factory floor. Substitute with leadership.

    b. Eliminate management by objective. Eliminate management by numbers and numerical goals. Instead substitute with leadership.

12. a. Remove barriers that rob the hourly worker of his right to pride of workmanship. The responsibility of supervisors must be changed from sheer numbers to quality.

    b. Remove barriers that rob people in management and in engineering of their right to pride of workmanship. This means, *inter alia*, abolishment of the annual or merit rating and of management by objectives (See Ch. 3 of "Out of the Crisis").

13. Institute a vigorous program of education and self-improvement.

14. Put everybody in the company to work to accomplish the transformation. The transformation is everybody's job.

Malcolm Baldrige National Quality Award Criteria

The Baldrige model is defined by the Baldrige Criteria, which is organized into seven categories and 17 items. The application summaries of recent Malcolm Baldrige Award winners can be found on the National Institute of Standards and Technology website: http://www.baldrige.nist.gov/Contacts_Profiles.htm.

> **Category 1: Leadership (70 points)**
> – How do your senior leaders lead?
> – How do you govern and fulfill your societal responsibilities?
>
> **Category 2: Strategic Planning (85 points)**
> – How do you develop your strategy?
> – How do you implement your strategy?
>
> **Category 3: Customer Focus (85 points)**
> – How do you obtain information from your patients and stakeholders?
> – How do you engage patients and stakeholders to serve their needs and build relationships?
>
> **Category 4: Measurement, Analysis, and Knowledge Management (90 points)**
> – How do you measure, analyze, and then improve organizational performance?
> – How do you manage your information, organizational knowledge, and information technology?
>
> **Category 5: Workforce Focus (85 points)**
> – How do you build an effective and supportive workforce environment?
> – How do you engage your workforce to achieve organizational and personal success?
>
> **Category 6: Operations Focus (85 points)**
> – How do you design, manage, and improve your work systems?
> – How do you design, manage, and improve your key work processes?
>
> **Category 7: Results (450 points)**
> – What are your healthcare and process effectiveness results?
> – What are your patient and stakeholder-focused performance results?
> – What are your workforce-focused performance results?
> – What are your senior leadership and governance results?
> – What are your financial and marketplace performance results?

The healthcare industry has embraced the use of the Malcolm Baldrige National Quality Award Criteria as reflected in the number of healthcare organizations submitting applications. In 2011, 40 of the 69 submitted applications were from healthcare organizations, and in 2012, 25 of the 39 submitted applications were from healthcare organizations. The positive impact of the use of the Malcolm Baldrige criteria in healthcare has been documented by John R. Griffith and Kenneth R. White in their paper titled "The Revolution in Hospital Management," as presented in the May/June 2005 issue of the *Journal of Healthcare Management*.[10] In October 2011, David Foster PhD, MPH, from the Center for Healthcare Analytics, and Jean Chenoweth, from the Center for Healthcare Improvement, and 100 Top Hospital Programs reported "Baldrige hospitals were significantly more likely than their peers to display faster five year performance improvement. Baldrige hospitals outperformed non-Baldrige hospitals on nearly all of the individual measures of performance used in the 100 Top Hospitals composite score."[11]

Summary

The skill set of the hospital management engineer is well suited to lead and support the quality and safety improvement initiatives that result in achieving new standards for performance accountability and excellence as reflected in these studies.

Endnotes

1. Henry Ford Health System, Malcolm Baldrige National Quality Award Application Summary, 2012, ii.
2. Sharp Healthcare, Malcolm Baldrige National Quality Award Application Summary, 2007, i.
3. Institute of Medicine, *To Err is Human: Building a Safer Health System* (Washington, DC: National Academy Press, 2000).
4. Malcolm Baldrige National Quality Award, *2011–12 Health Care Criteria for Performance Excellence*, National Institute of Standards and Technology, United States Department of Commerce, 2011, http://www.nist.gov/baldrige/publications/upload/2011_2012_ Health_Care_Criteria.pdf.
5. Deming, W.E., *Out of the Crisis* (Cambridge: Massachusetts Institute of Technology, Center for Advanced Engineering Study, 1986).
6. Juran, J.M. (1989) *Juran on Leadership for Quality: An Executive Handbook* (New York: The Free Press, 1989), 19–23.
7. Juran Institute, Inc., http://www.juran.com/publications/, December 14, 2012.
8. Malcolm Baldrige National Quality Award, *2011–12 Health Care Criteria for Performance Excellence*, National Institute of Standards and Technology, United States Department of Commerce, 2011, http://www.nist.gov/baldrige/publications/upload/2011_2012_ Health_Care_Criteria.pdf, 49.
9. Malcolm Baldrige National Quality Award, *2011–12 Health Care Criteria for Performance Excellence*, National Institute of Standards and Technology, United States Department of Commerce, 2011, http://www.nist.gov/baldrige/publications/upload/2011_2012_ Health_Care_Criteria.pdf, 52.
10. John R. Griffith and Kenneth R. White, "The Revolution in Hospital Management," Journal of Healthcare Management 50, no. 3 (2005): 170–190.
11. Davis A. Foster and Jean Chenoweth, *Comparison of Baldrige Award Applicants and Recipients with Peer Hospitals on a National Balanced Scorecard* (Ann Arbor, MI: Center for Healthcare Improvement, 2011).

Chapter 16

Six Sigma

Cristina Daccarett

Contents

In statistical terms, Six Sigma means that a process produces no more than 3.4 defects per million opportunities. In broader terms, Six Sigma is a highly structured data-driven methodology for problem solving and variation reduction. When following Six Sigma improvement projects, two separate processes can be followed, DMAIC (define, measure, analyze, improve, and control) and DMADV (define, measure, analyze, design, verify). The DMAIC process is used when an existing process needs to be improved, while the DMADV process is utilized when a new process needs to be developed. Although this chapter focuses on the DMAIC flow, the DMADV process is slightly similar with the difference being that the focus of the various phases is on understanding what is needed and developing a new process. DMAIC focuses on understanding the current state and improving it.

Define

The *define phase* is one of the most critical stages in the DMAIC flow. The focus of this phase is to understand the problem and build the foundations to ensure a successful outcome. It is important that this phase remains problem oriented. Root causes and solutions are identified later in the process.

During this phase, a *project charter* is developed. This document summarizes the findings from the define phase and serves as a reference tool in other phases of the project. An example can be seen in Figure 16.1. A typical charter includes a project title, a project plan, the team structure, problem

Project Charter		
Project Title: Preventing avoidable utilization of acute care services		

Project Team		Project Plan		
		Milestone	*Target*	*Actual*
Sponsor:	David Fonseca	Start of Project	1/9/2012	1/13/2012
Champion:	Cecilia Forero	End of Define	1/20/2012	1/19/2012
Leader:	Sarah Clifford	End of Measure	2/2/2012	2/6/2012
Team Members:	Marcos Yaar	End of Analyze	2/24/2012	2/23/2012
	Catherine Smith	End of Improve	3/16/2012	3/23/2012
	Brad Johnson	End of Control	4/6/2012	4/11/2012
	Angelina Braun			

Problem Statement: Chart audits of patients discharged between 7/1/11 and 9/30/11 demonstrate that 35% of patients who used acute care services postdischarge (emergency room or/and hospitalization) could have been prevented.

Goal Statement: Reduce the percentage of patients who experience a decompensation postdischarge that results in the utilization of acute care services. From 15% to 10% by 3/16/12.

Business Case: Designing targeted and effective interventions that aid in preventing decompensations can improve quality of life for patients and reduce healthcare costs.

Scope: All patients discharged from the hospital excluding those who have transitioned to hospice care or are in a transplant registry.

Customers and Stakeholders: Patients, family, providers, insurance

Signatures:

Sponsor _____

Champion _____

Leader _____

Figure 16.1 Project charter.

and goal statements, the business case, scope, and stakeholders. The title should be short but should describe the project. The project plan includes dates for milestones and a targeted completion date. A Six Sigma project team includes, at minimum, a sponsor, a champion, a leader, and team members. The *sponsor* has an executive leadership role and is responsible for selecting the project and supporting the team by eliminating barriers and solving cross-functional issues. The *champion* owns the process and has the ability to mediate issues across the organization and can create support systems. The *leader* is a black belt (a professional with thorough understanding of the Six Sigma philosophies, principles, and tools) who directs and guides the team throughout the DMAIC process. The *team members* are active participants in the process and have firsthand knowledge of the various stages of the process. The problem statement is a brief description of the problem while the goal statement is a brief definition of the target. Both of these statements should be specific, measurable, achievable, relevant, and time bound. An easy way to remember how to state the goal is to use the acronym SMART. The business case describes why the current situation is important or is no longer acceptable and details the financial justification for the project. The scope defines the boundaries for the project. The stakeholders are all those individuals who will be impacted by the project.

Six Sigma projects focus on the customer, and as such, it is important to keep in mind the customer's wants, expectations, and values throughout the project. During the define phase it is

Names	ARMI	Strongly Against	Moderately Against	Neutral	Moderately Supportive	Strongly Supportive
Clinic Director	A				X ⟶	X
Clinic Physicians	M			X ⟶		X
Clinic Nurses	M			X ⟶		X
Specialty Physicians	I			X ⟶		X
Hospitalists	R			X ⟶		X
Emergency Department Physicians	M			X ⟶		X
Emergency Department Nurses	M			X ⟶	X	
Unit Nurses	R		X ⟶		X	
Case Managers	R			X ⟶	X	
Inpatient Pharmacy	I			X ⟶	X	
Outpatient Pharmacy	M			X ⟶		X
Home Health	I			X ⟶	X	
Skilled Nursing Facilities	I		X ⟶		X	

(A)pprover: Approves team decision prior to moving forward

(R)esource: Individual whose expertise may be needed on an ad-hoc basis

(M)ember: Active participant of the team

(I)nterested party: Person who needs to be kept informed and whose support might be needed in the future

Figure 16.2   ARMI.

important to gather the voice of the customer. Collecting the customer's input through direct contact, focus groups, surveys, phone calls, and so on, provides an understanding of what the customer wants, expects, and values.

To clarify stakeholder involvement, a stakeholder analysis is developed during the define phase. The analysis first identifies the individuals who will be impacted or have control over the project, followed by categorizing their level of involvement as an (a)pprover, (r)esource, (a)ctive member, or (i)nterested party (ARMI worksheet). The last stage of the analysis is to determine each stakeholder's support toward the project, and the type of support they will need to provide to ensure the project's success. Refer to Figure 16.2 for an illustration.

Another important component of the define phase is to ensure everyone has the same understanding of the process. To achieve this, a high-level process map or SIPOC diagram is developed. An example is shown in Figure 16. 3. SIPOC refers to suppliers, inputs, processes, outputs, and customers. The SIPOC starts by listing the 4–6 key steps of the process. The inputs and their suppliers for each process step are then identified. Lastly, the outcome and their customers are listed for each process step.

Measure

The focus of the *measure phase* is to develop measurement systems to set a baseline for how the process is performing. To determine the primary metrics or key performance indicators (KPIs), it is important to review the voice of the customer. Based on what customers identify as being critical to

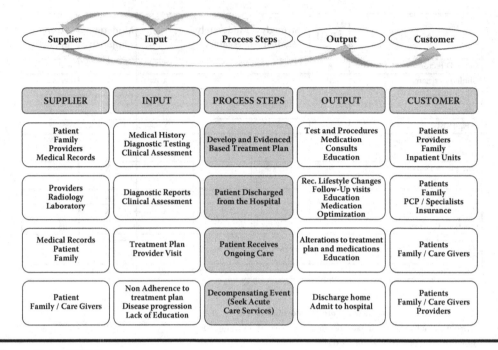

Figure 16.3 SIPOC.

quality, a measurable metric is defined and the data to be collected is then developed. For example, if patients desire to be seen by a physician within 10 minutes of arrival at a clinic, a KPI would be the percentage of patients who are seen by their physician within 10 minutes of arrival. The data to collect is the time between patient arrival at the clinic and first encounter with their physician.

Despite the important role data plays in measuring baseline and improvements, it can be very expensive and time consuming to gather the volume of data needed to draw statistically significant conclusions. There are guidelines to calculate the minimum data needed based on the variability in the data being collected and the precision required. However, if the minimum sample size seems difficult to obtain, evaluate other potential metrics with smaller sample size requirements that would still measure the performance of the process.

Another component of data collection is to ensure that the data being collected is valid and accurate. To evaluate potential bias or precision errors in the data, a measurement system analysis (MSA) should be completed. To guarantee that the data collection tool consistently measures the process, a gauge repeatability and reproducibility study (GR&R) should be completed. Calculating repeatability ensures consistent measurements regardless of the number of times the same person measures the process, while reproducibility ensures consistent data regardless of who is measuring the process.

Depending on the type of data being collected (continuous, count, or attribute) and the sample size, there are various methods to summarize and graphically represent the data. Continuous data measures a characteristic such as wait time and usually follows a normal distribution (although this assumption must be checked). Count data, as its name implies, counts things such as defects and follows a Poisson distribution if the process is in control. Attribute data classifies things such as pass/fail and follows a binomial distribution if the process is in control. To graphically represent these data, histograms or time series plots tend to be more useful with continuous or count data, while Pareto charts or 100% stacked bar charts work best for attribute data. Continuous data

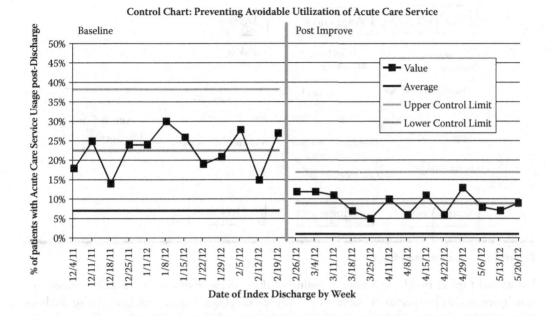

Figure 16.4   Control chart.

tends to be summarized using the average and standard deviation, while count data is summarized by defects per unit and attribute data by a percentage. Control charts are also commonly used in Six Sigma projects to track metrics over time. Data are plotted in time series, with a central line representing the average, and an upper and lower line representing the upper and lower control limits. Conclusions regarding the process variation can be drawn based on where the current data falls in relation to the control limits. Figure 16.4 contains the graph of a process pre- and postintervention. Improvements in the process can be seen by the decrease in the average and the decrease in the variation between the upper and lower control limits.

To further understand how the process is performing, a process capability analysis assesses the process's ability to deliver the customer's expectations. Depending on the distribution of the data, statistical software such as Minitab® can complete a capability analysis. The Six Sigma level is a common capability metric that generates a statistic that applies to all data and environments. The Six Sigma level is the Z value in the Z-table, and converts the percent defective of a process into a sigma level. Another common metric is *Cp*, a metric used to reflect the potential capability: the ratio between the width of the upper and lower customer specification and the width of the upper and lower process performance. Since the distribution of the actual process might not be centrally positioned to the specification of the customer, the actual capability metric, *Cpk*, is used to measure the position to the closest specification: the ratio of the difference between the process average and the nearest specification and three times the sigma. A Cp and Cpk value above 1.33 is acceptable while a value above 2 is excellent.

Analyze

During the analyze phase, critical factors and root causes are identified. As part of this phase, a process map or flowchart is drawn illustrating how the process currently performs. Once the team

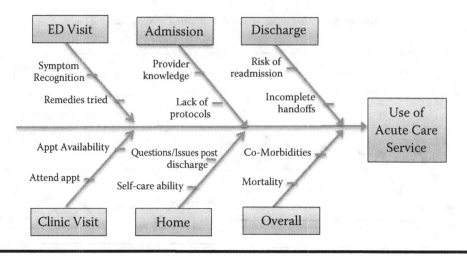

Figure 16.5   Cause and effect.

has gained further insight and understanding of the process, root causes are brainstormed and usually organized by themes or branches in a cause-and-effect diagram (an Ishikawa or fishbone diagram). An example can be seen in Figure 16.5. The next step in the analyze phase is to validate the causes identified and determine their effect on the process. Depending on the number of causes listed and the availability of resources, it might be necessary to prioritize what causes will be validated. Appropriate data is then collected and analyzed using graphical and statistical techniques. Some common tools to represent the data graphically include histograms, box plots, scatter plots, and Pareto charts. These graphical representations can provide theories that can be further investigated with statistical analysis such as hypothesis testing, analysis of variance, normality tests, correlation, and regression. Caution should always be used with statistics to ensure that the appropriate analyses are being used on the appropriately distributed data.

Improve

Based on the findings from the analyze phase, the improve phase focuses on brainstorming, prioritizing, and implementing the best solutions. The phase starts by having the team identify possible solutions through tools such as brainstorming and researching best practices and benchmarks. The team should then identify criteria to assess each solution. The most appropriate solution or solutions should be selected by a thorough prioritization exercise. As the solutions to be piloted are identified, it is important to complete a failure mode and effect analysis (FMEA) prior to the pilot. As part of this risk analysis, the process steps and their potential failure are identified, and a plan to mediate steps with potential failures should be developed. A focused trial of the solution is then completed, and data is collected to validate the performance of the solution and its effect on the KPIs.

Control

Once an effective solution is identified, the goal of the control phase is to ensure that the improvements gained throughout the project are sustained when the project closes, and if applicable, to roll out the solutions to other areas. The control phase is the most important and sometimes most difficult phase in the DMAIC process.

The key to sustaining improvements is having an ongoing measurement protocol and standardization. To achieve this, a control plan that includes a rigorous data collection system identifying who is responsible for collecting and reviewing the data needs to be developed. This plan should also detect changes in the performance of the process, and detail strategies for how to react when the changes are detected. Documentation should also be developed during the control phase to standardize the process and ensure that it is clearly written. The documentation of the new process should be simple, use illustrations when possible, and leave no ambiguity.

The control phase also focuses on celebrating and knowledge sharing. Lessons learned from the project should be shared with other areas in the organizations. This information sharing should not only be focused on outcomes, but also on explaining the process the team followed and major breakthroughs and challenges encountered. As part of the project's closing, it is also important to recognize the team's effort and celebrate their achievements during the control phase. Individuals involved directly and indirectly with the Six Sigma project need to be acknowledged and recognized for their contribution and accomplishments.

Chapter 17

Lean in Healthcare

Karl Kraebber

Contents

Many nurses, physicians and hospital administrators know four facts: (1) that most American hospitals are sick; (2) that they are crippled by inadequate and outdated management practices, unnecessary duplication of services, and astounding waste; (3) that hospitals generate many avoidable, often deadly, mistakes—including countless "near misses"; and (4) that it is in hospitals where the turnaround in healthcare costs and safety must begin.

—Louis Savary and Clare Crawford-Mason, *The Nun and the Bureaucrat*

Currently, the United States is dealing with an epidemic unlike any it has seen before. The problem is not like the early 1900s with influenza, or in the 1980s with AIDS. Today, the US healthcare system is suffering through an epidemic of waste. No amount of scientific and medical knowledge would have prepared the US healthcare system to cope with the serious problem of waste. Healthcare in the United States receives enormous amounts of resources; however, the current system is unable to provide "safe, effective, efficient, patient-centered, timely and equitable care (Bush, 2007)." Beyond health insurance and payment reforms driven by the federal government, something must be done within the current healthcare system to minimize waste, and at the same time satisfy all elements of the Institute of Medicine (IOM) Six Dimensions of Quality (IOM, 2001). In order to transform the healthcare industry, healthcare administrators looked to other successful industries and professional disciplines to gain knowledge. The automotive industry, utilizing industrial engineering principles, pioneered a methodology for reducing waste, improving quality, and enhancing safety while maintaining a systematic perspective called Lean thinking.

Lean Defined and History

The origins of the Lean methodology are heavily rooted in the work of W. Edwards Deming and Taiichi Ohno from the 1950s. In *Toyota Production System: Beyond Large-Scale Production* (1995), Ohno detailed the development and fundamentals of the Toyota Production System (TPS). The production system developed by the Toyota Motor Company is designed to provide the best quality, at the lowest cost, with the shortest lead time through the elimination of waste. The Toyota Production System (see Figure 17.1) is based on a foundation of operational stability including: visual management, standard work, waste elimination, and kaizen (continuous improvement). The mission of the production system is supported by two pillars, just-in-time (JIT) production and built-in quality (jidoka). Also central to TPS are waste reduction and respect for people. TPS is maintained through iterations of standardized work and kaizen driving toward continuous improvement.

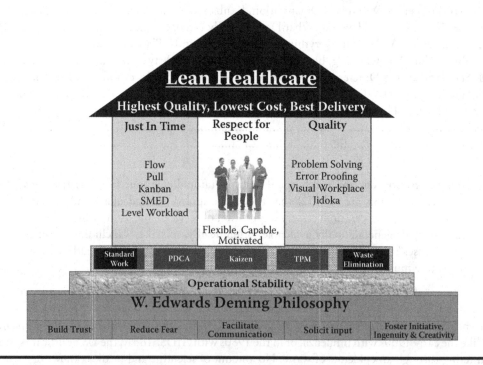

Figure 17.1 Altarum House of Quality image. (Copyright Altarum Institute and Steve Hoeft.)

The term *Lean* was coined by Womack and Jones as a result of years of studying the Toyota Production system. Womack and Jones later developed a 5-step thought process to guide managers through a Lean transformation that includes the following:

- Specify value from the standpoint of the end customer.
- Identify all the steps in the value stream.
- Make value flow toward the customer.
- Let customers pull value from the next upstream activity.
- Pursue perfection.

According to the Institute for Healthcare Improvement (IHI), Lean is centered on determining the value of any given process by analyzing the difference between value-adding and non-value-adding steps and eliminating those steps that do not add value to the process (IHI, 2005). Building upon the IHI definition, the Lean methodology also strives to identify the needs of the customer. A concise and healthcare-applicable definition for Lean is a system that is extraordinarily customer focused and responsive by ridding the entire system of waste.

Lean thinking is not a manufacturing technique, but instead a management philosophy applicable to all industries and services wishing to impact process, quality, and engagement. Traditional organizations function in isolated silos, managers direct employees, people are blamed for problems, and organizations are benchmarked for comparison (rather than improvement). Lean organizations function in an interdisciplinary problem-solving team, managers coach, and mentor employees, employees are accountable for root-cause problem solving, and waste is continuously eliminated driving toward organizational perfection (IHI, 2005). The central dogma of Lean may essentially do more with less, but equally important is respect for people. Lean principles can have dramatic effects on productivity, cost, and quality when integrated throughout an organization.

Lean thinking is certainly applicable to the healthcare industry in the United States, as many organizations have shown (Virginia Mason Medical Center, ThedaCare, University of Michigan, and many others). Lean focuses on the stakeholder satisfaction, efficiency, responsiveness to demand, cost reduction, revenue enhancement, quality, and patient safety—all key aspects of successful healthcare. Hospitals and health systems are engaging in Lean to become patient-centered (serving the patients as customers), emphasize clinical quality outcomes (outcomes are value), deploy the most advanced technologies possible (technology as tools), and to ensure efficiency and productivity.

Kaizen in Healthcare

Kaizen is a foundational element of the Lean philosophy. It is a Japanese word that means "change for the better" or "continuous improvement." Some may know Kaizen as a term used to describe a type of rapid improvement event; however, the Kaizen culture is much more than event style. Kaizen is truly an organizational culture, or even a change management philosophy, which promotes continuous improvement and implementation of sustainable change.

Improvement begins with the understanding that all organizations have flaws, defects, and undesirable effects of current processes, and that each of these provide opportunities for improvement and sustainable change. There has been a prevailing mantra in healthcare: "If it ain't broke, don't fix it." Lean and a Kaizen philosophy empower all stakeholders to examine all processes and envision a better way. This leads to the mindset, "It ain't broke, fix it anyway."

The best ideas for improvement are found within the people who do the work. They know the problems, often the best and most implementable solutions, and are eager to make improvement happen. Stakeholder engagement, buy-in, and sustained improvement are direct results of people who live and work with processes assessing the current state, designing an improved state, and being empowered to implement changes.

One of the key tenets of Kaizen is bias for action. The goal of a Kaizen culture is to not spend all of a team's time searching for a silver bullet or the perfect solution to every problem. Instead, it is an iterative cycle whereby problems are identified, improvements are made, and the impacts are evaluated. "Fast and good is better than slow and perfect," is the mantra of a Lean organization with a Kaizen culture.

The foundation of any Lean transformation is a Kaizen culture. A culture that seeks to continuously improve is one that identifies areas for improvement, analyzes process, and embraces change. If an organization wants to truly embrace the Lean methodology, they must understand the Kaizen culture necessary to transform the organization. People at all levels of an organization can participate in Kaizen, from the chief executive officer (CEO) down. The vehicle for Kaizen can be individual (quick and easy Kaizen), idea/suggestion boards, small group (departmental teams), or large group (value stream problem-solving teams). For healthcare organizations to successfully undergo a Lean transformation, Kaizen must become part of its new organizational culture. A new culture that studies processes and results, thinks systemically, and learns from every improvement project.

Seeing Work with New Eyes

In order to improve healthcare, it is imperative that clinicians and other professionals begin to see their work in an entirely different way. Gone are the days where individuals are blamed for process breakdowns and the status quo is tolerated. "This is the way we have always done it," is no longer an acceptable phase for explaining processes. Lean is about identifying and eliminating waste. The first part of that statement is equally important as the last. Much of healthcare knows where its waste is, but with its focus on providing patient care, is infamous for its workarounds to poor processes.

Process and Value Stream Mapping

When colleagues are brought together to discuss customers, processes, decisions, and outputs, work is able to be documented in a visual way, using process visualization tools that include process mapping, process flow maps (PFMs), and value stream maps (VSMs). Regardless of the process visualization tool, the challenge is engaging healthcare stakeholders in seeing work differently. One of the chief benefits of the IE in this work, besides the knowledge of Lean tools, is their ability to provide that outsider lens with which to examine a process. Lean improvement begins with current state process mapping and ends with a future state map.

Process mapping, often referred to as flowcharting, is either a visual representation of the workflow within a process or an image of the whole operation. It comprises a stream of activities that transforms a well-defined input or set of inputs into a predefined set of outputs. Similar to a process mapping, a PFM is a tool for breaking down a process into its individual component steps. It allows for the careful examination of each step in a process, its associated time to complete, the number or steps traveled to complete a step, and characterizes the type of action being done. Action designations within a PFM include operation, transportation, inspection, delay, and storage.

Value stream mapping (VSM) is the most essential Lean tool to provide understanding of current processes and how to improve them. Current state VSM documents the processes as they actually happen today (not based on a dusty policy and procedure) and highlight the undesirable effects caused by the current process. The future state VSM, based on an assessment of ideal future state characteristics developed after the current state mapping, documents the reengineered processes complete with improvement bursts required to implement and sustain the new future state. The current and future state VSMs set the stage for action plan development and subsequent individual Kaizen improvements, team-based small tests of change and any other Lean technique. A value stream map is useful for the following:

- Visualizing multiple process levels.
- Identifying exact sources of waste within the value stream.
- Providing a consistent and repeatable process for documenting healthcare processes and communicating about processes within healthcare organizations.
- Making visible issues with flow and pull for all up- and downstream processes.
- Facilitating discussion about how to eliminate the issues of the current state by reengineering the future state (eliminating root cause versus symptoms).
- Reinforcing systems thinking and team-based problem solving.
- Translating improvement opportunities (bursts) into an action plan.
- Demonstrating the connection between all seven flows (patients, providers, information, medication, supplies, reprocessed instruments, and equipment) within a healthcare organization.

Eight Kinds of Waste

Once the current process is analyzed using a VSM, the focus of the Lean work turns to waste elimination, but what work is actually waste? Work can be divided into three types: value added, business required nonvalue added, and non-value added (pure waste). Value-added work is any activity that transforms material or information into something that the customer cares about (or would pay for). Business required non-value-added work is any activity that is not necessary for the customer, but is required due to regulation, safety, and so on—patient registration is a typical healthcare example. Non-value-added work (pure waste) is any activity that is not satisfying a customer's needs or that they are not willing to pay for, such as waiting and transporting. This classification of waste is crucial to selecting the appropriate countermeasure to successfully and sustainably eliminate the waste from future state processes. In healthcare, waste is usually described in one of eight critical areas and can be represented with the pneumonic, DOWNTIME (see Figure 17.2 for healthcare examples):

- **Defects:** the effort involved in inspecting for and fixing defects
- **Overproduction:** production ahead of demand
- **Waiting:** waiting for the next production step
- **Not utilizing the creativity of staff:** not involving frontline staff in problem solving
- **Transportation:** moving products that are not actually required to perform the processing
- **Inventory:** all components, work-in-progress, and finished product not being processed
- **Motion:** people or equipment moving more than is required to perform the processing
- **Extra processing:** due to poor tool or product design, creating activity

Waste	Description	Examples in Health Care	Process Remedies at Virginia Mason Medical Center
Waste of overproduction	Producing what is unnecessary, when it is unnecessary, and in an unnecessary amount	Fragmented, parallel care: separate resident, attending, social services, pharmacy, and care management rounding cycles; making photocopies of a form that is never used; providing copies of reports to people who have not asked for them and will not actually read them; processing piles of documents that then sit at the next work station; cc's on e-mails	Multidisciplinary bedside rounds, with contemporaneous documentation and order entry by portable wireless computer; primary care physician flow stations incorporate many lean principles
Waste of time on hand (waiting)	Waiting for materials, operations, conveyance, inspection; idle time attendant to monitoring and operation procedures, rather than just-in-time supply or *pull production*	Patients waiting to see their physician; office staff batching test results for patients; waiting on the phone to schedule appointments; early-morning admits for surgeries that won't be performed until later in the day; waiting for support services such as internal transport; waiting for office equipment (computer, photocopier, etc.) to be repaired before being able to do work; waiting for a meeting that is starting late	Patients are advised at point of care when tests will be available, and test results are reported as they become available; emergency department physicians enter orders in the electronic medical record within 15 minutes of patient arrival
Waste in transportation	Conveying, transferring, picking up/setting down, piling up, and otherwise moving unnecessary items; problems concerning conveyance distances, conveyance flow, and conveyance utilization rate	Moving individual files from one location to another; moving supplies into and out of a storage area; moving equipment for surgeries in/out of operating and procedure rooms; patients receiving chemoradiation treatment traveling 1220 horizontal feet and 25 vertical floors per episode	Travel for chemoradiation reduced 55%, to 544 feet and 12 floors, by providing injections and dressing changes in radiation oncology department; instead of patients or supplies traveling to and from isolated process villages, the input proceeds through the operations in single-piece-flow in 1 short space

Figure 17.2 **Waste in healthcare.**

Continued

Waste	Description	Examples in Health Care	Process Remedies at Virginia Mason Medical Center
Waste of processing	Unnecessary processes and operations traditionally accepted as necessary	Hard copies of memos already sent by e-mail or posted on intranet; redundant capture of information at admission; multiple recording and logging of data; writing by hand, when direct input to a word processor could eliminate this step; producing paper hard copy when a computer file is sufficient; patients waiting for preapproval of urgent treatments	Hyperbaric oxygen indications negotiated with payers who have agreed to waive preapproval; redesign of chamber to allow emergency cases without canceling scheduled patients; eliminate medication lists on electronic medical records progress notes
Waste of stock on hand (inventory)	Inventory waste is when anything—materials, parts, assembly part—is retained for any length of time, including not only warehouse stock but also items in the factory that are retained at or between processes	Office supplies in hallways; expensive clinical supplies and implants that can be ordered on a just-in-time basis; charge slips piled up to be dictated; unnecessary instruments in operating room kits	Surgeons now accept only those instruments that are frequently used, or 25 instruments, in the operating room kit
Waste of movement	Movement that is unnecessary, that does not add value, or that is too slow or too fast	Physicians and nurses leaving patient rooms for common supplies or information	Common supplies are stocked in hospital, operating, and outpatient rooms, with visually controlled restocking system; computer access in outpatient examination rooms and wireless portable computers for inpatient rooms
Waste of making defective products	Waste related to costs for inspection of defects in materials and processes, customer complaints, and repairs; passing defects down to a coworker or patient, rather than the defect producer "feeling the pinch"	Iatrogenic illness; fixing errors made in documents; misfiling documents; dealing with complaints about service; mistakes caused by incorrect information or miscommunication; handwritten orders; sending out bills with an incorrect address	Ventilator-acquired pneumonia bundles decreased annual incidence from 40 to 5 cases; patient safety alerts; computerized clinician order entry

Source: Adapted from T. Ohno, *Toyota Production System: Beyond Large-Scale Production* (New York: Productivity Press Inc., 1995).

Figure 17.2 (Continued)   Waste in healthcare.

The first step in any Lean transformation (and project) is to understand the current state by conducting in-depth process or value stream mapping and assessing the current process for waste. The clear identification of waste in the current state is vitally important to challenging them in the future state. A redesigned future state follows with clearly defined opportunities for improvement that sets the stage for action plan development, waste elimination, iterative improvement, and sustained benefits. Waste elimination becomes much easier when problems are clearly identified using a team-based approach within the context of the entire system rather than the narrow scope of an individual or isolated department.

Waste Elimination

Lean arms healthcare clinicians and professionals with tools that assist in the elimination of waste, improvement of quality, decreasing of production time, and cost reduction. Waste elimination can be accomplished by using a number of Lean tools; however, it is important to remember that waste elimination in isolation just leads to more waste. Cherry picking Lean tools to solve individual problems does not promote systematic and sustainable improvement. The Lean "toolbox" includes the following: quick-and-easy Kaizen, cellular design, single piece flow, quick change-overs, standard work, error-proofing ("stop the line" or no defects passed downstream), 5S workplace organization, kanban/pull inventory systems, visual management and status boards, jidoka (autonomation), and total production maintenance (TPM). Two of the most fundamental tools for waste elimination in healthcare are 5S and Kanban to promote a visual work place.

Visual Workplace: 5S, Workplace Organization, Kanban

"A place for everything and everything in its place," is the mantra for 5S in Lean. 5S is a workplace organization tool used to eliminate waste and improve flow. 5S stands for sort, set in order, shine, standardize, and sustain. 5S is often performed as an initial part of a Lean transformation, whereby processes become more visible and identified waste is eliminated. Benefits of 5S in healthcare are: eliminates the need for searching, reduces probability of error, increases quality, improves productivity, expedites response time, improves staff morale, and enhances the professional image of an area. 5S drives a cleaner work environment and establishes a standardized organization of the workplace. 5S is a Lean tool that can set the stage for subsequent process improvements that have been identified during a VSM event and documented on an action plan.

1. Sort: What Do We Have and What Do We Really Need?

Sort involves the identification of what is required for work (necessary) and what can be removed from the workplace (unnecessary). Necessary items are then subdivided by how frequently the item is used (required for set in order). Unnecessary items are either discarded or red-tagged (see Figure 17.3). Red-tagged items are sequestered on a cart or in a designated area for review by colleagues from all shifts prior to final disposition. The red tag documents the item description, suggested disposition, date tagged, disposition date, and includes the name of the tagger. Figure 17.4 shows examples of overstocked and unnecessary items being sorted out of birth center patient rooms and clean utility storage closets at St. John's Hospital in Springfield, Illinois.

Red Tag: This item identified for disposal or permanent relocation.	
Item description	
Suggested disposition	
Today's date	
Planned date to disposition	
Concerns? Contact	

Figure 17.3   Red tag.

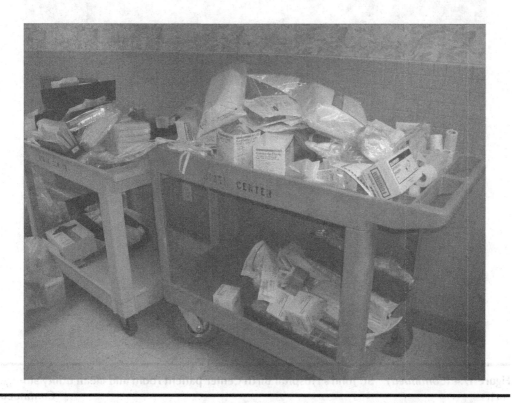

Figure 17.4   St. John's Hospital Birth Center patient room and clean utility storage sort.

Continued

Figure 17.4 (*Continued*)   St. John's Hospital Birth Center patient room and clean utility storage sort.   *Continued*

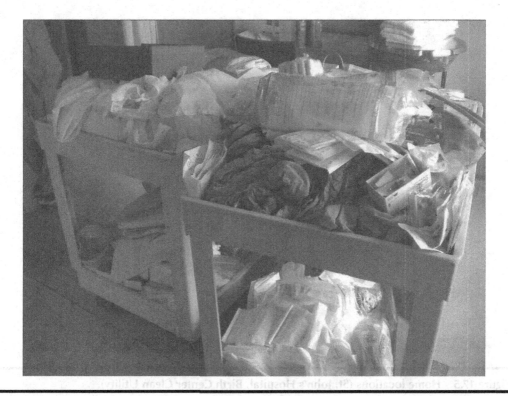

Figure 17.4 (*Continued*)   St. John's Hospital Birth Center patient room and clean utility storage sort.

- Potential failure point: The area looks good now (decluttered). Colleagues feel like lots of unneeded supplies and equipment were removed and there is plenty of extra space now. As a result, managers and leaders decide there is no need to go forward with the next four steps.
- Result: If a 5S event concludes now, freed up space will be squandered and unnecessary items will creep back into the area.

2. Set in Order: A Place for Everything and Everything in Its Place

Once supplies are reduced to only those necessary, our next "S" is to Set in Order, that is, arrange, organize, and create an address (home location) for everything that remains. Designate storage locations based on function and frequency of use of the item stored: frequently needed items should be placed close to the point of use; occasionally needed items should be placed in a central location in the department; and seldom needed (but required) items should be placed in a central location within the organization. All signage or labeling should be clearly visible and self-explanatory so everyone can identify at a glance where anything belongs (Figure 17.5). Information on the label should include item name, location address, quantity required, and a product barcode (if applicable). Labeling conventions and nomenclature should be standardized within the entire organization (Figure 17.6). Using a color-coding scheme (Figure 17.7) enhances the visual workplace and allows for ease of finding needed items. The goal of Set in Order is: easy to find, easy to use, easy to return.

Figure 17.5   Home locations (St. John's Hospital, Birth Center Clean Utility).

Figure 17.6   Standardized labels (St. John's Hospital, Birth Center Medication Room).

Color	Meaning	Symbol
Red	IV supplies/needles	
Yellow	Urinary supplies	
Brown	GI / Ostomy supplies	
Blue	Respiratory supplies	
Orange	ADL supplies	
Green	Dressing supplies	
White	Miscellaneous	

Figure 17.7   Color-coding convention.

3. Shine: Not Only Cleaning, but Seeing What Is Getting Dirty

This step in 5S is a deep cleaning of the area to establish a new baseline for departmental cleanliness. All surfaces, including floors, walls, ceilings, as well as equipment and furniture, should be maintained in like-new condition. Scheduled audits and routine cleaning of the area is done by any assigned colleague (not only housekeeping) because an unclean environment cannot produce quality care and be safe. Abnormalities are readily visible when a workplace is regularly cleaned and organized.

- ■ Potential failure point: The area really looks good now. It's clean and well organized. Colleagues are disciplined so there is no need to standardize. It will be self-sustaining.
- ■ Result: If a 5S event concludes now, improvements will be short lived, items and supplies will find new home locations, and cleanliness will not be top of mind.

4. Standardize: The Difference between a 3S Project and a 5S Way of Life

Step 4 transitions healthcare organizations from the active phase to the maintenance phase of 5S. Standardization starts with creating a 5S map (annotated floor plan or picture; see Figure 17.8) and schedule of responsibilities. The schedule of responsibilities clearly articulates what needs to

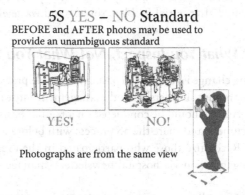

Figure 17.8   5S standardization image.

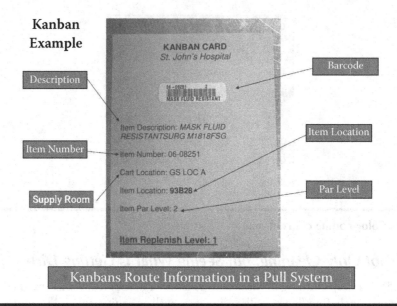

Figure 17.9 Example Kanban card from St. John's Hospital main operating room.

be done on a daily, weekly, and monthly basis to maintain order and cleanliness. Standard work documents should also be developed to capture 5S duties in a standardized format (used for new employee training and current employee remediation). A 5S checklist should be developed that identifies and defines what will be done. When and who is responsible is another tool to assist with standardization. It is the responsibility of everyone in a department to maintain the organized workplace and prevent regression to a cluttered and unorganized environment.

Another important tool of a Lean organization that supports a visual workplace and facilitates flow is Kanban. *Kanban* is a Japanese word that means "signboard." In a Lean organization, Kanban is a pull signal initiated by consumption from an upstream process or depletion to a defined replenishment point. Kanbans may be text pages, replenishment cards (Figure 17.9), or even empty bins. Either the card is placed at the reorder point or the par level is split in half between two bins (Figure 17.10). Kanban signals authorize production or delivery of required materials, supplies, and so on. Kanban allows a JIT environment to be set up; however, it requires level or balanced production and built-in quality (defect-free products). Kanban is a high-level Lean tool that is implemented after initial problem solving and waste elimination efforts.

5. Sustain: You Get What You Inspect, Not What You Expect

Since human nature during change is to revert to past comfortable practices, departmentwide promotion of discipline is paramount. Leadership and management must reinforce 5S responsibility, standards, and schedules. Audits should be conducted on a regular basis by designated colleagues. It is also important to document and share the 5S process with before-and-after 5S photo exhibits (Figure 17.11 and 17.12). Recognize those who participated in the event and share the outcome with other areas in the organization via hospital newsletters, management meetings, and whole hospital meetings.

When implementing 5S, colleagues can rapidly improve the workplace environment with a minimal expenditure. Most organizations report 5%–10% efficiency improvement in several

Figure 17.10   Example Visual Controls from St. John's Hospital main operating room.

Continued

months, 25%–50% reduction in inventory, 50%–100% reduction in time searching for needed items, and one-time supply cost credits. At St. John's Hospital, the birth center realized a 42% reduction in inventory (translating to $4,200 worth of supplies no longer on the shelves), a 50% reduction in the time required to find needed supplies, and a one-time supply credit of over $4,500. With the implementation of a Kanban replenishment system in the main operating room at St. John's Hospital, supply stockouts have virtually been eliminated, 7–8 daily trips to central supply have become (at most) 1–2 weekly trips, and all case carts are completed the day prior to the case due to proper supply availability. While change is often received with a sense of apprehension, participants in the 5S activities begin to taste change as something that can be positive and even fun, paving the way for a true Lean transformation in healthcare.

Benefits of Lean in Healthcare

Lean systems have the ability to provide far-reaching benefits to all stakeholders in the healthcare system. Lean provides healthcare organizations with a methodology to systematically improve the IOM Six Dimensions of Quality (IOM, 2001), including:

1. Safe: Improved safety; reduced errors
2. Effectiveness: 70% to 90% lead time reduction
3. Efficient: 50% to 80% inventory reduction

Figure 17.10 (*Continued*)   Example Visual Controls from St. John's Hospital main operating room.

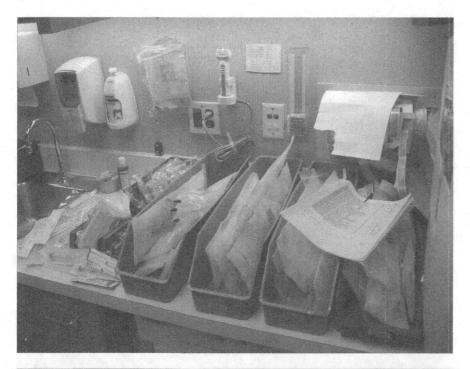

Figure 17.11 St. John's Hospital Birth Center Medication Room: 5S before and after.

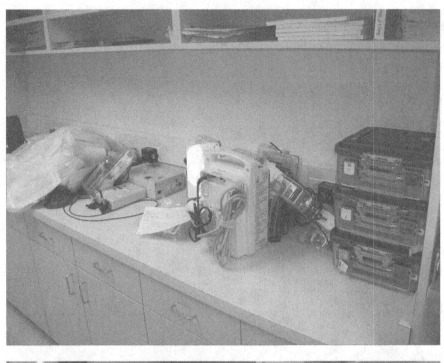

Figure 17.12 St. John's Hospital Birth Center Clean Utility Area: 5S before and after.

4. Timely: 50% to 100% productivity improvement
5. Patient or customer centered: Increased patient satisfaction
6. Equitable: Standard work; reduce rework

Lean allows for continuous improvement, waste reduction, error proofing, and employee engagement in healthcare. Other benefits of Lean in healthcare include improved patient and provider satisfaction; shorter wait times for patients; elimination of delays for all stakeholders; increased patient admissions and diagnoses; faster bed turn around; improved workplace organization, improved cleanliness and facility upkeep; better space and supply management; more streamlined administration processes; more efficient patient record and appointment processes; and timely delivery of care. Additional benefits to the application of Lean to healthcare include increased profits, increased time at the bedside for clinicians, reduction in errors and rework, and inappropriate procedures are reduced. In short, Lean helps improve the quality and safety of care, while reducing costs.

Lean systems are tried and true manufacturing and industrial engineering methodologies for process improvement and waste elimination. The healthcare industry in the United States continues to be inefficient and costly because of the large number of wasteful processes (e.g., redundant registrations steps, patient transportation, and inventory management) found within hospitals and health systems. The Lean methodology, under the watchful eyes of management engineers, provides healthcare organizations with cost-effective and customer-focused strategies and tools for waste reduction and quality improvement. The difficulty with Lean systems in healthcare is not the identification of Lean as a viable solution; it is the implementation of sustainable Lean systems.

> A system is a network of interdependent components that work together to try to accomplish the aim of the system. A system must have an aim. Without an aim, there is no system. A system must be managed. The secret is cooperation between components toward the aim of the organization. We cannot afford the destructive effect of competition.

—W. Edwards Deming, *The New Economics*

References

Bush, R. W. (2007). "Reducing Waste in US Health Care Systems." *Journal of the American Medical Association* 297(8): 871–874.

Deming, W.E. (1994). *The New Economics: For Industry, Government, Education*, 2nd ed. Cambridge, MA: MIT Press.

Institute for Healthcare Improvement (IHI). (2005). *Going Lean in Health Care*, Innovation series white paper. Cambridge, MA: Institute for Healthcare Improvement.

Institute of Medicine (IOM). (2001). *Crossing the Quality Chasm: A New Health System for the 21st Century*. Washington, DC: National Academy Press.

Ohno, T. (1995). *Toyota Production System: Beyond Large-Scale Production*. New York: Productivity Press Inc.

Womack, J. P., Jones, D. T., and Roos, D. (1991). *The Machine That Changed the World: The Story of Lean Production*. New York: HarperCollins.

Womack, J. P., and Jones, D. T. (2003). *Lean Thinking: Banish Waste and Create Wealth in Your Corporation*, 2nd ed. New York: Free Press.

Suggested Reading

Aherne, J. (2007). "Think Lean." *Nursing Management* 13 (10): 13–15.

Allway, M, and Corbett, S. (2002). "Shifting to Lean Service: Stealing a Page from Manufacturers' Playbooks." *Journal of Organizational Excellence* 21(2): 45–54.

Bhasin, S., and Burcher, P. (2006). "Lean Viewed as a Philosophy." *Journal of Management Technology* 17(1): 56–72.

Black, J., and Miller, D. (2008). *The Toyota Way to Healthcare Excellence: Increase Efficiency and Improve Quality with Lean.* Chicago: HAP.

Chalice, R. (2007). *Improving healthcare suing Toyota Lean production methods: 46 Steps for improvement* (2nd Ed.). Milwaukee, WI: ASQ Quality Press.

Fry, H. M., ed. (2008). *Advanced Lean Thinking: Proven Methods to Reduce Waste and Improve Quality in Health Care.* Oakbrook Terrace, IL: Joint Commission Resources.

Graban, M. (2012). *Lean Hospitals: Improving Quality, Patient Safety and Employee Engagement,* 2nd ed. New York: CRC Press.

Healthcare Performance Partners, "5-S Lean Healthcare Program," http://leanhealthcareperformance.com/page.php?page=5-S (accessed October 1, 2012).

Healthcare Performance Partners, "Kaizen," http://leanhealthcareperformance.com/page.php?page=Kaizen (accessed October 1, 2012).

Jimmerson, C., Weber, D., and Sobek II, D. W. (2005). "Reducing Waste and Errors: Piloting Lean Principles at Intermountain Healthcare." *Joint Commission Journal of Quality and Patient Safety* 31(5): 249–257.

Kim, C.S., Spahlinger, D.A., Kin, J.M., and Billi, J. E. (2006). "Lean Health Care: What Can Hospitals Learn from a World-Class Automaker?" *Journal of Hospital Medicine* 1(3): 191–199.

Liker, J. K. (2004). The *Toyota Way: 14 Management Principles from the World's Greatest Manufacturer.* Chicago: McGraw-Hill.

Liker, J. K., and Morgan, J. M. (2006). "The Toyota Way in Services: The Case of Lean Product Development." *Academy of Management Perspectives* 20(2): 5–20.

Nelson-Peterson, D. L., and Leppa, C. J. (2007). "Creating an Environment for Caring Using Lean Principles of the Virginia Mason Production System." *Journal of Nursing Administration* 37(6): 287–294.

Porché, R. A., ed. (2006). *Doing More with Less: Lean Thinking and Patient Safety in Health Care.* Oakbrook Terrace, IL: Joint Commission Resources.

Savary, L. M., and Crawford-Mason, C. (2006). *The Nun and the Bureaucrat: How They Found an Unlikely Cure for America's Sick Hospitals.* Washington, DC: CC-M Production, Inc.

Varkey, P., Reller, M. K., and Resar, R. K. (2007). "Basics of Quality Improvement in Health Care." *Mayo Clinic Proceedings* 82(6): 735–739.

Zidel, T. G. (2006). "A Lean Toolbox: Using Lean Principles and Techniques in Healthcare." *Journal for Healthcare Quality (Web Exclusive)* 28(1): W1-7–W1-15.

Chapter 18

Operations Analysis and Operations Research

Roger Gruneisen

Contents

Introduction

Operations analysis and *operations research* are approaches to decision making that incorporate math, science, and engineering principles to best plan and operate a system. Operations research is a very collaborative function and it is hard to set practice boundaries. The operational contexts to which operations research methods are often applied are those systems or organizations facing decisions to allocate scarce resources hoping to receive the best possible return. Operations research is often used to prescribe a solution to a complex issue that optimizes an organization's performance toward its goals. In other words, operations research puts science behind the tough decisions that have to be made under complex circumstances.

Operations research has its formal origins dating back to the British and US military during World War II. In the war, scientists and engineers were tasked with applying their skills to improve combat decision making and operations at the tactical, operational, and strategic levels. In war, operations research was applied to quantify what is often thought of as unquantifiable in order to improve, expedite, or gain confidence in decision making and planning. These decisions often involved allocating scarce resources, money, and personnel, to the varying battlefields to improve the war's outcomes for the allied forces.

Similar to combat operations, healthcare has its own unique challenges and variable operating environment. Healthcare is likewise faced with limited resources and important decisions must be made to meet the demands of a highly variable future. Operations research problems often are structured around quantifying future resource needs, like staffing or capital equipment, for predicted demands. Some operations research problems are more real-time decision models for end users and are tailored around enabling organizations to make better rapid decisions given analytical guidelines.

In healthcare, a great deal of operations analysis is conducted through mathematics, simulation, and other statistical modeling. Often, hospital process improvement initiatives are launched without a grasp of the connection to the larger healthcare system. This often results in improvement efforts that are focused with a limited scope. Operations research techniques like simulation can help identify and target processes where improvement efforts should be focused for the greatest value returns. As well, during the process of building an analytical healthcare model or decision support tool, a team can identify numerous opportunities for improvement, and thus the process of analytical modeling itself can help identify and focus improvement resources.

Better Demand Planning: Example 1

Hospitals have very dynamic patient demands because of the patient population, level of care offered, geographic barriers, and many other variables. One health system used a series of objective and subjective measures for determining nurse staffing for their inpatient units. The health system monitored the monthly average census of their nightly midnight census, the total number of days patients had stayed that month, and were using a series of benchmarks that offered insight into how other similar facilities staffed.

After the latest benchmarks came out, the health system executives realized that their inpatient units were seemingly staffed too heavily in comparison to their peers. The benchmark data showed they were staffed around the 60th percentile in comparison, and the health system set a target to be at the 75th percentile. The health system executives gave the order to get to the 75th percentile and left the execution of the order to the nurse management team.

Armed with only the average daily census (ADC), total patient days, and limited information on patient admissions, discharges, transfers, and acuity, the nurse management team did not know where to cut to make the 75th percentile. A rash decision could lead to patient safety and quality of care issues, but making no decision or refusing to reduce staff without strong evidence was not an option.

With today's electronic medical records (EMR) and admission, discharge, and transfer (ADT) records, an analyst or engineer can piece together the descriptive statistics for patient census, arrivals, and discharges by hour of the day, half hour, and more for any given unit (see Figure 18.1). Armed with the new information on census patterns, admission patterns, and discharge patterns, the nurse managers began to visualize that the staff allocation plans and staff scheduling changes needed to be more efficient. Rather than staffing to the patient unit's bed capacity, just in case the health system took on more patients, the nurse managers could now plan reduced staffing for certain times of the day, month, or even year.

With more information, the nursing leadership witnessed patient demand for what it was, variable throughout the day, week, and year. Equipped with the information, the nursing leadership began to estimate resource needs over a one-year period and started to work on other challenges like efficient daily scheduling.

Staff Scheduling: Example 2

The same health system that challenged its nursing management team to reach the 75th percentile of peer staffing did the same for its clinical laboratory. The health system executives found that

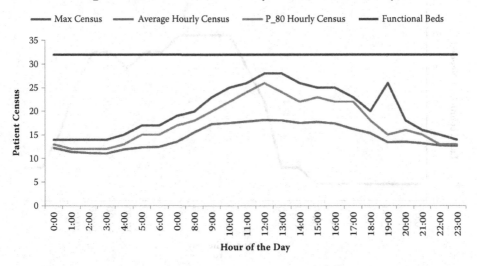

Inpatient Unit Census by Hour of the Day

Legend: Max Census — Average Hourly Census — P_80 Hourly Census — Functional Beds

Figure 18.1 Patient census descriptive statistics by hour of the day.

the lab was staffed around the 60th percentile compared to peers and wanted them at no less than the 75th percentile. The executives gave the direction to lab management to plan and execute the changes needed. The only way that no staff changes would be required was with sufficient evidence supporting the decision.

Like nursing, the lab also benefitted from having an analyst review the EMR and computer order entry (CPOE) system. The lab was a hybrid operation that supported some scheduled inpatient hospital test panels, urgent and emergent care tests, and some lesser test volumes from an area nursing home. The analyst and lab staff were able to review the lab demand curve much like in Figure 18.1. The lab then set about operationalizing what resources were needed to satisfy customer test demand (see Figure 18.2).

The lab decided that due to the nature of their work, they wanted to be staffed to handle demand 75% of the time during any given hour. The lab management realized that if they prioritized emergent and urgent care first, and monitored turnaround times of all other tasks, the risk of not completing work in a timely manner would be low. All other less-urgent work would be made up in the following shifts. At the same time, the lab management understood that staffing to a 75th percentile of test demand meant that 75% of the time, they had enough or too much staff on hand as well.

Given the lab's target resource needs by time of day, the lab manager needed to better schedule staff to no less than meet the planned service requirements. The lab manager was faced with scheduling decisions like whether to allow many different shift lengths—8 hours, 10 hours, 12 hours, or part-time 4 hours and numerous shift start times. The team was able to quickly realize with some analysis, that they were not meeting the demands as they previously thought (see Figure 18.3).

With an analyst's support, the lab manager could see the impacts of the different scheduling alternatives. With a basic Microsoft Excel programmer with Solver function, the analyst created an integer programming model for staff schedules. Based on discussions with the manager, it was determined that all staff did 8-hour shifts, but were open to other ideas. The lab manager was willing to examine any possible shift start time on any given hour of the day.

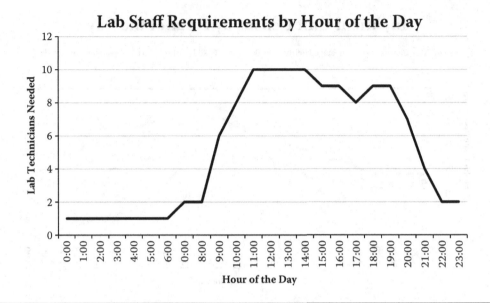

Figure 18.2   Staff requirements to meet 80th percentile of demand.

With the current state analysis in Figure 18.3, the team found that the current staff schedules were not meeting minimum requirements. In fact, the lab was overstaffed 13 hours of the day for a total of 37 extra staff hours per day. The team further found that for 4 hours of the day, the lab was understaffed for a total deficit of 9 staff hours. The mismatch of staff allocation was not the most efficient method for staffing. With integer programming, the team solved and understood what minimum staffing requirements were needed for a given day so that they would not be understaffed. The analysis accommodated the mixture of 4-, 8-, 10-, and 12-hour shifts with a shift start time beginning any given hour of the day. In general, the team found that as they added more shifts to the model, they could staff closer to the staff requirement target (see Figure 18.4).

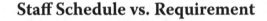

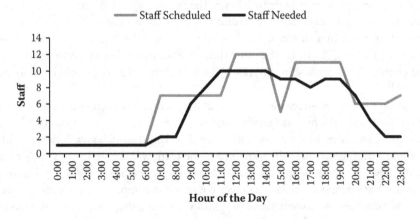

Figure 18.3   Current lab staffing by hour of the day versus the minimum staff needed.

Summary of Shift Scheduling Efficiency by Alternative					
Shift Lengths Allowed	Total FTEs Needed	Overstaff Hours	Understaff Hours	FTEs over per Year	Number of Different Shifts
Current State (four 8-hour shifts)	19.0	37	9	4.63	4
8-hour shifts	20.0	36	0	4.50	10
10-hour shifts	18.8	26	0	3.25	10
12-hour shifts	18.0	20	0	2.50	4
8- and 10-hour shifts	16.5	8	0	1.00	12
4- and 12-hour shifts	16.5	8	0	1.00	9
8-, 10-, 12-hour shifts	16.3	6	0	0.75	10
4-, 8-, 10-, 12-hour shifts	16.0	4	0	0.50	14

Figure 18.4 Results of programming model outputs.

Based on the analysis and results in Figure 18.4, the team identified that they could get by with the fewest working FTEs with the combination of 4-, 8-, 10-, and 12-hour shifts, but at a cost of managing 14 different shifts per day. As a next step, the team figured out which alternative was the most cost effective considering all costs. The healthcare system used the cost of an FTE at $60,000 per year, and the managerial burden to manage each additional shift was costed at $4,000. The incremental $4,000 was estimated on the cost of software, staff schedulers, and some incentive pay to motivate staff flexibility.

With the cost inputs, the lab manager and team could see the financial impacts of each alternative. Figure 18.5 highlights the decision-making table for determining which scheduling model was most cost effective.

In terms of cost, the lab manager found that a combination of 8-, 10-, and 12-hour shifts was the most cost effective and would allow him to reduce staffing by three productive FTEs per year.

Summary of the Costs of Scheduling Alternatives					
Shift Lengths Allowed	Cost of FTEs($)	Cost to Understaff ($)	Cost of Overstaff ($)	Cost Managing Shifts ($)	Efficiency Factor (%)
Current State (four 8-hour shifts)	1,140,000	67,500.00	277,500	16,000	75.9
8-hour shifts	1,200,000	—	270,000	40,000	79.5
10-hour shifts	1,128,000	—	195,000	40,000	82.8
12-hour shifts	1,080,000	—	150,000	16,000	86.7
8- and 10-hour shifts	990,000	—	60,000	48,000	90.2
4- and 12-hour shifts	990,000	—	60,000	36,000	91.2
8-, 10-, 12-hour shifts	978,000	—	45,000	40,000	92.0
4-, 8-, 10-, 12-hour shifts	960,000	—	30,000	56,000	91.8

Figure 18.5 Cost efficiency summary per scheduling alternative.

Space Planning: Example 3

Another health system was undertaking major facilities renovation and building. The health system had several outpatient clinics and needed to provide the facilities designers with the number of exam rooms needed for each clinic. One specialty clinic that had four exam rooms wanted no fewer than 8 exam rooms and rationalized that demand was going to increase by no less than 3% over the next few years, but no more than 15%. An initial assessment by the planners using average daily volumes and average process times estimated that the current number of rooms was adequate for future volume, but this was not accepted by the specialty clinic leadership. The clinic leadership was skeptical of using only averages and explained that they needed to prepare for more extremes.

With analytical support, the health system planners set out to use a Monte Carlo simulation to quantify clinic room demands that would account for real-world variation.

During the model-building process, the planners measured a series of key inputs and reviewed each with clinic staff. The main inputs for the current state model were (1) number of patient visits per day, (2) patient time in the exam room, (3) time the room is idle or cleaned between patients, and (4) predicted demand growth (see Figure 18.6). With these variables, the planners were able to simulate countless clinic days to understand how many rooms were needed to meet the demands of an 8-hour clinic day.

With the measured inputs and roughly 1,000 clinic days simulated, the team found that the clinic could meet patient demands 95% of the time with just 3 exam rooms, even with projected demand increases (see Figure 18.7).

The team also realized that 8 exam rooms were excessive given the current volumes. If the clinic were to use 8 exam rooms, the planners realized that utilization of the space was going to be less than 20% most of the time. Additionally, the costs to maintain 8 exam rooms wasted idle time, and space was cost prohibitive (see Figure 18.8). Armed with this mathematical evidence, the planners then worked on some operational changes within the clinic to reduce the variation that caused the need for additional exam room space and the feeling that more space was needed.

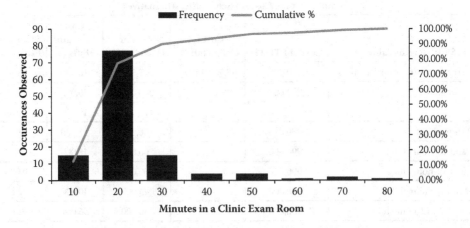

Figure 18.6   Patient visit time in exam room.

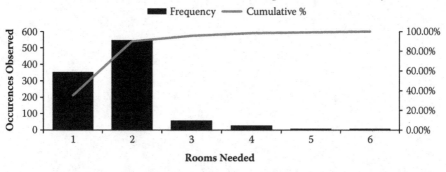

Figure 18.7   Distribution of rooms needed to meet variable demands.

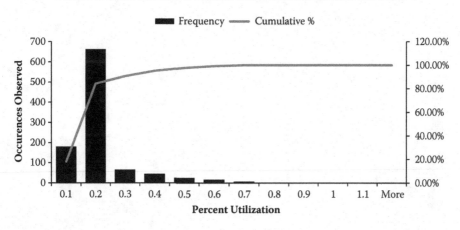

Figure 18.8   Space utilization with eight exam rooms.

Chapter 19

Data Collection, Analysis, and Presentation

Deborah D. Flint and Phil Troy

Contents

Introduction

Without data, it is impossible to be effective at improving healthcare processes. That is because without data, it is impossible to establish baseline measurements, determine and justify the processes that need to be improved, determine the best way to improve the processes, or determine if processes have actually been improved upon completion of improvement efforts.

To collect data effectively, it is important to use project goals to determine the data to collect. To structure this process, we suggest you think through and answer the following questions.

What Is the Primary Goal of the Project?

An example project goal might be to reduce patient waiting time in the ear, nose, and throat (ENT) clinic.

What Data Is Needed to Measure the Process with Respect to That Goal?

Without measuring the process with respect to the goal, we cannot determine how good or bad the current process is, or whether changes improve a process. Thus, in context of the example project goal, it is necessary to measure both before and after, at a minimum, the average patient waiting times that patients may encounter while at the clinic. In fact, it is advisable to look at the distribution of the observed data to determine the variation encountered in the process and to identify any outliers encountered. To determine where patients wait, it may be necessary to draw a flowchart of the process. (Please see Chapter 25 on Flowcharting.) Furthermore, since it can be very misleading to only look at averages, it is best to collect and look at a plot of individual waiting times at each point, to better understand whether all waiting times at all points of the process are long, or whether there are just a few waiting times, possibly at just a few locations, that are long. Are there any questions whose answers might help you address the goal(s)?

For this example, some questions to consider include:

a. At what points in the process do patients have particularly long waits?
b. Under what circumstances do patients have particularly long waits?
c. Do average patient waiting times differ significantly for different providers?
d. Do average patient waiting times differ significantly by day of the week?
e. Do average patient waiting times vary by appointment time?
f. Are average patient waiting times longer for physicians than for nurse practitioners or other providers?
g. Do new patient visits take longer than return or post-op patient visits?

Will Some Form of Modeling Be Required to Address the Goal(s)?

When it isn't straightforward to answer these questions, it may be helpful to model the process using statistical, queuing, or simulation models. This will, in turn, necessitate collecting the specific data needed by the selected model.

Data Collection

Once you've determined the data that is needed, structuring the data into tables can make it easier to collect. For example, patient visit wait times might be organized so that each row of the patient visit table corresponds to a patient visit and that the columns of the table correspond to characteristics of the visit and wait times during the visit (see Table 19.1).

Next, you will need to identify potential sources of data, which may include:

■ Ask staff if they keep logs or other records of needed data. If they do, determine if that data can help achieve the project's goals.
■ Check with IT. Ask your hospital's informatics group whether they already collect the data you need in their electronic health record system, or in other hospital systems such as the surgical information system, bed stay system, clinic appointment system, or radio frequency identification and real-time location systems (RFID/RTLS).
■ Collect it manually. One approach to collecting data is to use a legal pad, clipboard, and stopwatch, and note specific times observed during a process. A potentially more efficient approach may be to use a tablet or smart phone with apps such as FileMaker Go or

Table 19.1　Sample Data Collection Table

Patient Number	Visit Type	Provider	Day of Week	Date	Arrival Time	Appointment Time	Wait for Exam Room	Wait for Provider
1	New	Dr. J	Mon	1/21/2013	08:07	8:00	30	20
2	Ret	Dr. Y	Tues	1/22/2013	07:58	8:00	12	15
3	New	Dr. J	Mon	1/21/2013	08:10	8:30	18	12

HanDBase, which make it possible to create custom database tables. What can make the use of these apps more efficient is that the data they collect will already be in electronic form and thus preclude additional data entry. Because these database tables can include timestamp fields that you just need to click to capture the current date and time, and may also include lookup fields with lists of predefined responses, they can save even more data entry time.

When data is manually collected:

- Do not expect staff with other responsibilities to collect data for more than a few days due to the demands of their normal job responsibilities.
- Make sure the collected data is worth the extra effort required of the staff. It is always an added bonus if you can eliminate other work activities (such as manually logging or recording data) to be replaced with the desired data collection activities.
- Make sure that the staff fully understand what they will get out of their data collection efforts, and in particular, how this data will be used and how it can help them either improve their workplace or quality of work life.
- Provide the staff with specific data collection instructions both verbally and in writing. Also, spend time observing and collecting data while observing the staff record the same data to validate that the staff are properly collecting the data.

Regardless of the source of the data, one should keep in mind:

- Be knowledgeable on organization privacy regulations and be sensitive to not include patient name or demographic data on portable data collection devices to ensure patient privacy in case the data collection device is lost or stolen.
- Comply with all security requirements your organization has to make sure that Health Insurance Portability and Accountability Act (HIPAA) regulations are fully met.
- When collecting or transmitting data, make sure that secure networking is used or that data is adequately encrypted.
- Make sure that data on portable devices is properly secured in the event the devices are lost or stolen.
- Validate data, regardless of the source, before using it to make conclusions or recommendations.
- If there is more than one source of data and the data from the different sources need to be connected, make sure that there is a common field, such as patient number, staff number, or part number, in the data sources to be connected.
- Make sure that the collected data is precise; if you are trying to determine the distribution of time an activity takes, it is best that the data is not rounded.
- Make sure that the data is collected consistently; if data is collected in an inconsistent manner, it can negatively affect the results of the analysis. Note that there are measurement analysis tools in statistical software packages such as Minitab and Expert Fit that have been developed to help ensure data collection consistency when more than one staff member collects data.
- Make sure that enough data is collected, as without sufficient data, inferences made from the data may be incorrect. (See Chapter 27 on statistical sampling for further information.)

Analysis

The project's goals should drive the analysis to be performed. When analyzing data, keep in mind the importance of using the appropriate tools to help answer the desired questions in the most efficient manner. In other words, just because you have a chainsaw in your tool belt doesn't mean you need to use it to clip a tree branch!

For our example of the project with the goal to reduce patient wait time, let's take a look at some of the ways we can analyze the data.

- **Utilizing simple spreadsheet capabilities:** Using simple spreadsheet capabilities, we can graphically display the distribution of the data and quickly calculate the mean, median, standard deviation, and a 95% confidence interval of mean waiting times for each provider, for each day of week, and for different appointment types and appointment times. The graphical displays will often reveal anomalies that the numeric calculations will not. We can also use simple spreadsheet capabilities to test for statistically significant differences between providers, days of the week, and different times of day for appointments.
- **Utilizing statistical analysis capabilities:** Using analysis capabilities such as those found in SAS, SPSS, Minitab, and even Excel, we can do more advanced modeling, such as a first-order regression analysis where the dependent variable is the patient's waiting time and there are independent variables set to either 0 or 1 for each provider, for each day of week, for the time of the day of the appointment (e.g., early morning, late morning, early afternoon, late afternoon), for new patients versus return patients versus post-op patients. Then, by looking at the regression coefficients of the independent variables, we can identify those that significantly affect average patient waiting times. Should it be desirable to identify second-order effects we could also add products of these variables, though doing so would require more data samples. Note that similar analyses could be performed to identify factors involved in the time it takes each provider to see each type of patient.
- **Utilizing simulation modeling:** Because Chapter 31 is dedicated to simulation modeling, we just mention that using discrete event simulation software, it becomes possible to build models of the clinic processes. With these models, not only is it possible to evaluate what-if scenarios of the clinic to determine those that would be most beneficial to implement, it also becomes possible to semiautomatically or automatically optimize those processes with respect to dependent factors such as average patient waiting time, staff overtime, room utilization, and physician idle time. However, one should note that simulation models are only as good as the data used in the modeling. While wait-time data is not needed to build the model itself (but rather used when validating the modeling of the current situation), accurate data on arrival patterns and service times are crucial to ensuring that the model is realistic. Thus for our clinic example, we would need to know the patient arrival rate by provider, day of week, and time of day. We also would need to know the distribution of service times for the various processes during the patient's visit (e.g., service time by provider) for all appointment types (e.g., how long does it take provider A to service or treat new patients, versus return patients, versus post-op patients), as well as how long it takes for other processes encountered during the patient visit, such as how long it takes the receptionist to register the patient and how long it takes the nurse to obtain vital signs and history.

As a final note, the authors do not suggest using a queuing model for this project for three reasons. First, most queuing models require that the process being modeled be at least approximately in *steady state*, that is, that the characteristics of the process be unchanging in time, which is pretty unlikely to occur given that clinic processes start and stop each day. Second, developing a queuing model for processes with multiple steps that each require a different distribution of time, can be a very complex undertaking. And third, even if that undertaking is successful, the likelihood that management will have difficulty understanding the resulting complex mathematical model suggests that they will be less likely to accept the result of the analysis made with the model.

Presentation

As there is a considerable amount of published literature dedicated to presenting data and analysis by experts such as Edward Tuftee, Stephen Few, and Ed McMan to name a few, we present our favorite and most effective approaches.

Make Sure You Are an Expert in the Subject Matter

A good rule of thumb is that the ratio of what you present, relative to your understanding of the material you present, should be approximately one to ten. That way, when asked questions, you will be very likely to have the depth of knowledge to confidently answer them. But should you be asked a question for which you do not know the answer, indicate that you don't know the answer, and that you can pursue it after the presentation.

- **Customize the presentation to your audience:** The interests and level of knowledge of your audience should drive the level of detail of the presentation. For example, if your audience consists mostly of top management, or of individuals less familiar with the problem and approaches to be discussed, you should use less detail and provide the key points or takeaways.
- **Provide a one-page executive summary:** Often, a one-page executive summary is the only page of a formal report that most of your audience will read. Thus, the executive summary provides your best opportunity to highlight your key findings, conclusions, and recommendations. Be succinct and clear as to exactly what you want your audience to take away from your work. If you are presenting using slides, the executive summary can be more in the form of an outline with key points and findings listed as bulleted items.
- **For written reports, include appendices with more detailed information:** Even when the audience for the report consists of top management or of individuals less familiar with the problem or approach, they may wish to access and check the details of your work at their convenience. These appendices can include detailed tables, or graphs of trends, or cumulative results over time.
- **Present data and information in a clear and easy-to-understand manner:** In particular, always provide titles for charts, tables, and figures. Label horizontal and vertical axes of graphs and charts, provide column headers in tables, and identify the source of the data/information and the time period in which it was obtained. Also, after explaining the chart, table, or figure, point out the lesson to be learned from it or the key takeaway.
- **Presenting data in person:** If you have been requested to present the information to a group in person, find out where the presentation will take place and ensure that there will be computers and projectors that you can use to present slides. Without a projector, it is much harder for people to follow what you are presenting or explaining. However, there may be some instances where a projector or computer monitor may not be available. An example

may be where you are asked to come present information at a staff meeting and the staff are not able to leave the unit and do not have access to a conference room on the unit. In this type of situation, it can be helpful to provide handouts of key discussion points, charts, and graphs for the staff to refer to while you present.

■ **Presenting data via web without video:** This is perhaps the trickiest mode of presenting data since you cannot view your audience for body language cues. With remote access capabilities, presenting via GoToMeeting or other webinar formats is becoming increasingly common as it helps reduce travel expenses. If you are asked to present in this format, besides keeping all of the techniques provided in this section in mind, make sure you also tune in to verbal cues such as sighing, or tones of voice that may indicate uncertainty or questions, frustration, or appreciation for the presentation.

Presenting Data with Slides

When presenting data with slides, keep the following in mind:

■ Keep verbiage on slides to a minimum.

■ Do not read slides verbatim, but instead use high-level bullets to stay on topic and as memory triggers for details you'd like to present.

■ Use easy-to-read font types, large font size, and colors that provide good contrast between words and background so it is easy for all to see no matter where they are sitting.

■ Keep background graphics at a minimum. Do not use elaborate backgrounds that detract from the information you are trying to convey.

■ Determine how much time you have for your presentation and tailor your presentation accordingly. There will be a big difference between presenting a high-level 10-minute presentation at a board of directors meeting, versus giving a 45-minute presentation at a manager's staff meeting.

■ Practice, preferably with both a colleague and a voice recorder. Besides getting feedback from your colleague on where to strengthen your presentation, listening to your recording will help you see where you get stuck or where your wording is clumsy. You can then use this information to determine where you need to edit your presentation or practice it more.

■ Try to anticipate questions your audience may have. Think through some of the questions that you would have if you were hearing this presentation for the first time and then be prepared to answer them.

■ Dress professionally. Dress for the environment in which you will be presenting (business attire versus business casual), but never dress down for your audience.

While an entire book could be dedicated to the topic of data collection, analysis, and presentation, it is our hope that the information that has been provided in this chapter will help you and your colleagues improve healthcare delivery.

Chapter 20

Benchmarking

John T. Hansmann

Contents

Introduction

Have you ever asked yourself, "Is there a better way to do this?" Or, possibly, "There's got to be a better way to do this." Or, maybe, "I'm sure someone else has figured out a better way to do this." Those are three layman's phrases that describe the concept of benchmarking. This chapter will be focused on the topic of benchmarking, describing what it is, and providing practical tools and examples of how to successfully use the concepts of comparative analysis and benchmarking to improve your operations and overall performance.

Definition of Benchmarking

A benchmark is "(1) a point of reference from which measurements may be made or, (2) something that serves as a standard by which others may be measured or judged."[*] The concept of benchmarking in business dates back to at least the 1970s, but it was really brought to the forefront in the 1980s by Xerox Corporation. Xerox had lost a lot of their market share to other companies, and needed to do something different. Robert Camp, who led a number of Xerox benchmarking initiatives, defined benchmarking as "the search for industry best practices that lead to superior performance."[†]

Benchmarking provides information to help make more informed decisions about the business. It assists organizations to remain competitive and productive. It helps develop best practices. Benchmarking is an organized approach to determine if someone does something better than you, and to learn from them to improve your operations. It results in organizations seeking to become the best by identifying and implementing best practices.

Benchmarking in Healthcare

Formal, step-by-step benchmarking initiatives have been successful in many other industries. Healthcare has applied the concepts, but typically not as rigorously as other industries. The time and resources necessary to perform benchmarking typically have not been provided. The practice in healthcare tends to focus more on high-level financial metrics and less on the underlying processes or service and quality metrics. In most cases, a management engineer or process improvement professional gets an assignment from the hospital administrative team to reduce costs by using the provided comparative data, often called *benchmarking data*. The benchmarking data typically shows a large calculated *savings opportunity* that the administration wants to realize. The management engineer/process improvement professional needs to use a process adapted from the formal benchmarking steps used in other industries to realize any of the potential savings opportunity.

Keys to Successful Benchmarking Efforts

An argument could be made that any benchmarking effort, whether small or large, that created a learning opportunity and identified potential improvements was successful. But for any benchmarking initiative to be considered a success, it needs to include many of the following key components.

- ■ **Links to key business objectives, improvement initiatives, or strategies.** The time and effort necessary to complete a successful benchmarking initiative requires that it be done in support of key business objectives or strategies. Initiatives not linked to key business objectives dilute or waste necessary resources needed for critical projects.
- ■ **Good metrics.** The comparison data are the starting point for any benchmarking initiative. Without the data, the organization doesn't know where its potential opportunities are or who may be doing something better. And without the data, a baseline wouldn't exist against which to measure when any improvements are made.

---

[*] Merriam-Webster, http://www.merriam-webster.com/dictionary/benchmark.
[†] Robert C. Camp, *Benchmarking: The Search for Industry Best Practices That Lead to Superior Performance* (Wisconsin: ASQC Quality Press, 1989), 12.

- **Know your own processes.** An organization must know itself to understand its strengths and weaknesses prior to finding out about another organization. Knowing yourself helps determine the priorities to pursue first, and direct the analyses to the appropriate functions. Then when you partner with someone else, you can concentrate on the things that are important to the organization, focusing resources and expertise.
- **Structured approach for interviews, data collection, and fact finding.** This allows the organization's resources to be as efficient as possible, and utilizes everyone's time wisely. An organized, well-thought-out discussion or interview also shows your partner organization that you are serious about the process and respectful of their time. The focused effort minimizes "industrial tourism."
- **Propensity to action.** Once all the analytical work has been completed, and potential solutions developed, they need to be acted upon. Implementation plans with assigned responsibilities need to be developed. Action needs to be taken, adapting as necessary to make modifications to original plans. The good ideas need to be implemented for any results to be attained.
- **Manage/deal with change and transition.** With all change comes the need to manage the human side of the transition, the emotions, and the ambiguity. All change requires the understanding of the impact on the processes and people involved. While the actual change event or physical change has to be managed, the more difficult part it is to manage the transition of the people to the new change.

Benchmarking: The Eight-Step Process

Many organizations have developed their own x-step methodology to complete a successful benchmarking project. The commonality in all of them is that they follow the fundamental scientific method for problem solving. A generic eight-step approach to successfully complete a benchmarking initiative follows.

Step 1: Data Comparison, Internal, and External

A key attribute of benchmarking is the need for data to measure current and future performance. The first step of any benchmarking initiative is to collect data in your organization prior to looking outside at anyone else. Typical benchmarking/comparison analysis data compares like departments in operational metrics such as hours, dollars, and volume. Specific metrics, such as cost per unit of service (UOS), productive or paid hours per UOS, average length of stay (ALOS), salary/wage/benefits (SWB) cost per UOS, and supply cost per UOS are used. Some organizations include service level and quality metrics like CMS core measures in the analysis. Comparisons can be done at the hospital level, but should be done at the departmental level to provide actionable solutions.

Once an organization has collected data about itself, it needs to collect the same data from other organizations. These data may be obtained through public sources, or most likely need to be purchased from companies specializing in comparison data. The typical scenario involves the organization purchasing data from an external source that specializes in comparison data. In this scenario, data from the participating organizations are compared against each other. The value or success of comparison data revolves around consistent data definitions and having a *like comparison peer group*, or hospitals/departments that are similar in operations. The data definitions provide a map to determine which accounts to include or exclude, and specifically from where the different data elements originate. Included in the data definitions is the timeframe (annual, year to date [YTD], quarterly) of the data to provide a consistent comparison.

Comparison peer groups are typically decided by factors such as size of operation (e.g., bed size, number of patient days, number of procedures), patient type/mix, community populations, and/or geographic distributions. In many cases the data need to be normalized for wage differences (wage index) or patient mix (using case mix index [CMI]) or severity adjusted to include patient complexity in the comparisons. Additional operational characteristic details such as unit design (circle, square, X, H, I), unit storage (centralized vs. bedside), and available technology (automatic dispensing cabinet) refine the comparison even more. The point of the comparison is to select other hospitals that are as similar in operations as possible to which you can compare your hospital/department. The more similar the operations, the more any variances may be attributable to actionable differences.

Step 2: Variance Analysis: Identify Performance Variance and Potential Improvement Opportunities

The second step for a benchmarking/comparison analysis initiative is to analyze the comparison data and determine if a potential improvement or savings opportunity exists. This variance analysis calculates the difference between how one organization performs compared to another. The variance or potential savings opportunity is calculated by taking the difference in operating performance (e.g., productive hours per unit of service) between the two organizations and multiplying by the volume of the focused organization. This effectively calculates the focused organization's cost of operations using the comparison organization's cost structure and the focused organization's volume. In others words, it is measuring how much can be saved if the focused organization could operate at the other organization's cost structure.

Most comparisons use either quartile or percentile grouping methodology. Quartile and percentile groupings organize the comparison data in rank order from best to worst to identify a quartile or percentile for each hospital. In a quartile ranking system, the best or top quartile is the 1st quartile, the 2nd quartile is the next best, and so on. In a percentile ranking, the data are rank ordered from best to worst, with the percentile rank identifying the percent of hospitals that are worse on the list. For example, if a hospital is at the 75th percentile, its performance is better than 75% of the hospitals on the list.

Normally a high-level target is established to perform at the 50th percentile, 67th percentile, or 75th percentile levels. This is equivalent to the best and second-best quartiles. The methodology ultimately identifies a specific department or hospital as the target hospital. The target hospital is used to calculate the variance or potential savings opportunity. It is important that the comparison target is an actual hospital that is really performing at the identified level versus an average or other mathematical variance that is unattainable.

Many options exist to estimate an improvement goal for the department. The ultimate goal is to achieve the same or better performance as the target department, but in some cases that may not be realistic in the short term. Practice and experience show that in a short time period (defined as one year), it is rarely feasible to make changes greater than 20% of the total expenditure. Another concept that has been used to set the goal is to improve one spot in the rankings. This is especially useful in the case where the ultimate target may be a real stretch goal for the department. A third concept to set a goal creates a potential savings range, and is sometimes described using terms such as *conservative* and *aggressive* targets. However it is done, the point is to identify a hospital that is performing better than you. Improving one spot, being at the median of the list, or being better than 75% of the hospitals is much more realistically attainable than reaching the top of the list. This methodology also protects against comparing to a potential outlier that may not be attainable.

The table in Figure 20.1 shows typical comparison data and potential opportunity savings for Med/Surg nursing departments. It compares like departments using productive dollars and hours per patient day. The metrics are calculated for each department, and then rank ordered from lowest to highest productive hours per patient day. This example uses the percentile methodology, where the target performance is the 50th percentile, or better than 50% of the departments listed.

Many available tools provide graphical views of the data in addition to the table of numbers. The data displayed in Figure 20.1 show the departments aligned in ascending productive hours per patient day order. Organizing the data in ascending order allows clustering of hospitals/departments, which tend to indicate a consistent practice or performance, to be seen more easily.

In the example, the target hospital (50th percentile) is hospital R. Its hours per unit performance are 9.56 productive hours per patient day. The focus hospital is hospital N, running at 10.30

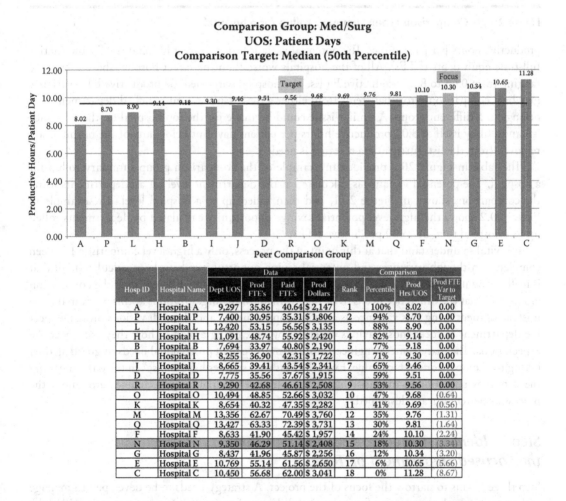

| Hosp ID | Hospital Name | Data | | | | Comparison | | | |
		Dept UOS	Prod FTE's	Paid FTE's	Prod Dollars	Rank	Percentile	Prod Hrs/UOS	Prod FTE Var to Target
A	Hospital A	9,297	35.86	40.64	$ 2,147	1	100%	8.02	0.00
P	Hospital P	7,400	30.95	35.31	$ 1,806	2	94%	8.70	0.00
L	Hospital L	12,420	53.15	56.56	$ 3,135	3	88%	8.90	0.00
H	Hospital H	11,091	48.74	55.92	$ 2,420	4	82%	9.14	0.00
B	Hospital B	7,694	33.97	40.80	$ 2,190	5	77%	9.18	0.00
I	Hospital I	8,255	36.90	42.31	$ 1,722	6	71%	9.30	0.00
J	Hospital J	8,665	39.41	43.54	$ 2,341	7	65%	9.46	0.00
D	Hospital D	7,775	35.56	37.67	$ 1,915	8	59%	9.51	0.00
R	Hospital R	9,290	42.68	46.61	$ 2,508	9	53%	9.56	0.00
O	Hospital O	10,494	48.85	52.66	$ 3,032	10	47%	9.68	(0.64)
K	Hospital K	8,654	40.32	47.35	$ 2,282	11	41%	9.69	(0.56)
M	Hospital M	13,356	62.67	70.49	$ 3,760	12	35%	9.76	(1.31)
Q	Hospital Q	13,427	63.33	72.39	$ 3,731	13	30%	9.81	(1.64)
F	Hospital F	8,633	41.90	45.42	$ 1,957	14	24%	10.10	(2.24)
N	Hospital N	9,350	46.29	51.14	$ 2,408	15	18%	10.30	(3.34)
G	Hospital G	8,437	41.96	45.87	$ 2,256	16	12%	10.34	(3.20)
E	Hospital E	10,769	55.14	61.56	$ 2,650	17	6%	10.65	(5.66)
C	Hospital C	10,450	56.68	62.00	$ 3,041	18	0%	11.28	(8.67)

Figure 20.1 Typical comparison data and potential opportunity savings for Med/Surg nursing departments.

Comparison Group Summary
Comparison Target: Median (50th Percentile)

Peer Comparison Group	UOS Selection	Prod FTE's	Paid FTE's	Prod Dollars	Dept UOS	Rank	Number of Peer Hospitals	Percentile	Prod Hrs/UOS	Target Hrs/UOS	Prod FTE Var to Target
Pharmacy Services	Doses	20.37	26.45	$ 1,480	3,380,700	21	21	0%	0.02	0.01	(7.08)
Lab Services	Billable Tests	39.78	43.90	$ 2,227	598,031	14	16	13%	0.15	0.13	(6.23)
Med Surg	Patient Days	46.29	51.14	$ 2,408	9,350	15	18	18%	10.30	9.56	(3.34)
Telemetry	Patient Days	45.51	50.90	$ 4,914	7,491	12	14	14%	12.64	11.77	(3.13)
ICU	Patient Days	29.84	30.62	$ 4,117	3,353	14	20	30%	18.51	17.39	(1.81)
HIM	Charts Processed	11.64	13.02	$ 530	45,614	11	14	21%	0.55	0.51	(0.86)
Central Serv/Purchasing	APD	7.35	8.11	$ 329	69,724	8	14	43%	0.23	0.21	(0.63)
Accounting/Payroll	Calendar Day	7.92	8.27	$ 412	365	9	14	36%	49.42	48.25	(0.21)
Quality/Risk/Infection	Calendar Day	5.16	5.38	$ 208	365	6	13	54%	32.16	33.29	0.00
Administration	Calendar Day	9.26	9.33	$ 361	365	6	14	57%	57.78	58.45	0.00
HR/Employee Health	Employees	4.54	4.66	$ 245	523	6	14	57%	18.07	19.82	0.00
Respiratory Services	Total PD	18.92	19.97	$ 1,089	41,694	4	14	71%	0.73	0.90	0.00
Nursing Administration	Total PD	6.88	8.03	$ 459	39,822	3	14	79%	0.27	0.34	0.00
ER Services	Visits	31.58	34.76	$ 1,145	22,739	4	27	85%	2.30	2.75	0.00
Imaging Services	Procedures	26.71	32.05	$ 1,607	51,023	2	18	89%	0.87	1.04	0.00
OR Services	OR Minutes	30.30	34.32	$ 1,607	283,337	1	19	100%	0.16	.21	0.00
Hospital Summary Total		**342.07**	**380.90**	**$ 23,198**							(23.29)

Figure 20.2 Comparison group summary rollup for a hospital.

productive hours per patient day. The potential variance to the target hospital is 3.34 productive full-time equivalents (FTEs). All of the hospitals worse than the target hospital show a variance ranging from 0.64 to 8.67 productive FTEs. The hospital with the 8.67 productive FTE variance may be a comparison error that stems from either a data issue or a mismatched department that belongs in a different group. A similar issue could be made for the top hospital on the list, since it stands all by itself at 8.02 productive hours per patient day. But before any of the hospitals are removed from the list, further data research is needed.

The table in Figure 20.2 provides an example of the comparison group summary rollup for a hospital. The potential variance is calculated at the department level for all departments using the comparisons shown in Figure 20.1, and then rolled up to a hospital level. The example in Figure 20.2 shows the high-level potential savings opportunity calculated by departments rolled up to a hospital total of 23.29 productive FTEs.

It is vital to understand that at this point in the process, only a high-level comparison has been completed. Although variances and potential saving opportunities have been calculated, all that is really known is that the focused organization is doing something different than the comparison group, and that the difference needs to be determined. Many organizations at this point make the mistake of identifying this variance as a savings opportunity, and through various means, expect the department to meet those savings potential by developing a plan of how they will meet the expectations. The management engineer/process improvement professional needs to guard against taking the comparisons at face value. Even the best data sources have "noise" in the data, meaning the data may still contain inconsistencies. The variance calculation will change throughout the process as better data are developed.

Step 3: Identify a Specific Area of Opportunity, the Focused Department or Topic

Step three begins to narrow the focus of the project. A strategy needs to be developed to manage and attain the real opportunity from the overall hospital variance. One strategy may utilize the internal and external comparisons to prioritize the focus. Figure 20.3 provides a tool that pictorially represents how a department compares to itself and to the external world. The star performers

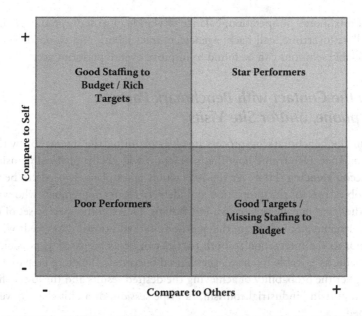

Figure 20.3 Tool for pictorially representing how a department compares to itself and to the external world.

compare favorably to internal trends and to the external world (upper right quadrant). The departments that compare favorably to their internal trends, but not so externally (upper left quadrant), are meeting their budgets but may have richer standards and potentially could be performing more cost effectively. The departments that are not meeting their budgets internally, but compare favorably to the external world (lower right quadrant) need to improve their operational performance. The poor performers in the lower left quadrant, do not compare favorably to their internal trends or to the external world. They have potentially significant improvement and savings opportunities, and should be the first group of departments on which to focus the benchmarking effort.

Another strategy may focus on the department with the largest variance. A third approach would be to focus on a department where the organization thinks success is assured, getting a *win* to help sell future initiatives. There is no wrong answer at this point, with the best answer being *just do something*.

Step 4: Identify the Comparison Department/Hospital

The comparison department/hospital, or benchmark partner, must be identified. Many factors exist to select the benchmark partner, but the first is their standing in the comparison data (e.g., median, best quartile, better than 75% of the hospitals). Once the list has been narrowed based on performance, other factors should be considered. A specific hospital may be chosen based upon intricate knowledge of that organization, its reputation, or general consensus that other hospitals strive to be like it. Characteristics such as bed size, geographic location, size of operation, patient mix, and payor mix may provide a better match. Completion of a survey to understand various operational characteristics may provide an even closer match.

The high-level comparisons (hours and dollars per unit) require drill down to another level of detail to understand daily operations, analyzing staffing levels, caregiver-to-patient ratios, utilization, skill mix, hours of operation, balance of workload to staff, productive hours, and use of premium dollars (overtime, call back, agency/contract labor), and so on. It is at this level of detail that actionable solutions can be found to improve overall performance.

Step 5: Plan the Contact with Benchmark Partner: Survey, Telephone, and/or Site Visits

The fifth step in the benchmarking process involves planning the interaction with the selected benchmarking partner. Determine how the interaction will occur: physically onsite or virtually via video or teleconferencing. However the interaction takes place, it needs to be well planned. Determine the objectives for the interaction and identify the team members who will participate. In some cases, the team may be one or two individuals. Develop the specific set of questions and additional data elements needed. Share the questions and additional data needs with the partner organization prior to the interaction so both parties can be as prepared as possible. All requests should be as specific as possible to ensure the desired outcome. The more prepared the organizations are, the higher the probability of achieving the desired results and the lower the chance that the interaction results in "industrial tourism," a gripe session, or a chit-chat conversation where nothing is learned.

Step 6: Perform Interviews/Site Visits

The sixth step of the process is to complete the site visit or video/teleconference interview. The team needs to operate like an investigator. Take notes and ask specific questions, clarifying if the answer is not initially understood. Don't be afraid to ask the obvious questions. Ask open-ended questions unless searching for a specific fact. Finally, continually ask *why*. You may not get the entire answer you seek until the *why* question is asked a few times. Be careful not to ask biased or leading questions.

Immediately after the visit or interview is over, the benchmarking team should hold a short debriefing session to recap what was heard. This provides an opportunity for further clarification, and to identify areas of confusion or follow up with the other organization.

Step 7: Review Findings from Contact; Summarize and Develop Action Plans to Implement Improvement Opportunities

A detailed debriefing session should be conducted within a few days (no more than a week) after the interview/site visit. Each team member should provide a short written summary of the information learned. The team should focus upon differences in practices. It is very easy to defend current practice and dismiss the improvement opportunities. Focusing on the differences helps to minimize the internal bias, allowing the learning to continue. Can the necessary changes be implemented to match what the other organization does? Should what they've done be implemented? The key at this step is to identify specific action items that can be implemented that will result in improved operations and lower costs. Return on investment and actual benefits and costs for each specific recommendation or change initiative need to be calculated. Criteria to use to determine which recommendations to implement include potential dollar savings, control (how much control of the change do you have), risk (patients, MDs, staff, payors), probability of success (short/long term, key players on board, is it doable), and resource requirements.

Step 8: Implement Action Plans and Monitor to Sustain Changes

The last step in the benchmarking process is to implement the changes and monitor to ensure the improvements are sustained. A project plan, along with timelines, goals/targets, and milestones needs to be developed. Identify key stakeholders, enablers/support components, and potential barriers. Transition and change management plans need to be developed. Ongoing success will be measured by the productivity management and financial reporting systems.

The goals of a benchmarking initiative are usually to reduce costs and improve operations. Initially, the objectives are to identify and implement a few best practices that will improve operations by reducing costs and providing improved service and quality to its customers. But as an organization delves further into the concept, secondary goals tend to surface. One key secondary goal is to identify areas in which the organization excels so they can be replicated across the organization. This cannot be overstated: it is important to know where your strengths are so they can be replicated as appropriate in the organization. Another important secondary goal is gaining benchmarking experience. As the organization matures in its benchmarking endeavors, the knowledge gained from earlier efforts will provide benefit for future projects. And finally, another desired secondary goal is to help build peer network contacts for the managers. Benchmarking provides the opportunity for managers to meet others and see how they do what you do. This network of peers over time provides the ability to query the group when future questions or issues arise.

Other Uses for Benchmarking/Comparison Analysis

Benchmarking should be used in conjunction with a robust productivity monitoring program. The productivity monitoring program provides a good internal comparison of how a department is performing against itself over time. But a benchmarking/comparison analysis allows the organization to see how it compares to the external world.

Benchmarking should be used in conjunction with process improvement initiatives. It can assist in the identification of process improvement projects and provide a measurement method to develop a better process when the existing process needs to be changed.

Benchmarking should be used in budgeting and other functions that require determination or allocation of resources. Utilizing benchmarking and comparison data in building a budget can provide stretch targets for an organization to meet.

Benchmarking should also be used as a strategic initiative, to design a new process or program. Understanding what someone outside the organization is doing may jump start a development exercise that is not meeting expectations.

Summary

Benchmarking/comparison analysis is a rigorous process applied in many industries to identify best practices and implement cost-saving ideas. The comparison data are vital, and must conform to consistent definitions and sources to ensure apples-to-apples comparison. The comparison peer groups need to be determined through like practices and operational characteristics. The high-level variances calculated prior to detailed drill down analysis only provide indicators suggesting that the focused hospital/department is doing something different than the comparison hospital/department. But once the real opportunity is determined, action plans must be developed to implement the recommendations to attain and sustain the expected results. The benchmark-ing/comparison analysis data and concept can be used with other initiatives in the organization. Keys to successful benchmarking initiatives include the analytical *science* part of the process, but depend as much on the *art* aspects. The search for best practices is a journey that is ongoing.

Chapter 21

Facility Planning: The Role of the Industrial Engineer

Amanda Mewborn and Richard Herring

Contents

What Is a Facility Plan?

Before a facility plan can be created, an organization must first have a mission, vision, and strategic plan. The mission describes what an organization does. Often, in healthcare, organizations have missions related to providing high-quality, compassionate care to patients. A vision describes why the organization does what it does. Many healthcare organizations are faith based, and therefore their vision may include references to fulfilling God's will or mercy on people. An organization's strategic plan outlines how the organization will go about accomplishing its mission and vision. The strategic plan typically includes details on growth plans to maintain viability. For example, a strategic plan may describe how the organization plans to become the primary provider of cardiac services for the community.

After a strategic plan is created, the next step is to develop a master facility plan. A master facility plan describes what facilities are needed to accomplish the strategic plan. Some of the components of a master facility plan include the following:

- Analysis of existing facilities, space, and land, to include:
  - How the space is utilized
  - Benchmarking the existing space against industry standards
  - Analysis of regulatory requirements, including zoning and any other factors that determine how the land or space can be used
  - Analysis of the mechanical, electrical, plumbing, and structure of existing facilities
  - Review of workflow within the existing space, including opportunities for gaining efficiency through changes to the physical space
- Plan or concept for how the facilities can be used in the future, to include:
  - Site plan for how the land and facilities can expand or be reused
  - Stack and block plans to demonstrate where departments will be located in relation to each other
  - Exterior building views showing building placement or expansion concepts
  - Plans for maintenance of facilities
  - Identification of required projects
  - A phasing or implementation plan showing project interdependencies
  - Estimates of project costs
- Sequencing/implementation plan detailing the phases in which the site and facilities can be modified or built

Master facility planning naturally leads to other types of analyses, such as understanding the following about the organization:

- Market and competitors, geography, and labor
- Brand and the opportunities for the facility to support or redefine the brand
- Organizational structure and how the structure may need to change with the strategic plan and changes to facilities
- Information technology and how changes may affect the organization, including facilities
- Operations and logistics

Ultimately, the master facility plan must support the organization's leadership in demonstrating that the implementation of the strategic plan and master facility plan will drive the largest gains for the organization, at the lowest cost and risk.

Some of the additional support that may be needed includes a detailed financial analysis that explores the availability of capital, plans for raising capital, and total cost of ownership analysis (what it will cost to operate and maintain the facilities). Sometimes, a cost–benefit analysis is necessary to help decision makers understand the options.

More detailed analyses may also be needed. For example, what is the cost of leasing space versus owning and building space? Operational variables may also be analyzed, such as whether to centralize or decentralize departments, and cross-utilization of spaces. Further, analyses may be needed to determine whether to renovate existing space or tear it down and rebuild. Some organizations also have options to buy existing facilities or space, and that option must also be considered.

As one may imagine, each master facility plan and the components are unique to the organization, and should be designed to meet the organization's specific needs. The organization or client is often referred to as the *owner* in architecture-related meetings.

Role of an Industrial Engineer in Facility Planning

An architect is usually the lead person in the development of a facility plan. Industrial engineers can support architects in facility planning in many ways.

Before the facility plan is created, an industrial engineer can support executives in an organization with the development of a strategic plan. Some of the questions that industrial engineers may analyze to support strategic plan decision making may include:

- How much of the market demand is the organization currently capturing?
- Where are opportunities to capture more market share?
- Who are the primary competitors?
- What service lines are underserved in the community?
- How profitable is each service line?
- Which conditions are at play in the market that may change the competitive landscape or profitability?

After the strategic plan is defined, industrial engineers may support architects with the master facility plan. During the analysis of existing facilities, space, and land, some of the work that industrial engineers can do includes:

- Observational studies to understand how the existing space is utilized. In Lean, this is called "going to the Gemba," meaning visiting the front line where work is happening to visualize and experience the environment and culture. Results of observational studies include opportunities that can be addressed with or without changes to the facility. For example, an observational study may identify a challenge created by a lack of information technology, which could be solved without changes to the facility. Other opportunities may require changes to the facility, such as excessive clinician travel distance to obtain supplies. In this example, the facility change may be creation of satellite storage closets for supplies to minimize clinician travel distance.
- Research on industry standards for space allocations for various settings, including office space, patient care units, and physician practices.
- Analysis of workflow in the existing space, including development of process flow maps of the current state operations. Identification of opportunities for improvement to workflow, through rapid improvement events or kaizen, as well as opportunities that require facility changes or longer-term projects.

During the phase where the plan or concept for the use of the facilities in the future is developed, industrial engineers can assist architects by:

- Developing process flow maps of future state operations. These maps provide detailed workflow specifications of how staff would like for work to happen, more efficiently, in the future. These maps can be used to understand critical working relationships, and determining placement of personnel, supplies, and work.

- Coordinating with architects in the development of the stack and block plans to ensure critical adjacencies are achieved, while minimizing wasted movement of personnel, supplies, and customers.
- Developing estimates of the impact of facility changes on personnel and supply expenses.
- Designing the sequencing plan detailing the phases in which the site and facilities can be modified or built, based on the impact to operations.

Other analyses that the industrial engineer can support during master facility planning include:

- Labor market analysis, answering questions about workforce availability; for example, how nursing or physician shortages will impact the organization
- Organizational structure and how the structure may need to change with the strategic plan and changes to facilities
- Information technology analysis, and proposal for changes to influence the organization's efficiency and quality
- Logistical analyses, such as supply chain and revenue cycle
- Cost–benefit analyses to identify the opportunities that have the best likely return on investment
- Engineering economy analyses such as the cost of renting versus buying versus building space

The industrial engineer's analytical toolkit can provide a lot of value in the master facility planning process. Furthermore, understanding the healthcare environment eliminates a steep learning curve, facilitating faster delivery of value to the customer.

How Are Industrial Engineers Involved Once a Facility Plan Is Created?

When speaking of facility planning, some people think only of the master facility plan components described earlier. Others think of facility planning as the entire architectural process. There are many additional components of the architectural process, and those pieces are described here.

Space Programming

The next phase after master facility planning is usually space programming. Space programming is a listing of all of the spaces, along with their sizes, that will be needed in a building. For example, the space program might specify 4 office cubicles that are sized at 4 feet by 6 feet for personnel in the medical records department. The space program also estimates the peripheral space that will be needed, for areas such as hallways, walls, and technical components (mechanical, electrical, and plumbing). Of course, the space program is heavily dependent on the planned workflow within the building. The space program is often compiled based on a series of interviews with the organization's personnel, and is therefore based on personal preference. This often results in more space than is needed, as well as a program reflecting operational silos where each person's or department's needs are met, without consideration for the facility as a whole or consideration of how the silos will operate together.

An industrial engineer can support more efficient space programming through development of future state process flow maps that integrate the silos and show how the silos will interact. For example, imagine a physician practice that will run a clinic out of a new building on Mondays and

Wednesdays, and work elsewhere the other days of the week. Within that same building, there may be another physician practice that will run clinic out of the new building on Tuesdays and Thursdays, and work elsewhere other days of the week. It may be possible for these two physician practices to utilize the same space in the new building, reducing the overall size of the building. An industrial engineer can assist by helping to standardize processes and spaces to facilitate both physician practices utilizing the same space.

Another example where an industrial engineer can assist is in simulation. Imagine that the two physician practices just mentioned decided that they both wanted to work out of the new building on Fridays. Simulation can be used to model the physicians' schedules and identify potential schedules where both physicians could use the space.

Operational analysis can also be used to identify the correct size of space needed. Continuing with the physician practice example, operational analysis may identify the correct number of exam rooms needed per physician.

Additionally, an industrial engineer could optimize the ratios that are utilized to estimate the support space needed in facilities. Improving the precision of these ratios would certainly result in better cost estimates. A cost estimate for the project is developed at the end of each phase of the architectural process. The estimate gains accuracy as the project becomes defined with greater detail in each phase.

Schematic Design

The next phase after space programming is schematic design. During this phase, the architect prepares diagrams of the buildings or spaces, to provide a general view of the components and scale of the building or project. This phase is based on information from the master facility planning and space programming phases, including the components and size of the spaces as well as the necessary adjacencies. The architect's plans may also be referred to as *drawings*, *schematics*, or *SDs* (for schematic designs).

An industrial engineer can support schematic design by optimizing the adjacency relationships. For example, it may be most efficient for radiology and laboratory to be closely located to the emergency department since these services are utilized heavily by the emergency department. Furthermore, the emergency department likes to be on the first level of the hospital for easy patient access. However, the site may not be large enough to accommodate all of these services on the first level. The industrial engineer can quantify the benefits of various adjacency relationships to help prioritize and place services. As an example, the quantification may reveal that there is more time-intensive patient movement to radiology than to the laboratory; therefore, radiology would be located on the first floor with the emergency department and laboratory would be located on another floor.

Another application of industrial engineering during the schematic design phase is the use of spaghetti diagrams to measure current movement of people and supplies. This information can be used to minimize travel distances of heavily traveled routes. Floor plans and designs for changes to the building can be analyzed and spaghetti diagrams created to measure the changes in the distances traveled, to identify the most efficient paths.

Industrial engineers can also help to interpret workflow plans into design implications. For example, the future state process maps may indicate that patients will be greeted at one central welcome desk when they enter the building. Without understanding this workflow, architects may plan for patients to enter the building at multiple locations, such as the emergency department, cancer center, and radiology. Having multiple entrances is costly for construction, traffic flow planning, and staffing. Additionally, more waiting spaces would have to be built at each of these separate entrances. Interpreting planned future state workflow into design considerations is an important role that an industrial engineer can play.

At the end of schematic design, the cost estimate from the space programming phase is recalculated and refined. Sometimes, if the cost estimate is not within the organization's range, the schematic design will be tweaked and refined to lower the cost estimate. The cost estimate is not very accurate at this phase, as details such as interiors are not determined at this point. Imagine the difference in the cost of installing all hardwood floors compared with linoleum in your home. Of course, the magnitude of the difference in cost for a large healthcare facility is huge, especially when considering all of the options for finishes. The analogy helps to understand part of the reason that cost estimates are not very accurate at this phase of the project.

Design Development

The next phase in the architectural process is design development or DDs. During this phase, the schematic design is fleshed out with more detail. Examples of details that are determined in this phase include development of the building infrastructure systems including mechanical, electrical, plumbing, and structure. The design of each individual space is also completed in detail in this phase. This includes placement of elements within the room including cabinets, lighting, switches, medical gases, furniture, medical equipment, and so on.

The industrial engineer's role in this phase remains similar to that in the schematic design phase: ensuring the design supports the workflow and interactions in the building. This phase provides more detail, though, so the industrial engineer can help with making design decisions around standardization. For example, should every room on a patient care unit be standardized and oriented the same way? Or, is it okay for the rooms to be mirror images of each other? Other details that are considered in this phase include specific placement of equipment and design of headwalls. For example, where should the medical gasses be located? Many of the questions in this phase can be answered in user group meetings. However, the industrial engineer can help to facilitate standardization across the facility. If user group meetings are the sole decision makers, a facility may find that each unit is designed so specifically to one patient population, it cannot be flexed to service another population easily. For example, patients in an intensive care unit require more medical gasses and space for medical technology than patients in a medical unit. However, it may be prudent to design the medical unit to have the additional space and medical gasses so that if the patient population becomes more acute in the future, the facility has the flexibility to convert the medical unit to an intensive care unit easily. Concepts such as these are important to consider early in the design process.

At the end of the design development phase, another estimate of pricing is completed. With further details, this will be the most accurate cost estimate provided yet. Some aspects of the design development may have to be redone to reduce the costs to within the budget constraints.

Construction Documents

The final phase of the design of a facility is construction documents, or CDs. During this phase, the designs from the design development phase are refined with further details. Construction documents provide a contractor with the necessary detail to provide the most accurate pricing estimate yet and actually construct the facility. Every detail is outlined in these documents, including what materials to use, size of materials, finishes, and so on. The construction documents usually include both a set of drawings as well as a detailed book of specifications.

The industrial engineer's role during this phase may be simply querying and answering any questions on user preferences or how things are used. For example, do the users prefer a solid glass door to patient rooms, a door with a window, or a solid door? Understanding how the users plan to work in the new space provides great information for designing to their needs.

Construction Administration

Now that the design is completed, the next phase is construction administration. During this phase, the architect administers the contract between the owner and the contractor. The architect observes the progress of the construction to ensure that it is completed according to the construction documents. The architect may be needed to clarify information or even make changes to the design as needed. Architects sometimes also review the contractor's bills to the owner, ensuring the owner is billed correctly for the construction. This phase ensures that the project comes to fruition. The industrial engineer doesn't have a specific role during this phase.

Add-On Services: Transition Planning and Move-In

There are add-on services outside of the traditional architectural process that the industrial engineer can do to ensure efficacy of the new facility. For example, the industrial engineer can assist the owner with transition planning. Transition planning involves creation of a plan to manage the transition from the current facility to the new facility. The plan is somewhat like a project plan in that it details all of the tasks that need to be completed to effectively transition to the new facility. The plan also outlines sequencing and timing of the tasks. A solid transition plan is essential to the successful move to a new facility. An industrial engineer is well positioned for this role, as it involves project management and integration of operations and facility. An industrial engineer can translate the operational plans and process flow maps into a methodology for implementing these operations in a new facility.

Another add-on service outside of the traditional architectural process is move-in. As the term *move-in* suggests, this is the phase when the owner begins to occupy the new space. An industrial engineer can coordinate the move-in process, identifying the necessary tasks, sequencing, and timing, and then executing on the project plan. Move-in within a healthcare environment can be extremely complex. Acutely ill patients dependent on multiple technologies and medications for life can be very challenging to move and there are high risks in moving them. How many and what kind of staff will be needed? An industrial engineer can also support the thinking through this process through tools such as failure mode effects analysis, or FMEA. This tool helps to identify all the possible events that could go poorly, and identifies ways to mitigate those events from happening or handling the events if they do happen. This can be very empowering to staff who may be scared to attempt moving critically ill patients. Additionally, this ensures patient and staff safety.

Add-On Services: Operational Planning

Many of the uses of an industrial engineer that have been described in the space programming and design phases actually represent an add-on service of operational planning. Surprisingly, operational planning is not one of the standard phases within an architectural project. However, architecture clearly has a close link with operations, and certainly the built environment influences the way people work in the environment. Organizations that choose to add operational planning usually insert this phase after or close to the space programming phase. In fact, operational planning and space programming can be done concurrently, maximizing the efficiency of meetings with users. Without operational planning, an organization risks designing a new facility that will not achieve the results desired.

Add-On Services: Sustainment

With all of the great work mentioned in all of these phases, it would be a waste (in Lean terms) to let operations slide back into old ways of doing business. The sustainment phase ensures that the efficiencies designed into the processes and facilities are achieved and sustained. Furthermore, an industrial engineer can train staff on efficiency principles, including Lean and Six Sigma. With this training, the organization can achieve true continuous improvement.

DECISION-MAKING SUPPORT

Chapter 22

Assessing the ROI and Benefits of New Technology

Dean Athanassiades

Contents

Management engineering involvement in cost justification of capital equipment dates back decades. However, the classic techniques used for cost justification and cost–benefit analysis of capital equipment do not always apply to assessing the return on investment (ROI) and benefits of disruptive technology, especially information technology. This chapter reviews classic cost justification methods and explains why those methods may not always be appropriate for assessing the return on investment and benefit of current-day disruptive technology. The chapter proposes techniques that management engineers can use to assess the return on investment and benefits of disruptive technologies.

Classic Techniques for Assessing ROI and Cost–Benefit Analysis

The management engineering body of knowledge contains substantial information about return on investment and cost–benefit analysis. For example, Holger George Thuesen authored the first edition of *Engineering Economy* in 1950. George J. Thuesen and W. J. Fabrycky published the eighth edition in 1993. A key premise of engineering economy (or engineering economics) is making project selection decisions using quantitative techniques based upon discounted cash flow analysis.

Engineering Economy

According to Thuesen (1992), when one compares mutually exclusive projects, the cash flow difference between the projects should be the basis for selecting the most desirable project (see Figure 22.1). More specifically, if one compares the cash flow from project A and from project B, if the cash flow from project B is superior to the cash flow from project A (B – A > 0), project B is the superior project. Conversely, if the cash flow from project A is superior to the cash flow from project B (B – A < 0), project A is the superior project. Thuesen (1992) further notes the importance of evaluating the *do-nothing* alternative cautioning that failure to do so could lead to investing in a project that yields a return below the minimum attractive rate of return. The chosen project is the one that maximizes present worth and has a rate of return above the minimum attractive rate of return.

Discounted Cash Flow Analysis

Acquiring new technology often involves committing substantial capital to a project. According to Lutz (1992), a capital expenditure involves an outlay of cash with expected future inflows spanning two or more years. Because it is impossible to predict the future with absolute certainty, one must consider multiple sets of alternative cash expenditures to identify the best option. In evaluating capital expenditures, one must consider (1) all costs and the time when each cost occurs, (2) all benefits and the time when each cash inflow occurs, (3) the economic life of each capital

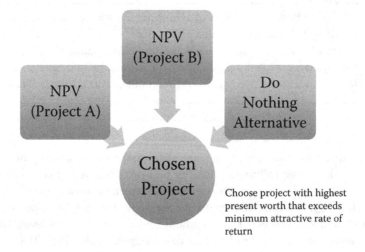

Project Selection based on Engineering Economy Analysis

Figure 22.1   Project selection based on engineering economy analysis.

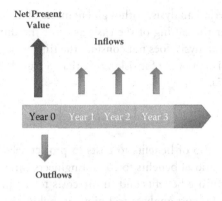

Discounted Cash Flow Analysis

Figure 22.2 Discounted cash flow analysis.

expenditure alternative, and (4) the interest rate that exists when each cost and inflow occurs that reflects the risk of uncertainty.

The economic life of a capital expenditure is the number of years during which the expenditure will return positive benefits to the firm. When performing a cash flow analysis, the engineer often constructs a cash flow diagram showing the positive and negative cash flows as vertical up and down arrows on a time line (see Figure 22.2 and Lutz, 1992).

When an engineer selects the appropriate interest rate for the analysis, a fundamental premise is that a dollar received or expended one year in the future has a lesser value than a dollar received today—the time value of money. The selected interest rate reflects the minimum interest rate that an organization expects to earn on its invested capital. The selected interest rate for the analysis may be adjusted upward reflective of the type of project and its risk. For example, an organization may elect to adjust upward the minimum interest rate for cost reduction projects (lower risk) by a different premium from a project to add a new product line or facility (higher risk) (Lutz, 1992).

Present Worth Analysis

The most common analytic techniques for comparing projects include present worth, future worth, rate of return, payback period, and benefit–cost analysis. Present worth compares the costs and benefits of a project using the current time (present) as the basis of comparison. If the present worth is positive (benefits exceed costs), the analyst considers the project as acceptable. If the analysis compares multiple projects, the engineer should select the project with the highest present worth. To use present worth, each project must have the same economic life. Future worth analysis is similar to present worth analysis except the analysis uses a future time as the basis of comparison. Rate of return analysis determines the interest rate where the cash flows from the benefits and the costs equal zero (Lutz, 1992).

Payback Period Analysis

Payback period analysis determines the time required to recover the initial investment using a zero interest rate. The capital expenditure alternative with the shortest payback period is the preferred alternative in the payback period analysis. Although engineers often use payback period analysis, this method fails to consider the timing of the cash flows or the duration of the cash flows. In other words, payback period analysis does not consider the time value of money. Because of these flaws, payback period analysis is a proxy for risk rather than a true decision support technique for selecting projects (Lutz, 1992).

Benefit–Cost Analysis

Benefit–cost analysis uses a ratio of benefits to costs in project selection. The chosen project is the one that has the highest ratio of benefits to costs. Engineers can use the classic present worth techniques in adjusting the future benefits and future costs to the present time for comparison. Engineers often use the benefit–cost analysis technique in public sector project analysis. A challenge comes from the valuation of the benefits and the costs. In classic present worth analysis, the benefits and costs represent quantifiable cash flows. In public sector analysis, the cash flows seek to estimate the benefits and cost to society despite an inability to measure benefits and costs from a financial accounting perspective. For example, if a new technology improves quality or patient safety, the benefit can be one of the most important benefits the project provides, even though putting a monetary value on that benefit can be very difficult. In addition, the types of projects analyzed using benefit–cost analysis often span decades making the estimates of the benefits and costs subject to significant variation (Lutz, 1992).

Evaluating ROI and Benefits of Twenty-First-Century Healthcare Technology

According to the Healthcare Financial Management Association, the purchase of new medical and information technology represented more than 50% of hospital capital spending in 2001. However, barriers to effective technology planning and purchase remain. For example, the direct financial benefits from new healthcare technology come from reimbursement and coverage decisions made by the federal government (Centers for Medicare and Medicaid Services), state agencies, commercial health plans, and other payers (Coye and Kell, 2006).

Disruptive Technologies

Organizations often use return on investment (ROI) analysis to justify investments in new technologies. For example, a healthcare organization considering the purchase of a new magnetic resonance imaging (MRI) scanner would consider purchase price, expected volume, and reimbursement rates, applying classic analysis to justify the project or to select the optimal project from a portfolio of competing projects. Disruptive technologies are those that change business models or affect the nature or flow of work within an organization. The effects of disruptive technologies on an organization are difficult to estimate, thus making it difficult to build a business case for the investment. For example, technologies like surgical robots, electronic health records, and computerized physician order entry systems all offer benefits to the healthcare system but have a great deal of uncertainty related to costs, revenues, and classic ROI (Coye and Kell, 2006).

In addition, external stakeholders can influence the economic evaluation of new technologies. Physicians influence technology purchases, especially when a physician is responsible for a significant volume of admissions, thus directly affecting the volumes related to the analysis. Consumers and patients also influence usage volumes through their choice of provider organizations. As technology providers direct more marketing to consumers, this trend will continue and grow. The actions of competitors can also affect usage volumes. The need to purchase a specific technology like a surgical robot may come from the need to keep up with competing organizations and support patient volumes that drive income (Coye and Kell, 2006).

Techniques for Evaluating Benefits and ROI of Disruptive Technology

Recognizing the differences between classic technology and disruptive technology, Menachemi and Brooks (2006) identified many challenges that exist when attempting to measure ROI for healthcare IT. They noted that a search of peer-reviewed publications yields few scientifically rigorous assessments. Menachemi and Brooks (2006) noted that many analytical tools exist for performing ROI analysis. However, a number of obstacles exist in applying these tools in healthcare IT.

Auditable, Quantifiable, Intangible Benefits

Building upon classic ROI and cost–benefit analysis, a useful technique for evaluating disruptive technology projects comes from segmenting benefits into those benefits that are auditable, quantifiable, or intangible. Auditable benefits appear on an income statement or balance sheet. Engineers can measure quantifiable benefits like improvements in productivity, employee engagement, or customer loyalty. However, those benefits do not appear on a financial statement. Intangible benefits are good for the organization and may benefit the community but are not directly measurable. One can visualize the hierarchy of benefits in a pyramid where the fundamental benefits are the auditable benefits. The quantifiable benefits go on top of the auditable benefits. The intangible benefits form the peak of the pyramid (Figure 22.3).

For example, the benefits produced by IT are dissimilar to benefits produced by other capital investments. In healthcare, capital investments like computed tomography (CT) scanners or MRI scanners produce a direct income stream from a billable service. Conversely, IT enables, improves, or enhances business processes. Traditional ROI methods are not effective in measuring the return on business processes. As another example, the improvements in a business process that come from IT investment often accrue across the enterprise, yet ROI analysis often focuses on measuring costs and benefits in specific cost centers (Menachemi and Brooks, 2006).

Another challenge in using conventional ROI comes from the paradox of benefits not accruing to the organization making the investment. For example, a hospital could invest in information technology that yields benefits for provider physicians or consumers who do not pay for the services. The authors noted that 90% of the financial benefits of IT investment accrue to payers and purchasers of care in the outpatient setting rather than to the party investing in the IT (Menachemi and Brooks, 2006).

Many of the benefits of IT do not directly translate into financial terms. As an example, electronic health records can improve the quality of care and computerized provider order entry systems can reduce medical errors. Both of these important benefits become difficult to dollarize on a financial statement. Finally, the most accurate measures of enterprise IT systems benefits comes

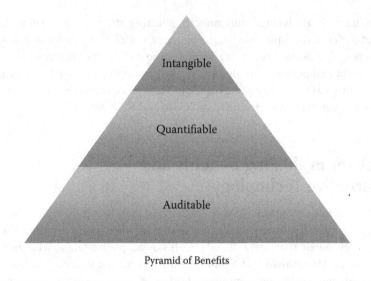

Pyramid of Benefits

Figure 22.3 Pyramid of benefits.

from retrospective analysis rather than prospective analysis during project selection (Menachemi and Brooks, 2006). In other words, if organizations limit project selection to projects with positive present worth based upon classic techniques, those organizations would not select projects involving disruptive technologies.

In the few published ROI studies, Menachemi and Brooks (2006) noted promising results. For example, in a five-year study of electronic health record implementations, the researchers found savings from reductions in drug expenditures, improved utilization of tests, improvements in charge capture, and decreased billing errors. The savings represented an excess over the costs of the system, thus providing a positive return on investment. In another electronic health record study described by Menachemi and Brooks (2006), the researchers measured key cost factors before and after implementation of an electronic health record (EHR) noting savings in spending and increases in revenue directly related to the implementation of the EHR. The savings came from reduction in transcription expenses, reduction in space requirements, and reduction in staff. The revenue increases came from improvements in coding. In another study described by Menachimi and Brooks (2006), a medical center attributed savings of almost $1 million from medical error avoidance. Another medical center reduced transcription costs by 50% and reduced drug costs stemming from formulary compliance.

Despite the lack of ROI studies providing financially auditable evidence of the benefits of healthcare IT, the potential quantifiable and intangible benefits of technology investments bear further attention. Several healthcare technologies offer the promise of improved patient safety including EHRs, computerized provider order entry systems (CPOE), and clinical decision support systems (CDSS).

Example: EHR System

EHR systems are essentially paperless medical records including interfaces with other healthcare information systems in the laboratory, pharmacy, imaging, and financial departments. The costs of electronic health record systems include the hardware, software, implementation, training, ongoing support, and temporary reductions in productivity. The costs accrue from fees paid to vendors as well as the cost of organizational personnel. For example, the cost of training could include vendor or consultant personnel who develop and deliver the training, but also include the time spent by system users attending training. With any new technology, and especially with a disruptive technology, the productivity of the users performing the business process will decline in the early phases of using the new technology. Organizations must acknowledge the learning curve and factor that into the benefit–cost analysis (Menachemi and Brooks, 2006).

Benefits coming from adoption of EHRs can be auditable, quantifiable, or intangible. For example, revenues can increase through improved charge capture, decreased billing errors, decreases in days receivables are outstanding, reduction in disallowed charges, and increased preventative care visits. As a result of the Health Information Technology for Economic and Clinical Health (HITECH) Act, healthcare providers can increase revenues by demonstrating meaningful use of EHR technology. In addition, EHR technology can aid organizations in avoiding costs. For example, the EHR can aid in eliminating duplicate tests (for which denial of reimbursement often occurs). Using the EHR reduces or eliminates the need for transcription services. Similarly, because the records are electronic, organizations avoid the cost of pulling and filing charts.

Deploying EHR technology can provide quantifiable benefits that are difficult to present on an income statement or balance sheet. For example, after full deployment, the EHR can aid in productivity by improving throughput by reducing "waste" associated with delays. Similarly, a well-implemented EHR can improve clinician satisfaction by providing clinicians with more time to spend with their patients. Finally, EHR deployment can provide intangible benefits that will not appear on a financial statement or are quantified but are still important. These benefits include improved quality outcomes like better infection control, improved prescribing practices, improved disease management, and improved immunization rates. Intangible benefits can also include improved patient safety. For example, it is difficult to quantify and monetize the benefits stemming from the ability of a provider to identify and contact patients affected by a drug recall. Other intangible benefits of an electronic health record could include improved patient education, improved coordination of care between providers, and better support for research. Ironically, one intangible benefit of an EHR is access to data supporting business initiatives. For example, a provider could use data captured in an EHR to negotiate with suppliers and payers for favorable terms, thus positively influencing auditable and quantifiable benefits.

Example: CPOE System

CPOE systems enable providers (often physicians) to enter orders into a computer rather than writing or dictating the orders. This introduces structure into the order entry process eliminating errors that stem from illegible handwriting, misunderstood instructions, or lack of relevant information. A key focus of CPOE systems is on medication orders because medication orders are a common medical mistake that causes the death of at least one person every day and injures over a million people each year in the United States (Menanchimi and Brooks, 2006). Avoiding medication errors has auditable, quantifiable, and intangible benefits. CPOE systems can be the enabler of achieving these benefits. As with EHR systems, the costs of electronic health record systems include the hardware, software, implementation, training, ongoing support, and temporary reductions in productivity.

Unlike EHR system deployments, in which cost savings come from reductions in labor (transcription avoidance) and increases in revenue (increased charge capture)—benefits that appear on an income statement, most of the benefits coming from deploying CPOE systems are quantifiable or intangible. Nevertheless, the benefits are substantial to the healthcare delivery system. Menachemi and Brooks (2006) noted that an adverse drug event costs at least $2,500 and adverse drug events occur in at least 10% of patient admissions. Evidence suggests that CPOE can reduce medical errors by 80%. Thus, CPOE can deliver a substantial quantifiable benefit in avoiding the costs associated with adverse drug events. CPOE facilitates compliance with formularies and dosing standards that can reduce drug expenditures.

Intangible benefits include standardization of the medication order process, eliminating unplanned variations that induce errors. Many CPOE systems provide means for customizing and personalizing the ordering process for individual physicians, thus increasing physician productivity and satisfaction. Deploying a CPOE system sends a message to healthcare consumers in the community suggesting the provider takes patient safety seriously, thus improving the provider's reputation in the community. As with EHR systems, some payers provide incentives, in the form of higher payments, to healthcare organizations using CPOE systems, thus offering potential revenue enhancements.

Example: CDSS

CDSSs are another example of a technology that offers significant benefit to society but may not demonstrate justification through conventional ROI analysis. A CDSS is a software package that aids in clinical decision making by matching the characteristics of individual patients to a knowledge base to provide patient assessments or care recommendations. The outputs of CDSS include alerts, reminders, and clinician work lists. The costs associated with CDSS are also similar to those for EHR and CPOE systems. The benefits of CDSS are rarely directly auditable and more often intangible or quantifiable. For example, Menachemi and Brooks (2006) note that CDSS deployment leads to reductions in length of stay, decreased drug cost, improved preventative care, decreased medication errors (often in conjunction with CPOE), and decreased time to ordering appropriate treatment.

Summary

Classic discounted cash flow analysis remains an excellent method of analyzing the benefits, costs, and return on investment of projects that have predictable and reliable future income streams. However, for disruptive technologies like healthcare informatics, management engineers should consider factoring nonfinancial and intangible benefits into the analysis.

References

Coye, Molly Joel, and Kell, Jason. (2006). "How Hospitals Confront New Technology." *Health Affairs (Project Hope)* 25(1): 163–173.

Lutz, Raymond P. (1992). "Discounted Cash Flow Techniques," in *Handbook of Industrial Engineering*, 2nd ed., ed. G. Salvendy, New York: John Wiley and Sons.

Menachemi, Nir, and Brooks, Robert G. (2006). "Reviewing the Benefits and Costs of Electronic Health Records and Associated Patient Safety Technologies." *Journal of Medical Systems* 30(3): 159–168.

Thuesen, Gerald J. (1992). "Project Selection and Analysis," in *Handbook of Industrial Engineering*, 2nd ed., ed. G. Salvendy. New York: John Wiley and Sons.

Chapter 23

Information and Technology Systems Analysis, Evaluation, and Selection

Mary Ellen Skeens

Contents

Introduction

By applying industrial engineering concepts to healthcare information technology, we have the potential to make a tremendous positive impact on healthcare organizations and patients. Practically every clinical department and functional area of a hospital is affected by information technology. All too often, the technology solution does not gain full adoption by the clinical end users. Many times the root cause of the project failure can be traced back to the systems analysis phase.

What is healthcare information technology? According to the US Department of Health and Human Services (HHS) Health Resources and Services Administration (HRSA), healthcare IT is defined as the use of computer applications to record, store, protect, retrieve, and transfer clinical, administrative, and financial information electronically within health care settings. The ultimate goal of health IT is to improve population health and the quality and efficiency of patient care.[1]

Define the Dream: What Problem Are You Trying to Solve?

Imagine a physician sitting in a coffee shop reviewing patient images on his tablet, performing quantitative analysis, and then reporting his findings back to the referring physician electronically. Now imagine what problem led to the implementation of the information technology. Perhaps the problem was lack of physician access to patient diagnostic data from anywhere at any time, aka mobility. Perhaps the problem was related to an unfulfilled need for advanced quantification toolsets and a standardized physician reporting language.

Consideration of implementing any information technology system should start with the definition of what problem needs to be solved. W. Edward Deming stated "A system is a network of interdependent components that work together to try to accomplish the aim of the system. A system must have an aim. Without the aim, there is no system."[2] Understanding the aim is critical in developing the system design. The system aim should be documented in the form of a detailed description of the problem statement. The problem statement should be tested against the organization's strategic objectives and mission statement. Is the problem affecting one or more objectives? Is a solution required to achieve success of the organization's mission? All too often, precious resources are spent investing in solutions that do not map back to the organization's needs.

Needs Assessment

A variety of techniques may be used in the needs assessment phase including workflow observation, interviews, surveying, brainstorming, Delphi method, and review of organizational policies. The problem statement is an input for the needs assessment process. A root-cause analysis of the problem should be performed during this phase.

The needs assessment process should include involvement of all key stakeholders, including those individuals with a vested interest in the success or failure of the project. The key stakeholder groups for an IT implementation project should include the following:

- **Executive sponsors** are responsible for creating the conditions to enable the project organization to function in the most efficient manner.
- **Departmental leadership** provide project resources; representation from impacted clinical departments, information technology, and finance should be included.
- **Physician champions** create enthusiasm and support for the implementation of the system, and help articulate and internally sell the system benefits.
- **Super users** are responsible for system configuration, subject matter expertise, and application training for end users.
- **End users** are the actual users of the system including physicians, technologists, nurses, and administrative staff.

If a key stakeholder is missed during this phase, it is likely to lead to missed needs and eventually a gap in the developed solution. It is essential that sponsorship at the departmental and executive leadership levels be secured for any major healthcare IT project. The stakeholder analysis may become the basis for the project organization chart (Figure 23.1).

The output of this process is a needs assessment report detailing the approach, findings, and results to be achieved. The approach should include a description of the information gathering methods applied during the needs assessment process. The findings should include the actual

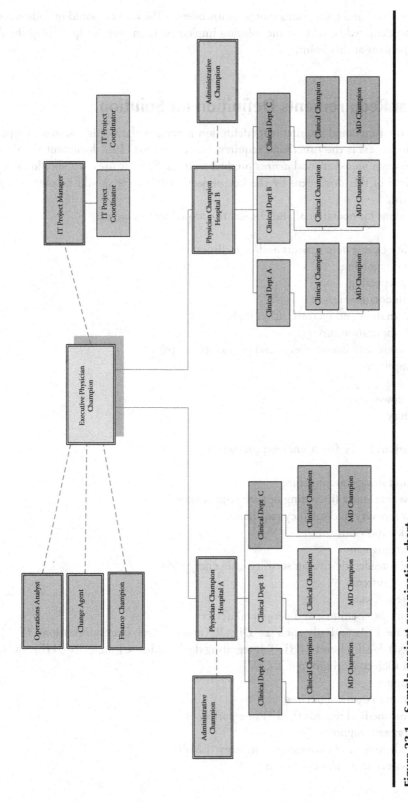

Figure 23.1 Sample project organization chart.

needs, current issues, and pain points that were uncovered. The results should include recommendations on the identified benefits of the solution implementation without specifying the detailed solution components at this point.

Functional Requirements Definition for Solution

The input to the functional requirements definition process is the needs assessment report. The output of this process is the functional requirements document. This document should include distinction between *must-have* and *desired* product features. Specific use cases should be included. Formal approval of this document by the key project stakeholders should be obtained prior to moving forward.

Considerations for operational and clinical functional requirements:

- Scalability (across departments and/or facilities)
- Statistical reporting
- Registry reporting
- Physician documentation
- Clinical analysis and quantification tools
- Clinical application support
- Privacy considerations (patients and physician groups)
- Customizability
- Ease of use
- System downtime
- Regulatory

Considerations for IT functional requirements:

- Server and storage architecture
- Business continuity (including uptime requirements)
- Disaster recovery (redundancy requirements)
- Network bandwidth
- User management
- Security considerations: user security, data encryption
- Operating systems
- Database software
- Workstations, monitors, and peripheral devices
- Healthcare IT standards such as Digital Imaging and Communications in Medicine (DICOM), Health Level 7 (HL7), Integrating the Healthcare Enterprise (IHE), and Clinical Context Object Workgroup (CCOW)
- Interfacing
- Integration to medical devices
- Electronic medical records (EMR) integration
- Vendor system support
- Patient identification management strategy (EMPI)
- Data conversion and/or migration

Workflow analysis is a useful tool in defining the functional requirements of a system. Mapping out the current state and the desired future state workflow allows the identification of changes in process and technology that will be required. Identifying change agents in the project initiation phase is instrumental in a successful implementation of any healthcare IT solution. Failure to focus on how the process change will be executed is a common reason for the failure of healthcare IT projects. One great resource for change management involving healthcare IT systems implementation is the Healthcare Information and Management Systems Society (HIMSS) Technology Adoption Framework.[3]

Modeling tools such as workflow and dataflow diagrams can be most useful in the requirements definition process (Figures 23.2 and 23.3). Including these visual representations in the functional requirements document may increase the document clarity.

Best Practices in Systems Evaluation

Healthcare information systems evaluation commences with an analysis of the solution alternatives. Alternatives may include a brand new system implementation, upgrade or expansion to an existing system, combination of multiple systems, or even doing nothing at all.

To gather information about relevant vendor systems, a formal request for information (RFI) process may be initiated and followed by a request for proposal (RFP).

The purpose of the RFP is to solicit proposals from vendors for a specific solution. This document provides insight into the solution supplier's capabilities and solution offerings. The functional requirements document becomes the input to the RFP document. In order to select the vendors to which you will submit the RFP, the key project stakeholders should review data sources such as KLAS or MD Buyline. The KLAS organization claims to assist healthcare providers in making informed technology decisions by reporting accurate, honest, and impartial vendor performance data.[4] MD Buyline claims to provide healthcare providers with quality, objective, evidence-based information to build confidence in the selection, acquisition, and management of healthcare technology.[5]

Once the RFP responses are received, they should be analyzed. The ability for each vendor to meet the must-have and desired requirements specified for the solution should be assessed. The financial solvency of the vendor should also be considered. It is important to investigate the vendor's implementation history for similar projects to assure they have existing processes and experience in performing the work that will be required.

Another system evaluation technique includes product demonstrations. Generally, the top few vendors are invited onsite to the healthcare facility for a demonstration of the product capabilities. Best practices include providing the vendors with a list of specified functions and questions to be reviewed during the demonstration. The key clinical stakeholders should participate in the demo and be given the opportunity for hands-on experience with the system. Immediately following each vendor demo, the attendees should be surveyed to gather their feedback on the systems. Often, a predetermined set of scoring criteria are used in this survey.

It is highly recommended to provide key clinical stakeholders the opportunity to attend site visits to comparable facilities actively using the systems under consideration for the evaluation of major healthcare IT system implementations. This is a great way to gain insights into lessons learned and best practices around the system implementation and daily use. If site visits are not a viable option, an alternative is contacting references to discuss their experiences.

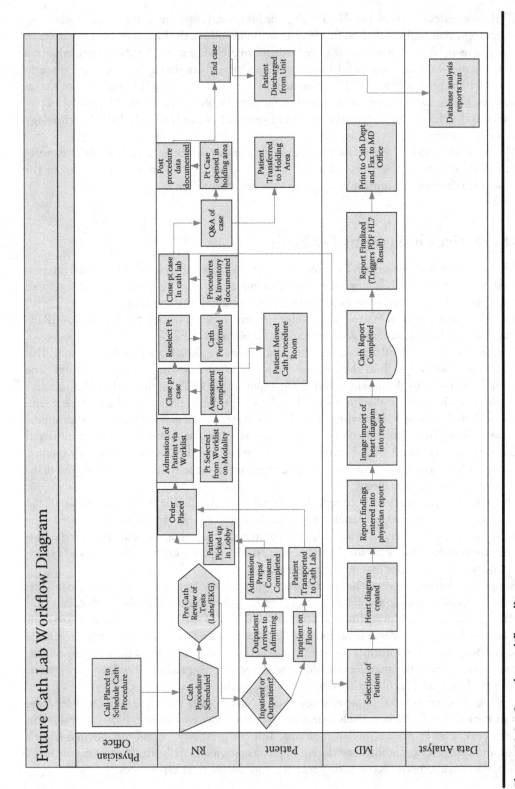

Figure 23.2 Sample workflow diagram.

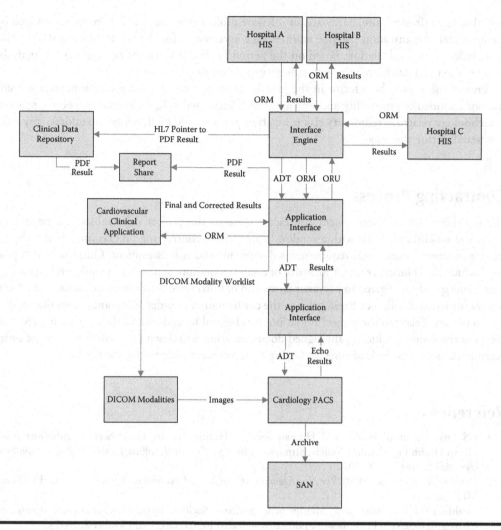

Figure 23.3 Sample dataflow diagram.

System Selection Techniques

Ranking of the systems should be based on a combination of the analysis of the RFP responses, product demo feedback from the project stakeholders, industry rankings of vendor solutions, feedback from references and site visits, as well as the cost–benefit and risk analysis of the solution alternatives. Some methodologies and tools that may aid in the systems selection process include the nominal group technique, prioritization matrices, Pareto charts, and histograms.

Performing a cost–benefit analysis of solution alternatives provides quantification of the system benefits and determination of the estimated return on investment of each solution. Financial measures such as the internal rate of return and the payback period should be calculated and included in the analysis. Quantifying soft benefits such as physician and patient satisfaction can be challenging, but these should also be considered for inclusion in the cost–benefit analysis. In calculating the overall solution cost, it is important to consider not only the third-party vendor quotation for the selected system, but the work effort that will be required by internal resources as well as any infrastructure, hardware, or software project components that are to be provided by the healthcare organization. Service maintenance agreements for the vendor system should also be included in this calculation. Based on the period of time defined in the cost–benefit analysis, consideration of a hardware refresh or storage expansion may be required.

Project risk should be a factor in the identification of a selected solution. Important considerations include the probability and impact of each identified risk. Risks may be people, process, or technology related. Preliminary risk mitigation plans should be developed to address any risks uncovered during this stage.

Contracting Process

The healthcare information system contract represents the project deliverables and negotiated terms and conditions of sale with a vendor. Inputs to the contracting process include the project charter statement, functional requirements document, and risk assessment. Outputs of this process include the solution contract inclusive of a sales quotation, statement of work, and terms and conditions specifying agreed to payment terms and defined system acceptance criteria. The formal project initiation should not begin prior to the confirmation of order acceptance from the vendor.

To prevent delays to the project initiation, it is helpful to understand the contracting requirements of the vendor including any signed documentation and down payments required for order acceptance as well as the lead time for having a project team assigned by the vendor.

References

1. US Department of Health and Human Services Health Resources and Services Administration, HRSA Health IT Adoption Toolkit, http://www.hrsa.gov/healthit/toolbox/HealthITAdoptiontoolbox/ (accessed September 28, 2012).
2. Deming, W. Edwards (2000). *The New Economics for Industry, Government, Education* (Second Edition). MIT Press.
3. Healthcare Information and Management Systems Society, http://www.himss.org/content/files/ ChangeManagementTFFramework.pdf?src=winews20110309. (accessed October 7, 2012).
4. KLAS, About KLAS, http://www.klasresearch.com/about/company.aspx (accessed October 2, 2012).
5. MD Buyline, About MD Buyline, http://www.mdbuyline.com/about/about-us#sthash.WCdlK0mv. dpbs (accessed October 4, 2012).

Chapter 24

RFI and RFP Process: How to Organize the Consultant Hiring Process

Adrienne Dickerson

Contents

Introduction

Once one makes the decision to hire a consultant, or consulting firm, there are many steps to be completed before the contract is signed. The request for information (RFI) and request for proposal (RFP) are two useful tools in the consultant selection and hiring process. Both of these documents, if properly used, can bring clarity and organization to a potentially complex decision. This chapter will cover many of the basics for using RFIs and RFPs such as:

- How to identify the initial list of potential consultants
- Outlining the project scope
- Preparing an RFI and RFP including typical questions and topics to cover
- Ideas for conducting the evaluation and decision-making process

Occasionally the terms of RFI and RFP are used interchangeably, and depending on the simplicity of the project in question, it may be sufficient to use one document for both purposes. In this chapter we will treat them as two separate steps. Also, the RFI/RFP process is not limited to consulting; it is often used for evaluating technology, supply partners, and other vendors. The focus of this chapter, however, will be on consulting services.

Difference between an RFI and RFP

The primary difference between an RFI and RFP is the level of detail and specificity related to your particular need. An RFI is more general and used in the early part of the evaluation process to narrow down the list of candidates before proceeding with more time-consuming comparisons. An RFI will include information such as company leadership, general employee skills, the range of projects and services, examples of successful projects, and other high-level information.

Once the field of potential consultants has been narrowed to a select few, it is time to implement an RFP. Ideally, the responses to this document should give you enough detail to make a final decision or narrow the field of candidates to your last few choices and to invite them for an in-person meeting. As such, the RFP will include information such as project governance structure, specific team members who would be utilized for your project, project length, internal resource time requirements, examples of the consultant's work on the same type of project, and possibly client references.

Getting Started: What to Look for in a Consulting Partner

Often the most difficult part of starting the RFI/RFP process is determining what your requirements will be from your future consulting partner. These requirements will determine many of the questions and information that you will want in your request. There are many factors to consider as you evaluate potential candidates:

- **Needs and goals:** What is your desired project outcome? The clearer and more defined you can be about your project, the more specific you can be in your information requests.
- **Budget:** The size and budget of your project may limit you to smaller "boutique" consulting firms or even individual consultants as opposed to a larger group practice. Alternately, you may be facing a deadline or have a project scope that requires the large-scale response offered by a larger consulting firm.
- **Organizational culture:** What sort of culture does your organization have? Think about how you want the consultants to fit into your current culture. Or maybe you are looking to shift your internal culture as part of your outcomes.
- **Capabilities and skill gaps:** Consider why you are hiring consultants. Is it to compensate for skills lacking in your current workforce? Are you looking for the consultants to work side by side with your employees, training them in the process? Or are you looking for independent workers to come in and complete the work with little or no assistance from your staff?

Once you have answered the above questions, you should have an idea of what you are looking for in a consultant. Now is the time to develop your first list of potential companies based on their advertised skill set, referrals from other organizations or colleagues, and any other sources you may have. You will continue to refine the list of consultants during the RFI/RFP process.

Scope of the Project

All of the above topics tie in very closely to perhaps the most important aspect of your project—scope. Scope is, at its simplest level, what the project should accomplish and with what (or how many) resources. Understanding project scope is critical to hiring an appropriate consultant, determining your budget and timeframe, and other aspects of your RFI and RFP. A common problem, which can often be avoided by thorough and mindful upfront work, is *scope creep*. Scope creep is the phenomenon of project expansion while the project is underway and is often subtle (hence the term *creep*).

Going through the more formal process of creating a project scope document may assist with the task of not only outlining scope but also managing it. The more specific you can be about defining measureable tasks and outcomes, the better able you are to both hire for and monitor your project. Once you have completed outlining your scope, you should be able to use it to determine which companies should submit an RFI.

Items to consider as you are outlining the scope of your project:

- **Desired results:** Is there a tangible (or intangible) result that is the desired outcome? Or is the project more open ended, based on time available or some other metric?
- **Out-of-scope Items:** It is often helpful to anticipate as many related issues that may arise as part of your project and determine not only what is *in* scope, but what is *out* of scope. This is critical in complex projects to keep costs and deadlines under control.
- **Metrics:** If there are measurable metrics, you should go ahead and plan for developing baseline measures and the desired improvement goals as part of your outcome or project management.
- **Scope management:** Very complex projects may need a formal scope management plan to address how and who will determine if items are in or out of scope as the project progresses.

RFI/RFP versus Contract

One last topic to review before getting into the details of the RFI and RFP documents themselves is the requirements you will want in the contract. Once you select your vendor/consultant there will be a contract development process (in fact, you may even go through this process with more than one final candidate before you ultimately make your decision). The contract will contain general information and legal wording (agreement terms) pertinent to general consulting engagements, as well as information specific to your project only. Some items you will typically find once you get to the contract phase are:

- **Payment arrangements:** This includes not only the dollar amount agreed upon for services, but also payment milestones or gates and at-risk payment options (often based upon consultants receiving pay or extra pay as a percentage of measureable outcomes such as reduced expenses or increased revenue).
- **Acceptance criteria:** The contract should clearly indicate the required outcome of the engagement, and therefore denote the conclusion of the project.
- **Termination clause:** This section will specify how and under what conditions either party may terminate the contract and any payments or penalties that may be due, including the timing of the termination and notices required.
- *Other requirements:* These will be specific requirements that apply to your situation and organizational rules.

RFI Topics

Earlier in this chapter, we gave a brief introduction to the contents of an RFI and RFP, and now we will review the specific items you should consider. Keeping in mind that the RFI is the more general of the two documents, here are some items that will be helpful to include in the RFI to help in the earlier phases of the decision-making process.

- **Capabilities/projects:** An RFI should ask for general information about the types of projects and services offered by the company. The referenced projects do not have to be exact copies of your needs, but should have a similar outcome or scope.
- **References:** Ask for a sample of the company's clients that you can contact for more information about their experience with the consulting firm. References are an excellent way to evaluate some of the "softer" criteria you are looking for, such as organizational or individual culture, working styles, and so on.
- **Lead time/availability:** This information may or may not be available or even required at this point in the process. However, if you have a specific scheduling need, such as an immediate start time, short turnaround, or an imminent deadline, it would be best to communicate that in the RFI as it may exclude some of the potential candidates and help narrow the field.
- **Staff information:** At this point in the process, you should not expect information on the specific consultant or team that may be assigned, but instead receive a general overview of staff backgrounds and their capabilities. Biographical information on the executive team is also usually included. Include questions about any specific skill sets that you are looking for such as Lean, Six Sigma, statistical analysis, or other required capabilities.

Once you have received a response to your RFI from the potential company, you will need to go through an evaluation to determine which candidates will be included in the next step in the process. There are several ways to determine who should continue in the evaluation process. Consideration should be given to what can and cannot be compromised in the project, which companies seem the best fit culturally, and other basic criteria such as budget or timeline requirements. The main goal of this process is to have a manageable list of candidates to review in more detail for the final selection.

RFP Topics

The consultant candidates who remain in consideration should now be a relatively small number so you can review them in sufficient detail and still make a timely decision. Also keep in mind that a well-crafted RFP will give the consulting company enough information to determine if they are a good fit for your needs. If not, they can excuse themselves from consideration, saving both of you a lot of time and effort. A thorough RFP should include at least the following information:

- **Specific examples/references:** The consulting company should be asked to provide examples of the same or similar project work performed for other clients. Details provided for these projects should include contact information for references, specific results similar to what you are looking for, and other relevant decision points such as timeline or client requirements.
- **Internal staff time:** Often there can be a significant difference in how much of your and your internal staff's time the consulting company will require to complete the project. Make

sure you get sufficient clarity about expected internal staff requirements, including executive participation, which will be needed from the potential candidates.

■ **Consulting team biographies:** At this point it is reasonable to expect the potential consulting groups to give you the proposed team members names and background information about their skill sets that are specific to your project. Again, if you have specific skills in mind, make sure you include those in the RFP.

■ **Budget:** If you have specific budget information about the project, you should consider sharing that with the potential candidates. That gives the candidates a chance to determine if they can provide the required work for the available budget. This strategy will also provide a set of final candidates that are comparable in cost, which allows a better comparison of the value and/or services that will be offered. Alternately, you can leave the budgeted cost open ended and be more specific about services needed if you want to see a range of bids.

Using the RFI/RFP process, you should have obtained the majority of the information needed to make a decision. Once you have narrowed down the potential candidates to a significant few, an onsite visit should be scheduled. Each candidate can then present and discuss the services that they intend to provide. Much like interviewing an employee, you can gain a lot of knowledge by meeting with the consultants in person. This will allow you to make an informed decision about which consultant makes the best sense for the project and your organization. As mentioned above in the contract section, you may also choose to move on to the contracting phase with one or more of the potential companies.

Summary

In conclusion, the RFI/RFP process requires time and planning on the front end of a project, but it is time well spent that will result in a better match of your needs and the consultant hired. The work detailed in this chapter is part of good project planning and execution and can be customized to fit your particular situation as needed. In addition, there are many resources at your disposal where you can obtain more information and more detail on what was covered in this chapter. Many project management training programs teach this process in more detail. Also, there are online resources, documents, and templates available using a simple web search.

FUNDAMENTAL TOOLS AND METHODS OF THE MANAGEMENT ENGINEER

V

Chapter 25

Flowcharting

Ryan Elizabeth Wood

Contents

Imagine a group of coworkers within a hospital department, sitting down in a meeting with the goal of making improvements to the patient and staff process flow for an appointment or treatment. As they begin to discuss the process, they start to realize that they each have a different understanding of how the process flows and what each person does in the process. They cannot begin to develop ideas for improvement if they are not clear on exactly what is currently occurring within the workflow.

One of the most beneficial tools that can be used for bringing a group together to understand a process, as well as develop a new process or identify potential improvements, is a flowchart. Flowcharting also allows individuals or groups to understand complex processes, identify start and end points of a process, reveal problems or delays, understand optimal process steps, and leverage opportunities for improvement. A flowchart outlines the sequential steps in a process, the relationship between the steps, the individual or group responsible for or involved in each step, and decision points with their associated process steps.

Steps in a Flowchart

Particular shapes are used in creating flowcharts to demonstrate different types of steps, such as a rectangle for a regular process step and a diamond for decision points. These shapes assist a group

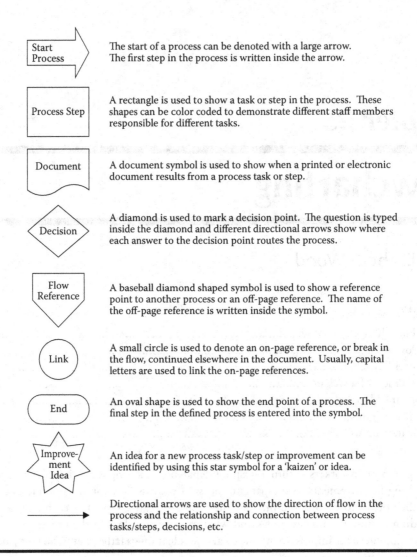

Figure 25.1 Flowchart Symbols and Descriptions.

in understanding the structure of a process and how it flows. Descriptions and uses for each type of flowchart symbol are provided in Figure 25.1.

Types of Flowcharts

High-Level Flowchart

A high-level flowchart, as demonstrated in Figure 25.2, focuses on the major steps in a process at a macro level. This may be used to understand the starting and ending points of a process and the major groups involved or major tasks within the process. More detailed flowcharts may be developed based on each step in a high-level flowchart or based on a grouping of steps in a high-level flowchart.

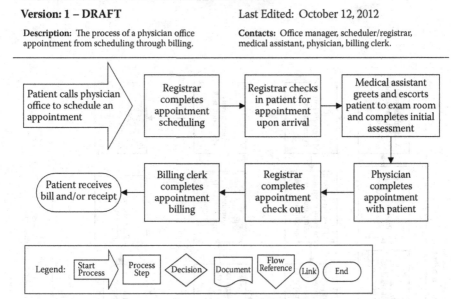

Figure 25.2   High Level Flowchart.

Detailed Process Flowchart

Detailed process flowcharts, as shown in Figure 25.3, provide micro-level details about each step or task within a process. These types of flowcharts are most useful for determining what is currently occurring in a process, identifying inefficiencies or bottlenecks, and developing potential improvements.

Value Stream Map

Value stream mapping is a specific tool used within a lean process improvement project. It is a combination of outlining the major steps and people involved, listing the detailed tasks within each step, following the flow of material, and demonstrating length of time and data outcomes within the process. Value stream mapping can be used to integrate metrics or data into the process, as well as identify areas of waste or non-value-added steps.

In addition to following the standard steps in designing a flowchart, value stream maps also include some additional details (see the legend in Figure 25.4 for an example of each shape).

- Wavy or crown-shaped boxes are used to show the people involved in each process step, either bringing data into the step or receiving data as an outcome of the step.
- Process data boxes are used to show metrics for each process step. The data included here is processing time (time required prior to the start of a step), delay time (time spent waiting or delayed in between steps), and percent effective (percent of time the step is complete and accurate as designed).
- The movement of material throughout the process is demonstrated using the document symbol and directional arrows.

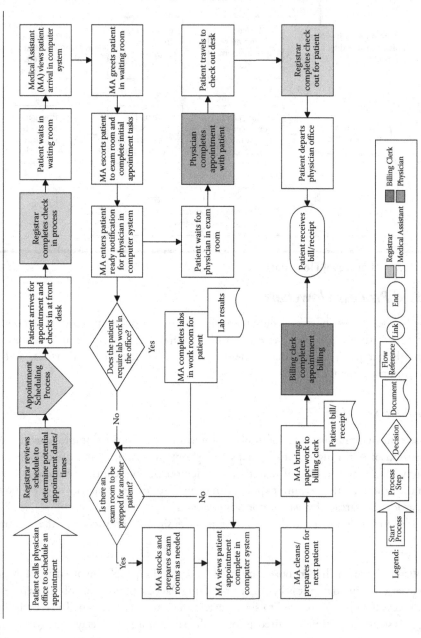

Physician Office Appointment: Medical Assistant Flowchart

Version: 2 – REVIEWED   Last Edited: October 30, 2012

Description: The Medical assistant role within the process of a physician office appointment from scheduling through billing.

Contacts: Office manager, scheduler/registrar, medical assistant, physician, billing clerk.

Figure 25.3   Detailed Flowchart.

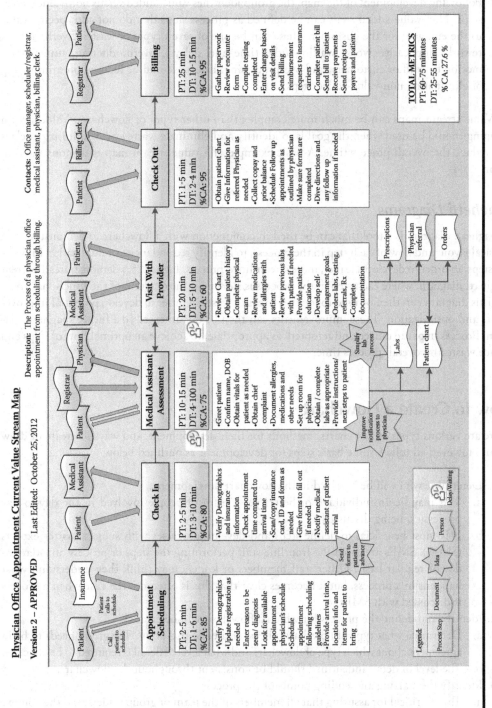

Physician Office Appointment Current Value Stream Map

Version: 2 – APPROVED   Last Edited: October 25, 2012   **Description:** The Process of a physician office appointment from scheduling through billing.   **Contacts:** Office manager, scheduler/registrar, medical assistant, physician, billing clerk.

Appointment Scheduling

PT: 2-5 min
DT: 1-6 min
%CA: 85

- Verify Demographics
- Update registration as needed
- Enter reason to be seen/ diagnosis
- Look for available appointment on physician's schedule
- Schedule appointment following scheduling guidelines
- Provide arrival time, location info and items for patient to bring

Send forms to patient in advance

Check In

PT: 2-5 min
DT: 3-10 min
%CA: 80

- Verify Demographics and insurance information
- Check appointment time compared to arrival time
- Scan/copy insurance card, ID and forms as needed
- Give forms to fill out if needed
- Notify medical assistant of patient arrival

Medical Assistant Assessment

PT: 10-15 min
DT: 4-100 min
%CA: 75

- Greet patient
- Confirm name, DOB
- Obtain vitals for patient as needed
- Obtain chief complaint
- Document allergies, medications and other needs
- Set up room for physician
- Obtain / complete labs as appropriate
- Provide instructions/ next steps to patient

Improve notification process to physician

Visit With Provider

PT: 20 min
DT: 5-10 min
%CA: 60

- Review Chart
- Obtain patient history
- Complete physical exam
- Review medications and allergies with patient
- Review previous labs with patient if needed
- Provide patient education
- Develop self-management goals
- Orders labs, testing, referrals, Rx
- Complete documentation

Simplify lab process

Check Out

PT: 1-5 min
DT: 2-4 min
%CA: 95

- Obtain patient chart
- Give Information for referred Physician as needed
- Collect copay and prior balance
- Schedule Follow up appointments as outlined by physician
- Make sure forms are completed
- Dive directions and any follow up information if needed

Billing

PT: 25 min
DT: 10-15 min
%CA: 95

- Gather paperwork
- Review encounter form
- Compile testing completed
- Enter charges based on visit details
- Send billing reimbursement requests to insurance carriers
- Complete patient bill
- Send bill to patient
- Receive payments
- Send receipts to payers and patient

TOTAL METRICS
PT: 60-75 minutes
DT: 25-55 minutes
% CA: 27.6 %

Labs

Patient chart

Prescriptions

Physician referral

Orders

Legend:

Process Step

Document

Person

Idea

Delay/Waiting

Figure 25.4   Value stream map.

■ Ideas for improvement that may arise during the development of a current state map may be documented in the star-shaped symbol. The group will expand upon these ideas during the brainstorming portion of a process improvement or lean project.

■ Following development of the map, the group identifies value-added versus non-value-added steps. Non-value-added steps can be defined as process steps that do not add specific value to the end goal for the customer. These can be one of seven types of waste: Overhandling, rework, duplicative work, waiting (idle time and delays), overproduction, unnecessary motion by staff or customers, and overprocessing. Efforts should be focused on minimizing or eliminating non-value-added steps.

Value stream maps can be much more complex than other types of flowcharts. Value stream mapping should be used when the goal is to identify and eliminate waste and to minimize delays and reduce the overall process time. A basic example of a value stream map is demonstrated in Figure 25.4.

Spaghetti Diagrams

A spaghetti diagram is a tool that can be used in conjunction with a flowchart to demonstrate the physical layout and flow of each step in the process, to identify redundancies or duplication in physical steps, in order to develop a leaner, more streamlined process. Figure 25.5 demonstrates a current spaghetti diagram, where each step in the process is shown on the diagram of the functional area.

This diagram can then be used to identify areas of waste in order to develop potential improvements and optimization. These improvements can then be documented in a future spaghetti diagram. Process steps are moved and rerouted, as appropriate, to achieve an optimal flow of steps and reduce waste and overall process time.

How to Create a Flowchart

There are various types of flowcharts, methods for their development, and ways to create or draw them. However, all follow some basic steps for development as outlined below.

1. Determine who will be involved in the flowchart development.
    a. This may be an individual, or better yet a team of people involved in the day-to-day process(es) being discussed.
    b. It is most beneficial to define steps and develop processes with subject matter experts (SMEs). SMEs are often the frontline staff performing the steps or process on a day-to-day or regular basis. Other staff members or leaders may think they understand what happens in a process, but it becomes clear that this is often not the case when a process is discussed with SMEs.
2. Identify and define the process for which a flowchart will be created.
    a. Determine what type of flowchart will be created at this point. The group needs to be in agreement about which type of flowchart and what level of detail is required to be effective.
    b. The level of detail indentified should be consistent throughout the flowchart.
3. Identify the starting and ending points of the process.
    a. This is critical for assuring that all members of the team or group understand the context and extent of the process being discussed.

Spaghetti Diagram: Physician Office Appointment

Version: 3 – APPROVED   Last Edited: September 25, 2012

Description: The process of a physician office   **Contacts:** Office manager, scheduler/registrar,
appointment from scheduling through billing.   medical assistant, physician, billing clerk.

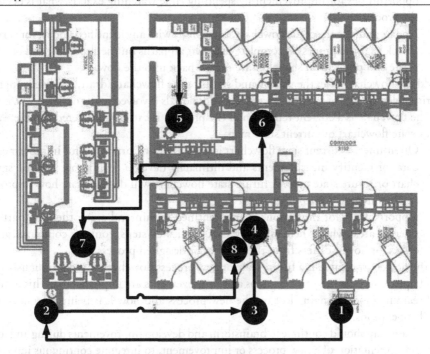

Patient Appointment – Medical Assistant Process
1. View patient arrival in computer system
2. Greet patient in waiting room
3. Escort patient to exam room and complete initial appointment tasks
4. Enter patient ready notification for physician in computer system
5. Complete medical preparation tasks (lab work, etc.) for patient
6. Stock and prepare exam rooms
7. View patient complete in computer system
8. Clean /prepare room for next patient

Figure 25.5   Office Visit Spaghetti Diagram: Current Process.

4. Define each step in the process sequentially in words and place in the appropriate shape, as demonstrated in Figure 25.1.
   a. Brainstorming can be used to list all the steps or major tasks in the process.
   b. It is most effective to outline the process on flipchart paper or a dry erase board in front of the group so that all can visualize the process and analyze if all steps have been included. The flowchart is then drawn electronically (and on paper) afterward.
   c. It is also important to identify who or what role is responsible for each step. This can be identified using words within the step description and/or by using different colors.
   d. Process data boxes should be included in the development of value stream maps.
5. Review the process with all involved individuals in the process, most importantly the aforementioned SMEs, to ensure that the flowchart accurately reflects the process.

  a. Another technique to make sure the flowchart is an accurate reflection of the identified process is to observe the process in person, making notes about the flow and who
is performing each step. Observation is also a highly effective way to identify potential
opportunities for improvement by spending time watching exactly what is occurring in
the process.

  b. Update and/or correct the flowchart accordingly with any identified updates or corrections.

  c. Check that the process is complete and that all paths on the flowchart end at an appropriate end point (oval shape) or are routed back into the flow.

6. Add the flowchart title, the version and status of the flowchart (draft, reviewed, approved), a
written description of the process, and the individuals involved in the design of the flowchart.

7. If the flowchart is a current reflection of the process, it can be considered complete as a current state flowchart or current state map.

  a. Oftentimes, a current state flowchart is used to brainstorm ideas for improvement, track
data, or identify measurements and ultimately develop an improved future state flowchart or future state map. A future state flowchart will demonstrate how improvements
can be integrated into the process.

  b. Opportunities for improvement are identified within and along the flowchart by considering areas where there may be waste, duplicated steps, complex communication processes, or how it differs from the optimal or designed process.

8. If the flowchart created is a future state or new process flowchart, it is continuously reviewed
and updated as the new process steps and improvements are implemented. This ensures that
all team members remain clear on the new process and how it is being integrated into the
daily operations.

  a. The group should continue to brainstorm and develop improvements during and following
implementation of a new process or improvement, to integrate continuous improvement.

9. If a spaghetti diagram will be developed for this process, the flowchart developed is now
used to identify the location of occurrence for each step in the process.

  a. The process steps should be numbered in order to identify each step on the diagram.

A flowchart is a meaningful way to design and demonstrate the steps in a process. As a visual
tool, it is highly effective as a clear and concise model of a process being developed or improved.

Chapter 26

Value Stream Mapping in Healthcare

Bart Sellers

Contents

This chapter looks at value stream mapping (VSM) for healthcare. Value stream mapping is a key tool used in Lean. A value stream is the value and non-value-added flows and processes required to deliver a good or service from the supplier to the customer. VSM was originally developed as a visual tool for representing the current and future states of material and information flows in a manufacturing environment with the aim of identifying and eliminating delays and waste. A simplified VSM of patient and information flow for a surgical patient is shown in Figure 26.1.

The VSM shows patient flow from primary care physician to return from surgery, electronic and manual information flow, delays represented by the tombstones, process boxes with data tables, and cloudbursts representing a process or flow problem.

VSM differs from traditional process mapping in several ways, including:

- Provides a high-level view of the entire system from supplier to customer (customer is defined below)
- Highlights delays (flow stagnation)

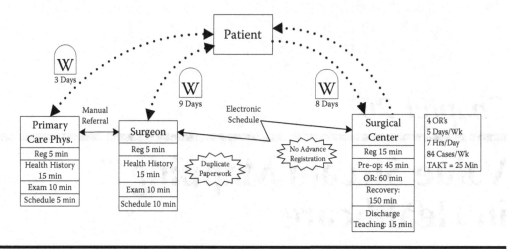

Figure 26.1 An example of a value stream map for a surgical patient.

- Helps to identify other problems in addition to delays
- Provides a roadmap for improvement
- Engages and involves key stakeholders through participation

It is beyond the scope of this chapter to cover all the details, symbols, and other conventions of VSM. However, the main steps are listed below:

1. Define customer requirements
2. Identify and show connections for key process steps
3. Show data attributes for the process steps
4. Determine time between process steps and identify other non-value-added delays
5. Identify waste other than delays
6. Prioritize improvement opportunities
7. Develop an improvement plan

Rother and Shook developed an excellent reference for VSM in their workbook *Learning to See* [1]. This book thoroughly describes the *know-how* and the *know-why* of VSM. Their workbook includes a simple case study that demonstrates the application of symbols, measurement, and steps for developing a VSM. Anyone attempting to apply value stream mapping should study *Learning to See,* or a similar book on the subject *and* preferably be trained by someone experienced in VSM in the same industry.

VSM and Lean

Womak and Jones describe the importance of the value stream in Lean improvement. From their book Lean Thinking: Banish Waste and Create Wealth in Your Corporation: "Lean Thinking can be summarized in five principles: precisely specify value by specific product, identify the value stream for each product, make value flow without interruptions, let the customer pull value from the producer, and pursue perfection" [2].

The first five principles or steps are done in a continuous improvement cycle. Identifying value and mapping the value stream in steps 1 and 2 set the stage for actual improvement in steps 3 through 5 as the value stream moves toward the ideal state or "perfection."

VSM and Healthcare

There are many important distinctions between manufacturing and healthcare in applying VSM. Beyond material and information flow, there are other types of flow that may be important to the customer depending on the situation. These flows include:

Patient
Providers
Information
Instruments
Medication
Equipment
Supplies
Processes

While manufacturing typically consists of linear flows of material and information, healthcare processes can flow in linear, parallel, and even in reverse directions.

There is no recognized standard for VSM. As an example, swim-lane diagrams have been incorporated into healthcare maps. An effective VSM doesn't need to follow a set format but it should readily communicate key flows, delays, and waste. Typically, there are more value streams in healthcare organizations than in similarly sized manufacturing plants. A large hospital can provide services for dozens of distinct patient types, each of which can be considered a separate value stream.

Identifying who the customer is and what they value is often a challenge. The customer may be the payer, the patient, the provider, or even the community. Patients may value intangible or ambiguous aspects of healthcare over price, speed, or quality. VSM may have limitations where value is difficult to define, but it should always be specified by the customer.

Many of the delays and waste in healthcare are difficult to see compared with manufacturing where excess inventory, scrap, and customer returns can be readily seen. Waste and delays in healthcare often happen behind closed doors, in the middle of a procedure, or even after a patient has been discharged. Other significant delays and waste happen so infrequently that they can rarely be seen. A greater reliance on information systems is often necessary to *see* the value stream in healthcare.

VSM at the Project Level

VSM in healthcare is frequently used as a project tool in 3- to 5-day improvement events or workshops. At the project level, a team is typically chartered by senior leadership to make a specific improvement in a particular area. A team leader, often with a facilitator or coach, defines key metrics and flows in advance of the event, and defines the beginning and end points of the VSM.

The team leader may decide to draft a VSM before meeting with the team or wait until the team is formed so the VSM can be done as a group activity. The team should walk the value stream if possible to visualize the key processes and see the waste and delays. The team then identifies the waste and delays in the VSM that can be improved during the event and identify opportunities for future improvement. Depending on the complexity of the improvement, the team may develop a future state map showing the expected improvement. The team then makes improvements during the event and the VSM is progressively updated. At the end of the event, the future state or updated VSM becomes the new current state and another cycle of improvement in planned.

VSM at the Service Line Level

VSM can also be used as a strategic planning tool for entire clinical service lines or major administrative processes. Applied at this level, a VSM is used to identify and prioritize future projects within a value stream, and forms the basis for developing a future state plan. Based on high-level opportunities, the organization's senior leadership charters a value stream owner to develop a strategic improvement plan. The value stream owner is typically a service line leader over a major service or support or administrative function. The primary difference between a value stream owner and a service line leader is that the value stream owner is responsible for delivering beginning-to-end value to the customer as the value stream crosses the many different functions in an organization. The VSM activity is planned in advance where flows, key processes, and necessary support functions for the VSM are defined. The VSM activity should include team members from all the important cross-functional and support organizations the value stream crosses to generate buy-in and support for future improvement. Executives and physician leaders should also be involved in the event as their participation can provide direction during the activity and generate support and ownership for the future improvement events. At the end of the activity, the team should identify the key areas for improvement for the next planning horizon. This could be identifying and planning 5 to 6 improvement events that will be worked on in the next 12-month period. The VSM is progressively updated along with the strategic plan as improvement events are completed. Healthcare organizations with mature Lean systems often have a command room where the entire organization's VSM is posted along with work plans. The VSM and work plans are continuously updated as progress is made.

The Ideal and Future State

Many organizations develop an ideal state and future state VSM as part of an improvement activity. The *ideal state* is what the value stream would look like if there were no problems, constraints, or limitations impacting flow or value to the customer [3]. Teams struggling to envision an ideal state should ask the question, "What would this value stream look like at Disneyland?" This approach gets team members to start thinking out-of-the-box and begin to explore innovative countermeasures.

Different than the ideal state, the future state should describe what the value stream can *realistically* look like in the next few days, weeks, or months, depending on the complexity and urgency for improvement. The future state is used to develop the value stream improvement plan, along with the work plan that details the sequence, schedule, and accountability going forward [1].

Recommendations for VSM

1. Include key stakeholders in drawing the VSM. Perhaps the biggest benefit of VSM is in engaging key stakeholders. This is particularly important when value streams cross service lines.
2. In any VSM activity, it is important to identify the type of flows that are to be included as an early step and to limit the number of flows to avoid making the VSM overly complex.
3. Walk the value stream. Rarely does anyone understand all the details of an entire value stream. Walking the process generates buy-in and understanding for everyone involved.
4. Don't worry about the format of the VSM; focus on understanding and communication. A VSM is only effective when it readily communicates delays and waste.
5. Use VSM as a roadmap that is progressively updated as improvements are made and as the value stream changes.
6. For the facilitator, there is no substitute for experience. Start with small value streams and build on that experience.
7. Do not VSM discrete processes. There are other tools and techniques such as job breakdown sheets and spaghetti diagrams that are much better suited for improving individual processes.
8. It is important to realize that while VSM can be effective in seeing problems and making the case for improvement, it is not a structured improvement methodology all by itself. For some value streams, it is enough just to *see* the problem before starting improvement. For other value streams, root cause analysis, data collection, process capability analysis, and a series of experiments are needed for improvement. In these cases, a more structured approach with application of other tools is needed to make effective and lasting improvements.
9. Develop a business case and key measures prior to starting a VSM. A project charter should be used to define the scope and the business case to guide the VSM activity.
10. Include Takt time and process capacity measures in the VSM. Takt time is defined as the available production time divided by the quantity of customer demand for the same period. Imbalances between customer demand and capacity of individual processes are often the most critical driver of delays and waste.
11. Do not try to value stream map everything. The 80/20 rule or even the 90/10 rule applies to VSM. Remember that each improvement cycle is aimed at moving toward, but not necessarily achieving, perfection.

Role of the Industrial Engineer in VSM

Although VSM is not the unique domain of industrial engineers, industrial engineers and other improvement specialists can have an important role in how the tool is used. The industrial engineer should focus on developing expertise early on in the organization's implementation of Lean, and this is only done through practice and training. By developing competence and confidence in VSM, the industrial engineer will find himself in demand as a resource in improvement efforts at all levels of the organization.

The industrial engineer should focus on facilitating, not leading, the VSM activity. Leading is for the value stream manager or the person who "owns" the process and who will be "living" in the VSM going forward. It is important that this person have complete buy-in and understanding of the VSM. The industrial engineer should closely coordinate with the value stream manager or team leader in preparing for a value stream activity.

While VSM is not an analytical tool, analysis is often helpful in drawing the VSM. Some data elements for the VSM may conveniently be captured through existing data systems. This can help streamline the process. Analysis should never be used as a substitute for going and seeing the value stream.

Conclusion

Although developed for manufacturing, VSM has been adapted for use in healthcare. VSM has proven to be a practical and powerful tool for pictorially identifying waste and delays in delivering goods and services to customers. Developing a VSM is a vital step in the Lean continuous improvement cycle as its use identifies what the customer values and the waste and delays in providing that value before improvement efforts are begun. VSM can be used at the project level as a first-step improvement tool and as a strategic planning tool to develop long-term improvement plans. Effectively leading or facilitating VSM events takes considerable experience, especially since VSMs are frequently developed in real time in front of large groups. The greatest benefit of VSM is in communicating and developing buy-in and agreement from stakeholders and providing a roadmap for ongoing and future improvement.

References

1. M. Rother and J. Shook, *Learning to See* (Brookline, MA: The Lean Enterprise Institute v. 1.3, 2003).
2. J. Womak and D. Jones, *Lean Thinking: Banishing Waste and Creating Value in Your Corporation*, 2nd ed. (New York: Free Press, 2003).
3. B. Hamilton and P. Wardwell, *e² Continuous Improvement System* (Boston, MA: GBMP, Inc.).

Chapter 27

Statistical and Mathematical Analysis in a Healthcare Setting

Roque Perez-Velez

Contents

Introduction

This chapter will discuss the topic of statistical and mathematical analysis in a healthcare setting. The author will share his experience with dealing, analyzing, and studying data from various healthcare systems, and how to explain trends to a nontechnically oriented audience. If the reader is interested in the basics of statistics or learning more about this topic, the author recommends Kurtz,* Walpole and Myers,† or Montgomery and Runger.‡

So, what is statistical and mathematical analysis? First, we need to define several terms. We, as engineers or managers, are concerned with two types of problems: summarizing, describing, and

---

* M. Kurtz, "Engineering Economics," in *Standard Handbook of Engineering Calculations*, 2nd ed., ed. T. G. Hicks (New York: McGraw-Hill Book Co., 1985).
† R. E. Walpole and R. H. Myers, *Probability and Statistics for Engineers and Scientists*, 4th ed. (New York: Macmillan Publishing Company, Inc., 1989).
‡ D. C. Montgomery and G. C. Runger, *Applied Statistics and Probabilities for Engineers*, 2nd ed. (New York: John Wiley& Sons, Inc., 1999).

exploring data or using data to infer on its nature. Mendenhall and Sincich[*] define descriptive statistics "as the branch of statistics devoted to the organization, summarization, and description of data sets." Furthermore, in our profession we need to understand the type of data we are working with. Vining[†] classifies statistical analysis as "either enumerative or analytic studies. Enumerative studies tend to assume that the data come from a static process. Analytic studies tend to assume that the data come from a dynamic process that changes over time."

Also, Boslaugh[‡] offers that "the practice of statistics usually involves analyzing data, and the validity of the statistical results depends in large part on the validity of the data analyzed." She asserts that "this means that at some point between data collection and data analysis, someone has to get her hands dirty working directly with the data file, cleaning, organizing, and otherwise getting it ready for analysis." Finally, Peck and Devore[§] assert, "statistics involves collecting, summarizing, and analyzing data. All three tasks are critical. Without summarization and analysis, raw data are of little value, and even sophisticated analyses can't produce meaningful information from data that were not collected in a sensible way."

With this in mind, we can define *statistical analysis* as the collection, management, organization, summarization, analysis, and description of data sets by means of a statistical software program or other similar methods.

Perhaps the reader has heard the term *structured data analysis*. Is this a different analysis or is it associated with the *statistical analysis* defined above? First, structured data analysis is defined as the statistical analysis of structured data sets such as results from surveys, multiple-choice questionnaires, or other arranged data sets. By definition, structured data analysis is a subset of statistical analysis. Some examples of this methodology are regression, Bayesian, cluster, and algebraic analysis.

The author defines mathematical analysis as the study of stochastic, continuous probability and Markov chain analyses as a subdivision of the work performed during statistical analysis. The parameters calculated with statistical analysis are used as a foundation, in stochastic or Markov chain analyses, to further study any healthcare system, such as an emergency department's patient flow.

Commonly Used Descriptive Statistics

In this section, the author defines and provides examples of the most commonly used descriptive statistics: mean, standard deviation, median, mode, minimum, and maximum. First, we will define the statistics that are used as measures of central tendency followed by the measures of dispersion.

The *mean*, commonly called the *arithmetic mean*, is the average of a set of values. The mean is used as a measure of central tendency. Suppose we have a family medicine practice clinic with weekly patient load as shown in Table 27.1.

We can calculate the mean as:

$$(52 + 57 + 57 + 61 + 44)/5 = 54.2$$

[*] W. Mendenhall and T. Sincich, *Statistics for Engineers and the Sciences*, 3rd ed. (San Francisco, CA: Dellen Publishing Co., 1992).

[†] G. Geoffrey Vining, *Statistical Methods for Engineers* (Pacific Grove, CA: Brooks/Cole Publishing Co., 1998).

[‡] S. Boslaugh, *Statistics in a Nutshell* (Sebastopol, CA: O'Reilly Media, Inc., 2012).

[§] R. Peck and J. L. Devore, *Statistics: The Exploration and Analysis of Data* (Boston, MA: Brooks/Cole Publishing Co., 2012).

Table 27.1 Weekly Patient Load

Weekday	Patient Load
Monday	52
Tuesday	57
Wednesday	57
Thursday	61
Friday	44

The arithmetic mean formula, as expressed in summation notation, is shown in Equation (27.1):

$$\mu = \frac{1}{n}\sum_{i=1}^{n} x_i \tag{27.1}$$

When the values are ranked in ascending or descending order, the median, mode, minimum, and maximum are the middle value, the most frequently occurring value, and the lowest and the highest occurring values, in that order. The median is a better measure of central tendency than the mean for data that is asymmetrical or contains outliers, while the mode is most often useful in describing ordinal or categorical data. Continuing with the clinic example above, the patient load, ranked in ascending order, is: 44, 52, 57, 57, and 61. The minimum is 44, the median is 57, the mode is 57, and the maximum is 61. The median is formally defined as the $(n + 1)/2$ values for odd numbers or average of the two middle values for even numbers.

Please bear in mind that, in perfectly symmetrical distribution such as the normal distribution, the mean, median, and mode are identical while in asymmetrical or skewed distributions, these three measures will differ.

A common measure of dispersion for continuous data is standard deviation. It describes how much the individual values in a data set vary from the mean. The formula for the sample standard deviation is shown in Equation (27.2):

$$s = \sqrt{\frac{1}{n-1}\sum_{i=1}^{n} (x_i - \bar{x})^2} \tag{27.2}$$

So, what will the standard deviation be for our family practice clinic example? Let's see:

$$s = 1/(5 - 1) \times [(44 - 54.2)^2 + (52 - 54.2)^2 + (57 - 54.2)^2 + (57 - 54.2)^2 + (61 - 54.2)^2] = 6.53$$

Another measure of dispersion is the percentile, of which quartiles are a subset. When an ordered set of data is divided into four equal parts, the division points are called quartiles. The first or lower quartile, q1, is a value that has approximately 25% of the observations below it and approximately 75% of the observations above. The second quartile, q2, has approximately 50% of the observations below its value. The second quartile is exactly equal to the median. The third

Table 27.2   **Weekly Patient Load**

Pediatric Unit Daily Census							
31	20	18	30	20	27	22	15
13	19	17	15	24	24	27	18
23	21	25	22	21	19	30	25

quartile, q3, has approximately 75% of the observations below its value. The first and third quartiles can be calculated as $(n + 1)/4$ and $3(n + 1)/4$ respectively, where n is the number of observations. The interquartile range (iqr) is calculated as (q3 – q1). Also, the smallest and largest values are calculated as q1 – 1.5 (q3 – q1) and q3 + 1.5 (q3 – q1), respectively. These metrics are extensively used in the creation of box plots or commonly known as box-and-whiskers plots. Tuffery[*] indicates that it can also be used to compare two populations, or to detect the individual outliers that must be excluded from the analysis to avoid falsifying the results.

Suppose that we have a pediatric unit where the management engineer is conducting a staffing analysis. The engineer wants to know the estimated daily census for any given day. One way for the engineer to understand the census dispersion for a particular day is to calculate the sample's percentiles and subdivide it into quartiles. Table 27.2 shows the census for 24 days.

For this example, the median, after sorting in ascending order, is 22. The minimum and maximum values, respectively, are 13 and 31. The first and third quartiles, using the formulas presented above, are 19 and 25, respectively. These values give the engineer a pretty good perspective in relation to the spread or dispersion for the daily census.

These metrics are widely used to analyze any process or system within the healthcare environment no matter if the data is nominal, ordinal, interval, continuous, or discrete. The use of metrics, such as the mean and standard deviation, is the foundation of statistical process control (SPC), Total Quality Management (TQM), and Six Sigma methodologies, which are discussed in another chapter of this book.

Now, the author has noticed that when presenting statistical analysis, on occasions where the audience's background is diverse (nontechnical to technical), the audience is likely to mistakenly believe that the values for the mean and standard deviation are equal to quartiles. Figure 27.1 shows how these two metrics compare.

Data Visualization

Statistical analysis results must be presented in meaningful ways, specifically if the audience is diverse. It should be presented in a simple and clear but concise method. Care must be taken when visualizing data to present an unbiased picture. Ryan[†] stresses that "much care must be exercised in the use of graphical procedures, otherwise, the impressions that are conveyed could be very misleading." There are methods that are appropriate for displaying essential information in large data sets and there are methods for displaying small data sets. Methods for displaying small data sets include, but are not limited to, tabular displays, steam-and-leaf displays, control charts, scatter plots, frequency tables, bar charts, pie charts, and dot plots. Common methods for displaying

---

[*] S. Tuffery, *Data Mining and Statistics for Decision Making* (West Sussex, UK: John Wiley & Sons Ltd., 2011).

[†] T. P. Ryan, *Modern Engineering Statistics* (Hoboken, NJ: John Wiley & Sons, Inc., 2007).

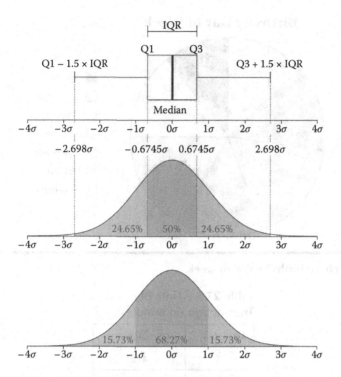

Figure 27.1 Graphs illustrating mean and standard deviation.

large data sets include, but are not limited to, histograms, box plots, Pareto charts, line and regression charts, and bivariate and multivariate charts. For extremely large data sets, the most recent analysis method is called data mining.

The following is a discussion of several examples of displaying data sets of various sizes.

Pie charts are broadly used to display small data sets with a small number of workable groups. Pie charts are the simplest and most commonly used to depict nominal data, such as limited-option questionnaires. Ott and Longnecker[*] provide simple guidelines for constructing pie charts. They recommend choosing "a small number (five or six) of categories for the variable, and to, whenever possible, construct the pie chart so that percentages are in either ascending or descending order." Figure 27.2 depicts a local hospital's percentage of births by day of week in a pie chart.

Bar charts are widely used to display small to medium-size data sets. The chart consists of two axes, horizontal and vertical, arranged on a small number of workable groups, that visually represents magnitude. A simple example would be for a clinical laboratory's manager to respond to a question related to length of time per transaction for a pneumatic tube transport system. Table 27.3 summarizes the number of transactions per time frame.

Figure 27.3 shows the same data plotted using a bar chart.

By using similar data to that presented in Table 27.2, the management engineer can plot the daily census, by day of the week, for a pediatric unit. This will enable the engineer to better visualize any patterns in daily census. This large data set is from the results of a dynamic simulation

---

[*] R. L. Ott, and M. Longnecker, *An Introduction to Statistical Methods and Data Analysis* (Belmont, CA: Brooks/Cole, Cengage Learning, 2010).

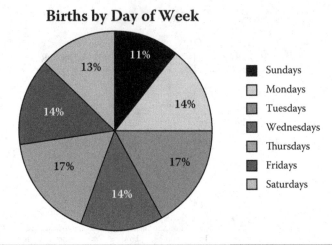

Figure 27.2 Pie chart: births by day of week.

Table 27.3 Time per Transaction (in minutes)

Minutes	Transactions
1	472
2	346
3	85
4	36
5	7
6	4
7	1
8	1
9	0
10	0
Over 10	0

where the engineer ran 182 weekly replications with 1,274 data points. Figure 27.4 depicts box plots of daily census by day of week.

Sanderson[*] explains that "the ABC Analysis Technique is a widely used tool that management uses to categorize materials and components into workable groups. The ABC Analysis is the application of Pareto's principle of analysis and segregation to the inventory investment." Pareto's analysis is based on the premise that 80% of investment is concentrated in group A while the other 20% is distributed among groups B and C. This same technique is useful when analyzing data in a healthcare setting.

---

[*] G. A. Sanderson, "Inventory Control Records and Practices," in *Production and Inventory Control Handbook*, ed. J. H. Greene (New York: McGraw Hill Companies, Inc., 1997).

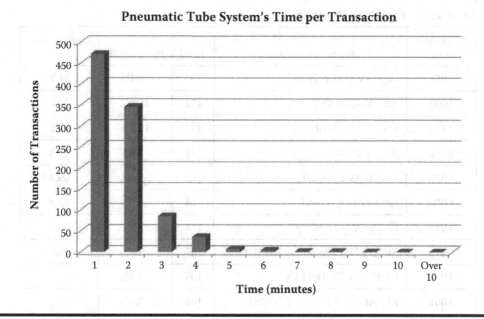

Figure 27.3 Bar chart.

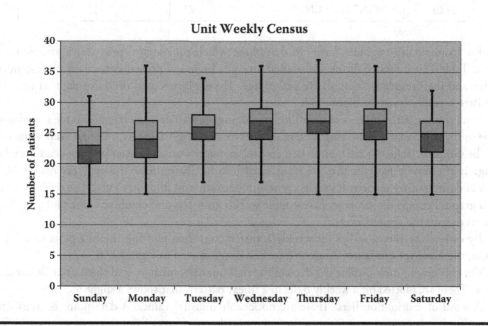

Figure 27.4 Box plot graph.

Table 27.4 Radiology Procedures

Procedure Number	Procedure Name	Total	Percentage	Cumulative %
1060	HEAD W/O CNTRST	750	24.1%	24.1
1005	ABD W/CNTRST	492	15.8%	40.0
1225	PELVIS W/CNTRST	492	15.8%	55.8
2000	ABD 1 VIEW	231	7.4%	63.3
1055	CHEST W/CNTRST	185	6.0%	69.2
1000	ABD W/O CNTRST	114	3.7%	72.9
1045	CHEST W/O CNTRST	114	3.7%	76.6
1410	MULTI-PLANAR REFORMATIONS	107	3.4%	80.0
1056	CHEST W/CNTRST EXT	105	3.4%	83.4
1002	RENAL STONE W/O CNTRST	102	3.3%	86.7
1215	PELVIS W/O CNTRST	102	3.3%	90.0
1080	HEAD W/&W/O CNTRST	42	1.4%	91.3
1085	MXFACE 1 PJ W/O CNTRST	39	1.3%	92.6
1025	BIOPSY 30-60 MINUTES	30	1.0%	93.5
1015	ABD W&W/O CNTRST	24	0.8%	94.3
1255	C SPINE W/O CNTRST	21	0.7%	95.0

For example, an engineer wants to determine which radiological procedures are requested most. Table 27.4 shows 16 of the 43 most common radiological procedures, sorted in descending order, and their respective cumulative percentage. The engineers used this large data set to create the Pareto graph shown in Figure 27.5.

Data mining is the process of handling, managing, and analyzing extremely large sets of data. Due to the complexity of working with huge or extremely large data sets, such data sets must usually be sampled. Take, for example, a bed control manager wants to better prognosticate how bed usage is affected by patients that are transferred into his institution. The manager may want to look at daily transfer reports. It may become cumbersome and difficult to visualize daily transfers on a graph. Perhaps the manager may sample weekly transfers and combine a box plot and linear graphs to gain the desired effect.

By estimating the quartiles for weekly transfers and then plotting the box plots in a linear graph, the manager can better prognosticate bed usage as seen in Figure 27.6.

On this graph, each bicolor bar depicts the first quartile, median, and third quartile for each week. These are plotted on a weekly basis in a linear pattern that shows a slight increase.

A word of caution: outliers. These are noticeably unusual values. A data point is considered an outlier if it is more than 1.5 times the interquartile range away from the nearest quartile. The reader must detect outliers, but there are no general rules on how outliers should be handled once

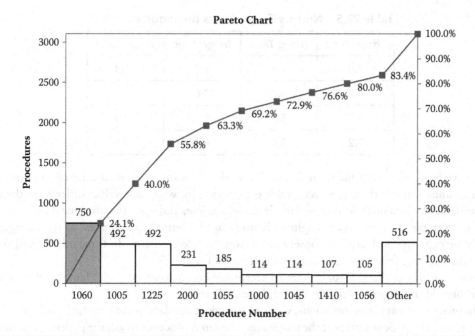

Figure 27.5   Pareto graph.

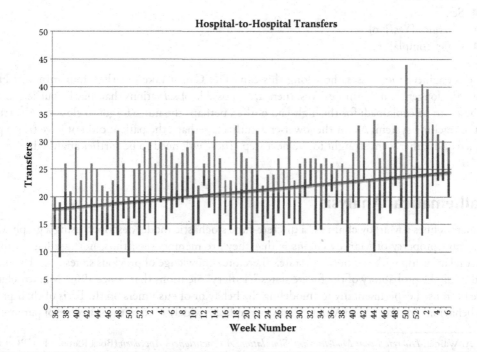

Figure 27.6   Data mining: box plot and linear graph.

Table 27.5 Nursing Triage Times (in minutes)

Triage Time	Triage Time	Triage Time	Triage Time
0.0	0.1	1.2	1.4
4.5	6.7	7.6	4.8
5.3	5.9	6.2	4.9
7.2	5.6	6.1	25.6

they have been detected. One thing is certain: we do not want to automatically reject them. We want to understand if there is an acceptable explanation for why these values differ from the rest of the data. Outliers often lead us to further study, analyze, and operationalize the data.

For example, a management engineer is studying the nurse triage process at the emergency medicine department. Gathering observations from the electronic medical records (EMR) database, the engineer found the data excerpt depicted in Table 27.5.

Are there any outliers? If so, is there an acceptable explanation for these? Finally, what can be done? Should the engineer keep or discard these outliers?

In order to answer these questions, we need to look at the data in context. Let's look at the triage process. The patient arrives at the triage area; the nurse proceeds to ask the patient a minimum of six questions:

- Name
- Social Security number or medical record number
- Date of birth
- Sex
- Allergies (Yes/No)
- Chief complaint

The engineer must assess how long this can take. Can it take less than four minutes? How about any longer than 8 minutes? Yes, there are 5 possible observations that may be outliers. Some of these can be explained: for the high-end outlier, perhaps the nurse forgot to close out the triage on the tracking system. As for the lower-end outliers, perhaps the patient did not have triage performed and rather went straight to the next step. These will need to be further analyzed.

Mathematical Analysis

Wainer[*] defines a Markov chain as "a discrete-time stochastic model described using a graph. One important property of Markov chains is that they are memory-less; thus, no state has a cause–effect relationship with the previous state. Therefore, knowledge of previous states is irrelevant for predicting the probability of the future states." Tuffery[†] mentions that "since 1962, Markov chains have been used experimentally for modeling the behavior of customers on the basis of their previous behavior." Markov chain Monte Carlo methods are widely used in the inference of parameters

[*] G. A. Wainer, *Discrete-Event Modeling and Simulation: A Practitioner's Approach* (Boca Raton, FL: CRC Press, Taylor and Francis Group, 2009).
[†] Tuffery, *Data Mining and Statistics for Decision Making*.

estimated by statistical analysis. Also, Markov chains are used for modeling techniques where time and variables are discrete.

Continuous probability models, specifically the normal distribution, are used extensively to quantify the risks in these decisions and to evaluate ways to collect the data and how large a sample should be selected. Also, we work with continuous probability distributions due to their close relationship with histograms. Montgomery and Runger[*] explain that a "histogram is an approximation to a probability density function. For each interval of the histogram, the area of the bar equals the relative frequency (proportion) of the measurements in the interval. The relative frequency is an estimate of the probability that a measurement falls in the interval."

Exploratory Data Analysis

Martinez and Martinez[†] grant that "John W. Tukey [1987[‡]] was one of the first statisticians to provide a detailed description of Exploratory Data Analysis (EDA). It is mostly a philosophy of data analysis where the researcher examines the data without any pre-conceived ideas in order to discover what the data can tell him about the phenomena being studied."

EDA utilizes an assortment of methods to maximize insight into a data set, uncover underlying structure, detect outliers and anomalies, and test assumptions. EDA strongly relies on these methods in order to analyze, detect, and present data sets and their characteristics. Examples of these methods are charts, diagrams, histograms, scatter plots, and box plots. Runkler[§] emphasizes that "data can often be very effectively analyzed using visualization techniques" such as EDA. He states that "data distributions can be estimated and visualized using histogram techniques."

Church[¶] accentuates that Tukey's EDA "approach to data analysis is highly visual. Graphs are used to store quantitative data, to communicate conclusions, or to discover new information." Finally, Iversen[**] stresses that EDA "is a more modern form of inductive reasoning with an emphasis on looking at the data before formulating hypotheses or theories. EDA facilitates the researcher's ability to detect patterns and relations in the data. Tukey described how the exploratory phase must precede the confirmatory phase of data analysis, and presented several new visual and quantitative methods of exploring data" discussed in this chapter.

Conclusion

The information covered in this chapter will help the reader to understand some basic dos and don'ts in regards to statistical analysis and how to clearly and concisely present these to a diverse audience with various degrees of understanding of statistics. Maindonald and Braun[††] emphasize

---

[*] Montgomery and Runger, *Applied Statistics and Probabilities for Engineers.*

[†] W. L. Martinez and A. R. Martinez, *Exploratory Data Analysis with MATHLAB* (London, UK: Chapman&Hall /CRC Press UK, 2005).

[‡] J. W. Tukey, *Exploratory Data Analysis* (Reading, NY: Addison Wesley Inc., 1987).

[§] T. A. Runkler, *Data Analytics* (München, Germany: Springer Vieweg, 2012).

[¶] R. M. Church, "How to Look at Data: A Review of John W. Tukey's Exploratory Data Analysis," *Journal of the Experimental Analysis of Behavior* 31 no. 3 (1979): 433–440.

[**] I. H. Iversen, "Tactics of Graphic Design: A Review of Tufte's the Visual Display of Quantitative Information," *Journal of the Experimental Analysis of Behavior* 49, no. 3 (1988): 171–189.

[††] J. Maindonald and W. J. Braun, *Data Analysis and Graphics Using R: An Example-Based Approach*, 3rd ed. (New York: Cambridge University Press, 2010).

that the engineer must "ensure that the analysis and graphs reflect any important structure in the data, to think about the science behind the data, that the aim should be an insightful and coherent account of the data, placing it in the context of what is already known. Ensure that the statistical analysis assists this larger purpose."

The author emphasizes understanding the origins of the data, the results from statistical analysis, and to further analyze and study, not only the science behind the data, but the logic behind it as well. The reader must be able to answer the question: "What does this statistical analysis tell me?" Also, the author emphasizes that the reader be able to understand what the data say and be able to communicate, in an efficient, clear, and unbiased manner, the message being delivered by the analysis.

Chapter 28

Human Factors

Cristina Daccarett

Contents

Human factors is a multidisciplinary field that studies the human body and its cognitive strengths and limitations to develop tools and devices that enhance performance and increase safety and user satisfaction. *Ergonomics* is a field frequently included when referring to human factors. Historically, ergonomics referred to the study of factors only related to physical activity, but this definition has been broadening blending human factors with ergonomics.

Although human factors have been used extensively in industries outside of healthcare, its use in healthcare settings has been minimal. Despite this, errors from machines, materials, and methods have significantly decreased because they are being designed with safety in mind, with extensive quality testing and based on evidence-based practice. Although focus should still be placed on human–machine interactions, greater focus needs to be given to the understanding of how the human brain, behavior, and abilities are impacted by processes and the environment.

Healthcare providers have a sincere commitment to providing the best care possible and to do no harm. Unfortunately, aspiration, expertise, and competence do not always prevent harm when the processes designed fail to understand human capabilities. Human factors help mitigate this by focusing on two main areas, how humans process information and nonpsychological issues. As part of information processing, the science looks at visual and auditory systems, perception and cognition, decision making, display processing, and controls. Nonpsychological issues relate to workspace layout, strength, physiology, and stress.

In healthcare, there are some human factors that have a higher effect in the safety of patient care. These include cognition, distractions, physical demands, and the environment.

Cognition

Cognition is a group of mental processes that give humans the ability to process information and apply knowledge. It includes memory, attention, decision making, and problem solving. When processes are designed, limitations need to be considered and tools must be developed to mediate these shortcomings. For instance, instead of asking a provider to remember the ten items that need to be collected to insert a central line maintaining the sterile field, develop a checklist with the items needed. A change to make the process even more human-friendly would be to have the items located within proximity in the storage area. The ideal process would be to develop a kit that contains all the needed supplies, limiting the number of items the provider needs to remember to one item.

Distractions

Despite best efforts, high noise levels and interruptions are becoming inevitable in healthcare organizations. These factors are frequent causes for distractions causing providers to divert their attention to items other than their main area of focus. Unfortunately, there are situations where the effect of distractions cannot be minimized, such as when a pharmacist performs the final check to a medication dispensed. To limit distractions, a visual signal can be developed to alert others not to disturb the pharmacist during this critical check. An example of this visual signal includes a color mat for the pharmacist to stand on when performing the final check.

Physical Demands

Physical demand refers to the stressors that impact human physical capability, technical skill, and cognitive ability. Frequently, individuals underestimate their limitations, overestimate their capabilities, and have difficulty identifying their physical constraints. Failing to recognize the effect of lack of sleep, performing tasks outside the scope of practice, or taking on too many tasks are examples of physical demand. Another example is when a provider underestimates their physical ability to handle a patient. Protocols have been developed to safely lift patients and failing to follow them can cause injuries and musculoskeletal disorders to providers.

Environment

Environment refers to factors associated with the setting such as lighting, sound, and temperature. When including human factors in healthcare, considerations should be given to ensure that the conditions facilitate the delivery of safe, effective, and efficient patient care. Unfortunately in healthcare, improvements to the environment are often constrained by older facilities that were not designed with flow and human factors in mind. This can be seen, for instance, in inpatient care units that have significantly small storage units and a high number of items to store. A very busy and messy storage area can create errors due to delays in finding the appropriate product, or accidentally taking the wrong item. To mediate the challenges caused by small storage areas, storage rooms could be organized by placing the commonly used items within reach, including labels and color bins to identify products and limiting the amount of product stored to what is absolutely needed to operate for a specific period (a shift, 24 hours, a week, etc.).

Increasing the use of human factors in healthcare will result in significant improvements to the quality and the safety of care delivered, and will positively impact patient and employee satisfaction. As processes are being designed and modified, a human factors "expert" can provide great guidance and highlight opportunities. It is also important to include the knowledge of individuals who are closely related to the process and are performing the task on a daily basis.

When errors or near misses occur, a root cause analysis can help determine if the cause was related to human factors, and if that is the case, processes should be redesigned with considerations to prevent them. Keep in mind that it is always preferable to redesign a process, rather than add an additional inspection step.

Chapter 29

Using Human Factors Engineering to Improve Root Cause Analysis Efforts

Bridget O'Hare

Contents

Root Cause Analysis

A root cause analysis, or RCA, is an investigation of an accident or near-miss accident to learn what factors contributed to the event. A typical root cause analysis in healthcare is a methodology or process used to find out what went wrong, and more importantly, what contributed or caused a medical error or near miss that produced harm or could have caused harm to a patient. In addition to the discovery of the root cause(s), a plan of action is developed to mitigate the risk of the event happening again. A successful plan of action to prevent the reoccurrence of the medical error or opportunity for error will include human factors engineering principles and practices.

The primary reason that an RCA is used in healthcare is to identify what caused or likely caused a medical accident so that efforts can be made to prevent the medical accident or reduce the risk of the event in the future. Healthcare providers are committed to helping patients and doctors take an oath to "First do no harm." Healing, not harming, the patient is a healthcare practitioner's primary passion. Practitioners expect perfection in patient care and their life is dedicated to helping their patients to heal.

The vast majority of healthcare workers are conscientious and they carry the weight of errors with them always. Those healthcare workers directly involved in a medical accident, or those at the "sharp end of the knife" are often referred to as the second victim. The staff and employees involved in healthcare accidents are highly motivated and deeply moved to make changes to prevent the same mishap from happening again. Part of a healthcare worker's healing process, when they have contributed to an error, is to be part of the process to change or prevent another medical accident. They are often powerful members of an RCA team when they are part of a nonpunitive and transparent environment. An organization that focuses on learning from errors so that they are not repeated is more likely to improve safety.[1]

A second reason for conducting an RCA is to prevent an accident reoccurrence because such errors are costly to an organization and ultimately to individual practitioners, increasing both dollar and time costs for malpractice insurance, claims, and legal settlements. Intangible factors and loss of market share are also a concern when harmed patients and their families share the personal impact of medical errors with their families and friends.

A number of techniques and tools are often used in an RCA to determine what happened or what went wrong, such as employee interviews, walkthroughs of the environment where the event or near miss opportunity occurred, flowcharting the process of what actually occurred, flowcharting the process of what normally happens, flowcharting the process of what should occur, compiling patient timelines, and reviews of the patient's medical record documentation. The information gained from the review provides information, which when compared to what normally happens or should happen,[2] will often highlight what went wrong and what contributed to the error or near miss. It is beneficial to include individuals in the investigation who were not directly involved in the event, and also those who were present at the time of the event or near miss. A robust investigation will include an experienced interviewer and someone with a background in human factors engineering.

Human Factors Engineering

The incorporation of human factors engineering in a root cause analysis helps the team create robust action plans. This is an essential ingredient to minimize and prevent errors from repeating. The principles and practice of human factors engineering (HFE) focus on understanding human limits, (e.g., cognitive, auditory, visual, etc.) in the design of systems, interactions, and processes. By using these principles and incorporating them into action plans, HFE helps to design or redesign better systems that make it possible and easier to do the right thing and impossible or difficult to do the wrong thing.

Several examples of the successful implementation of human factors engineering have been used in other high-risk, high-reliability environments for more than four decades. The aviation industry, for example, has successfully reduced the opportunity for error or an airplane crash and the National Transportation Safety Board (NTSB, 1990) estimates that a passenger boarding a US carrier has over a 99.99 percent chance of surviving the flight. Healthcare has begun to implement actions aimed at preventing medical errors and injuries to patients using the power of human factors engineering to create forcing functions and system engineering changes in the design of equipment and work processes to prevent bad outcomes.

A research study was performed in healthcare to address two near misses and one sentinel event that resulted from poor handoff communication of critical cardiac alarm information. HFE was used to improve the response time to (tend to) the patient and it improved the communication and the timeliness of response to life critical telemetry alarms at a 1,061 bed tertiary care hospital with 264 telemetry monitoring system channels.[3] In contrast, the research also pointed out that standardization of the process and education efforts alone using a pager to communicate cardiac alarms did not show a change in pager response time. Standardization and education of the alarm communication process using the one-way communication of an alpha-pager was compared with a new bidirectional communication badge.

The use of a communication badge with bidirectional communication fostered a closed loop of communication or handoff of information from the centralized telemetry technician with the nurse caring for the patient. There were no sentinel events or known near misses following the implementation of the communication badge compared with previous periods of similar duration where two near misses and one sentinel event occurred.

The communication badge featured hands-free operation, voice activation, and an automated escalation pathway to support human-to-human contact. The badge had a significant impact on alarm management for the nursing areas. "The direct communication functionality of the badge significantly shortened the time to first contact, time to completion, and rate of closure of the communication loop in both the pilot and study phases. Median time to first contact with the communication badge was 0.5 minutes, compared to 1.6 minutes with the pager communication (p < 0.0003). Communication loop closure was achieved in 100% of clinical alarms using the badge versus 19% with the pager (p < 0.0001)."[4] Previously, the alarms went into a queue of pages awaiting response with a one-way communication device. The badge had the advantage of fostering human voice-to-voice interaction and the power of intonation to communicate the criticality of the cardiac alarm and these features were perceived to be factors in reducing the alarm response time. The improvement in response time was used as a measure of the clinical information handoff. By supporting the timely closure of the alarm, the new process allowed both the telemetry technicians and the nurses to focus on the priorities at hand rather than having incomplete alarm notifications waiting for a confirmation call. Use of the improved communication tools and processes, thus getting to the patient faster, could positively influence patient outcomes.

At a large multihospital system, human factors engineering principles were used in a "never means never" initiative to prevent operations on the wrong surgical site, wrong patient, and the prevention of unintended retained foreign objects.[5] One HFE component included adding a forcing function, or a bright orange towel with the words "TIME OUT" inscribed for every surgical procedure. Human memories are fallible and sometimes there are errors of omission when individuals believe that they have performed a task when, in fact, they have not. The towel was used as a mental trigger to help them remember to perform the timeout. This is a critical safety check or confirmation of the correct patient, the correct site, and the correct procedure. The towel was incorporated into the sterile surgical packages so that it was present during presurgical preparation of supplies and equipment in the operating room. The towel was consistently placed over the knife or instruments on the Mayo stand or over the surgical site. It would be difficult to ignore the "TIME OUT" message because the act of moving the towel to perform the next step in the surgical process, or incision, would require the surgeon to look at the towel to get to the scalpel or surgical instrument.

Another example of HFE used in the never means never initiative was the order of the timeout, which incorporated cognitive psychology and the known hierarchy that exists in the surgical environment. From prior events and near misses, it was known that staff would not always question the surgeon if the surgeon began the timeout and said, for example, "This is Jane Smith and we are going to perform a left arthroscopic knee procedure." Staff might assume the surgeon was in charge and that they must know the procedure that they are performing or that they had intentionally changed course if that is not what they believed to be true about the procedure. The remaining members of the surgical team would nod in confirmation, but they did not always participate in an active way, nor were they cognitively engaged in the timeout process. Because they were not cognitively engaged or fully present, there was not a true double check of the correct patient, correct site, or correct procedure during the timeout process. By having the surgeon initiate, but not call out the procedure details until after all other members of the surgical team confirmed their scripted role, two things began to happen. First, the staff perceived that the surgeon supported the timeout process by initiating it. And second, by considering the known hierarchy that often exists in the perioperative environment and having the surgeon speak up last in the scripted roles, intentional redundancy was facilitated rather than impeded. This technique to ensure full team cognitive engagement should minimize the risk of an incorrect procedure or incorrect patient.

Another HFE practice helped to standardize counting practices and reduced the number of unintended retained foreign objects. The hospital system standardized the method for counting used sponges by implementing the consistent use of sponge counting bags (that hang from an IV pole) and implementing a standardized, two-person counting process, recording the count information on a preformatted white board to account for used surgical sponges and reconcile them against the baseline count. Better human factors engineering controls existed as each used sponge was placed in its own unique bag and the operating room team was able to see what had been separated and counted. The new process aids human visual limitations by making it possible for the entire perioperative team to clearly see the sponges against a darker background. The sponge-counter bags were hung at the appropriate line of sight for the standing surgical team members. Previous counting practices included placing previously counted, rolled sponges on the floor on disposable towels. The counting practices varied and the accountability of used sponges was even more difficult when shift changes occurred prior to the completion of a surgical case.

A root cause analysis is a tool that is used to determine what contributed or caused a near miss or harm to a patient. The incorporation of HFE practices and principles in the RCA action plans is a helpful mechanism to eliminate and minimize repeat events or near misses. Because it specifically takes human factors and fallibility into account, HFE has been shown to create better controls and improved patient care practices, which further limit the risk of adverse patient outcomes due to medical errors.

Endnotes

1. M. D. Winokur and Kay Beauregard, R.N., "Patient Safety: Mindful, Meaningful, and Fulfilling," *Frontiers of Health Services Management* 22, no. 1 (2005): 17–28.
2. David Marx, "Just Culture," Outcome Engenuity, 2011, http://www.outcome-eng.com/.
3. Kimberly Bonzheim, Bridget O'Hare, et al., "Communication Strategies and Timeliness of Response to Life Critical Telemetry Alarms," *Telemedicine and e-Health* 17 (May 2011).
4. Kimberly Bonzheim, Bridget O'Hare, et al., "Communication Strategies and Timeliness of Response to Life Critical Telemetry Alarms," *Telemedicine and e-Health* 17 (May 2011), 241.
5. Kathleen Harder, PhD, University of Minnesota, designed the safe surgery process together with the author, et al, at Banner Health, Never Means Never Initiative, 2009–2012.

Chapter 30

Throughput and Cycle Time Reduction

Ben Sawyer and Alyn Ford

Contents

Introduction

Three management engineering tools provide approaches to significantly improve inpatient throughput in hospitals. They are as follows:

    A. **Value Stream Mapping** may be described as reducing waste and variability in the processes of care

    B. **Queuing and Smoothing** involve prioritization and load balancing

    C. **Constraint Theory** establishes processes to ensure on-time, complete, and correct (OTCC) activities

    This chapter will examine how hospitals can apply these process engineering principles to meet the needs of patients and the organization, improving patient care by eliminating waste and through waste-reducing cycle times.

Most other industries have already adopted process engineering principles or logistical control systems, demonstrating how management engineering science optimizes throughput. Healthcare and hospitals, however, have been slow to apply these concepts of logistical control to patient throughput, despite proven success in other economic sectors. There are five root causes of healthcare process inefficiency that can be mitigated through an integrated hospital operations system approach leveraging organizational mindset, throughput methodology, and logistical control system technology.

1. The fragmentation and variability associated with isolated, discrete, functional and operational areas at hospitals (often referred to as *silos*)
    - Groups unintentionally work at cross purposes or in parallel functions
    - Poor coordination and ineffective handoffs
2. Lack of real-time performance information
    - No meaningful 24/7 process and cycle data is available.
    - Performance data that does exist is retrospective, lagging information— often too late for managers and caregivers to act on and improve efficiency while the opportunity still exists.
3. Lack of prioritization, queuing, and coordination of simultaneous demand across limited resources
    - Diagnostics and service departments schedule outpatients and work inpatients to meet 24-hour rounding cycles by physicians, rather than managing demand consistent with priorities and demands of the patient and the system flow. This elevates the tyranny of the urgent to become prioritized over what is most important for orchestrated patient care.
4. Push rather than pull processes
    - Patients are pushed to nursing units rather than being pulled by demand triggers from the emergency department (ED) and other admission areas into the most appropriate bed placements.
    - Push processes persist throughout the patient care stay into postdischarge environments of care.
5. Artificial creation of peak system load
    - Batch processes, like predetermined discharge time frames, unnecessarily create demand for the services of many people at the same time, as well as a backlog of patients waiting for appropriate care or attention.

Value Stream Mapping: Reducing Waste and Variability in the Processes of Care and the Artificial Creation of Peak System Load

Consider the traditional process flow of hospital operations: admitting patients, providing care, and discharging them (ideally without readmission for 30 days). Within these processes, consider the examples of role fragmentation and variability. A physician calling to admit a patient may interact with an admission clerk, a bed manager, and a house supervisor. When the patient gets to the nursing unit and progresses through their clinical and therapeutic care events, the fragmentation and variability of roles and processes multiplies and the conflicts grow in number and continue through to their discharge from the hospital. Postdischarge coordination also represents highly variable and fragmented coordination, left largely up to the patient and their family to navigate.

Specialized health professionals serve inpatients throughout their hospital stay. These professionals know and apply their specific expertise to identify urgent or life-threatening conditions. They are typically not asked to consider the bigger picture—the efficient, optimum coordination of care for all patients. As a result, healthcare tends to organize itself very quickly around urgent, acute needs but has much more difficulty organizing its efforts to satisfy longer-term, less acute requirements.

The lack of efficiency in a system organized around urgency becomes most evident in the transitions of care. Whether the transition occurs because a patient's nurse has been called away unexpectedly or as a result of multiple resources arriving at the patient's room at the same time to perform different tasks, the inefficiency is readily apparent.

Batching happens with many activities in hospitals as a reactive response to inefficient throughput. For example, attempting to get all patients discharged by 11 a.m., while correct in its intent, can overwhelm available resources. The volume of discharge demand can easily create gridlock and further delays for patients as they wait to go home. Value stream mapping identifies the key milestones in the patient's stay and provides the foundation for optimizing the process steps needed to most efficiently manage a patient's stay in the hospital. Optimizing the process eliminates redundancy and rework, generating system capacity and eradicating unnecessary process batching.

Value stream mapping is the critical first step in the process of improving patient throughput. Once the hospital staff and leaders identify and map all the process steps and transitions of care across the entire inpatient stay, steps can be eliminated or established to ensure the patient is receiving the optimal amount of care and rest.

Queuing and Smoothing: Prioritization, Queuing, and Coordination of Simultaneous Demand and the Management of Demand

There are two keys to prioritization and load balancing. First, the organization must understand its goals and the steps to achieve them. Second, the organization needs an enterprisewide system that can provide real-time process and cycle data for patient throughput.

Edwards Deming is arguably one of the fathers of system thinking. To quote him:

> "What is a system? A system is a network of interdependent components that work together to try to accomplish the aim of the system. A system must have an aim. Without an aim, there is no system. The aim of the system must be clear to everyone in the system ..."[1]

It is the *aim* that Deming coined that drives an understanding of priority. It aligns activities and filters out efforts that do not satisfy the aim of the system. Most hospitals and healthcare systems lack a clear system aim, and thus struggle to address important and urgent needs in an optimized way. Establishing a system aim does not mean abandoning core strategic imperatives such as profitability, patient safety, clinical quality, leadership, and stewardship.

To better understand the system aim, consider this one established by the Medical Center of Central Georgia in August 2011: "Patients 1st, Pursuing Perfection."[2] Medical Center of Central Georgia aligns and focuses activities around this concise, elegant system aim—at any point, when any activity or priority is in question, staff and caregivers refer and adhere to the guidance of the system aim. Their activities must be in the best interests of the patient and should not be redundant or a result of rework, driven by poor-quality efforts.

Most healthcare organizations prioritize as follows: (1) emergency demands and (2) everything else. Based on this prioritization, diagnostic and therapeutic service departments schedule outpatients first and then work inpatients in as time slots allow. Once things are scheduled, however, they are at the mercy of emergent issues that can disrupt schedules at a moment's notice. Service departments do not typically have visibility to patients' length-of-stay targets or their discharge requirements. As a result, patients are worked in on a first-come, first-served basis or in response to a call from the nurse or physician demanding that their patient be seen as soon as possible because of a perceived overriding need or urgency. This logistical disarray substantially obstructs patient flow.

To highlight the effect of queuing and smoothing, consider a hospital that has a fully operational electronic medical record (EMR) and computerized physician order entry (CPOE) system. Let us assume in this example that there are 300 patients in this hospital and every patient has received a perfect history and physical (H&P) and an ideal plan of care (POC). Let us also assume on any particular day, there are three orders pending for each patient after the morning rounds with his or her physician. This will equal 900 total orders that the diagnostic and therapeutic departments must service.

Which patients will get their orders executed first? There are several things a system should be able to consider to prioritize and decide effectively, such as:

■ An overriding system aim
■ The severity of injury or illness of the patient
■ Intensity of services required
■ Age of patient
■ Imminent discharge status

If the hospital cannot intelligently account for these and other factors, it almost certainly cannot efficiently and effectively manage the simultaneous care demands of all 300 patients.

Most importantly, this is not a clinical problem. The clinical decision making has already been completed. This is, instead, a logistical problem requiring prioritization, queuing, and simultaneous demand coordination across limited assets.

Constraint Theory: Establishing Process and Subprocess Parameters to Ensure OTCC Activities

Process operators must have a clear understanding of what defines the start and end of a process. Many other industries have embraced the concept of OTCC, reflected in familiar service guarantees. Couriers guarantee delivery by 8:00 a.m. or 10:00 a.m. the next business day. Consumer product manufacturers provide us with expiration dates so we are guaranteed the freshest product experience possible. These predictable service outcomes result from OTCC process measures, which reduce variability and maximize the overall customer experience.

Healthcare workers learn appropriate procedures for their specific clinical responsibilities and obtain certification in their area of expertise when they are proficient and meet a specified standard of ability. They are not, however, trained on OTCC processes related to patient flow and care transition handoffs across the healthcare enterprise, which directly impact length of stay and readmission rate performance.

When considering established OTCC measures for patient throughput, performance measures are only looked at in the aggregate. Length of stay (LOS), for example, has an aggregate

OTCC measure established by the geometric mean length of stay (GMLOS) for a particular diagnostic related group defined from the patient's presenting condition. There are not, however, subprocess OTCC measures that break down the detailed process expectations for front-line workers. Consequently, care delivery organizations have not been successful managing to the aggregate LOS targets. Frontline care providers and associated service departments need real-time information on how they are performing their subprocesses relative to the expectations that have been set as OTCC.

So what system or systems can a healthcare executive or frontline worker rely on to get the real-time process and cycle data necessary to understand what is going on right now in their operation or in their efforts to provide optimized patient care? This information is not available from the clinical systems, nor is it available from the revenue cycle systems. Any data that does exist is either in departmental applications, like the emergency department, within perioperative services, or it is manually collected. As a result, most information within the healthcare enterprise tends to be incomplete and retrospective or, as is often the case for frontline workers, nonexistent. When workers lack real-time process and cycle data, it is like trying to drive a car by looking into the rearview mirror. When the information is absent, the only thing to be done is to manage your immediate needs without regard for the objectives of the enterprise. The result for many hospital executives is that trends are often occurring long before they know about them, and they lack the tools to correct performance issues in a meaningful way. Process control systems require an integrated software suite that not only provides visibility to the progress of patients through established OTCC milestones but also does this in a manner that draws OTCC performance at the front line into alignment with the OTCC goals at all levels of this organization.

Process or Logistical Control Methods: Management Engineering's Answer to Controlling and Substantially Reducing Cost of Healthcare

Payors have been demanding more efficient care for decades. These expectations have largely landed on doctors, nurses, and affiliated clinical professionals to resolve. As a result, advances in the quality and efficiency of clinical care have been realized. Why then has the cost of care continued to rise?

The care coordination model used by hospitals and health systems has not changed much in the last fifty years. Healthcare has remained a system of individual practitioners focused on and certified in very specific areas of expertise, which has perpetuated a system of discrete, uncoordinated activity across people and service areas—also referred to as *silos*.

Deming said that all system components must work together to achieve system goals. Any management engineering project that only addresses one element of the system will ultimately be at the mercy of the parts not being addressed. Unless throughput and flow are addressed as a system issue, discrete performance improvement projects can simply chase the bottleneck bubble around the healthcare enterprise.

With healthcare approaching 20 percent of our gross domestic product, payors are seeking significant cost reductions with simultaneous dramatic improvements in the quality of care. As the healthcare economy progresses, the ultimate target will be to improve health system quality performance by up to 50 percentage points while simultaneously reducing waste and process inefficiencies by 40 percentage points. That is a tall order, but not unlike what other economic sectors have had to achieve.

An integrated hospital operations system approach leveraging organizational mindset, throughput methodology, and logistical control system technology can overcome the root causal factors impeding the transformation of healthcare operational performance and result in dramatic improvements in quality, patient safety, patient throughput, and predictive service performance on par with other economic sectors.

Endnotes

1. W. Edwards Deming, *The New Economics for Industry, Government, Education*, 2nd ed. (Cambridge, MA: MIT Press, 1993).
2. Used with the permission of the Medical Center of Central Georgia, November 26, 2012.

Chapter 31

Simulation in Healthcare

Tarun Mohan Lal and Thomas Roh

Contents

Introduction

As healthcare costs continue to rise and providers move toward optimizing the care delivery processes with the Institute for Healthcare Improvement (IHI)'s triple aim of improving patient experience, improving health of populations, and reducing costs as the eventual goal, the ability to assess trade-offs among resource utilization, service, and operating costs is becoming more and more important. Simulation, successfully applied in other industries, is an industrial engineering methodology that provides the ability to assess such trade-offs and is now gaining traction in healthcare. This chapter discusses the use of simulation modeling in studying and improving health systems. The chapter will cover the basics of discrete event simulation model development, and its common applications in healthcare.

Definition of Simulation and Its Importance and Growth

The term *simulation* refers to imitation or enactment of a future event. Simulation in healthcare sometimes refers to physical simulation in which education centers are set up for training care providers to practice real patient care in an artificial environment. In a medical context, the words *model* and *simulation* can have several meanings and are beyond the scope of this chapter. The focus of this chapter will be on an analytical computer simulation technique known as *discrete event simulation* that is often used by management engineers or operations research experts to evaluate, optimize, and improve care delivery processes. In this technique, historical data are used to imitate or simulate the operations of various kinds of healthcare systems to provide an approximation of future outcomes. As an example of simulation, consider a hospital that is contemplating a decision to add beds in the intensive care unit to reduce the time that a patient must wait to be moved into an inpatient unit. It is not certain that adding more beds would truly reduce the congestion in the system, and even if it does, the number of additional beds required to make this a financially viable option is unknown.

A healthcare system is often referred to as a *system of systems* due to multiple components that are both operationally and managerially dependent. There is also a high level of variability, making them stochastic in nature. When the relationships that compose the system are simple, it is possible to use simple mathematical methods to obtain exact information on questions of interest and provide an analytical solution. However, for complex systems such as most healthcare processes, with multiple moving parts, deterministic methodologies do not give the desired accuracy. The use of simulation is crucial in order to estimate the desired characteristics.

Simulation is used when the proposed change cannot be implemented without a significant change in practice that might be too disruptive or too expensive. It can be used to justify improvements or to find the bottlenecks in a system without a huge investment. Going back to the example of additional beds in the ICU, for example, it would certainly not be cost effective to add beds and then remove them later if it does not work. However, discrete event simulation could throw light on the question by simulating the operations of the hospital as they are currently and as they would be if the number of beds were increased.

Example: Major Applications in Healthcare

Application areas for simulation in healthcare are numerous and diverse. The following is a list of some of the problems in healthcare for which simulation has been found to be a useful and powerful tool.

- Hospital operations
  - Bed occupancy and utilization
  - Staffing analysis
  - Operating room scheduling
  - Patient flow analysis
- Emergency department
  - Patient triage and its impact on resource needs
  - Number of beds needed
  - Patient flow from emergency department to hospital inpatient units
  - Staffing analysis

- Outpatient clinics
  - Patient scheduling policies
  - Workload balancing
  - Facility analysis of lobby size, number, and design of exam room space
  - Equipment utilization
- Call center
  - Patient appointment scheduling office staffing needs
- Healthcare supply chain
  - Blood platelets usage and optimal inventory levels
  - Pharmaceutical needs demand and inventory levels

The above list provides examples of some common application areas in different components of healthcare delivery systems and is not meant to be exhaustive. Further information can be found in numerous articles on applications of simulation methodology in healthcare.

Steps in a Simulation Study

Although simulation is becoming a very widely accepted methodology in healthcare, its usefulness and implementation is very dependent on the process used to build the models. It is important to keep in mind that, like any scientific method, simulation modeling is most successful when attention is paid to the process of building a model that includes statistical experimental design to budget and personnel management. This section outlines the recommended framework to be adopted in building simulation models as described in Figure 31.1.

The very first step in a simulation study is to define the specific problem and associated goals and metrics. The project can then move forward into data collection and early statistical analysis of the data. At this point, one starts conceiving how the model is going to be built, what further information might be needed, and maps out the flow of the system. Building the model is a phase that is entwined with the analysis. The analysis drives some of the things that the modeler can and cannot do in building the model and sets the quantitative guidelines. The other part of model building is the art of reproducing actual processes, rules, behaviors, and policies in an artificial model.

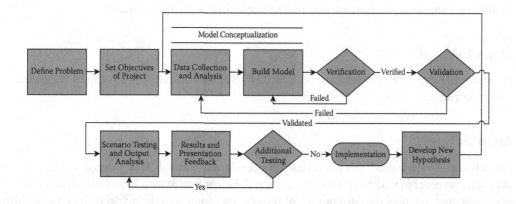

Figure 31.1   Phases in a simulation study.

After the model is built, the simulation needs to be verified. Verification is checking the coding of the simulation and ensuring that the inputs are producing the intended outputs. Validation is ensuring that the simulation model closely resembles the real-life system. If either test fails, you have to go back and change the model. Once an agreed upon model is developed, the simulation is used to answer what-if questions and output comparable metrics. The results are then presented and feedback is gathered. Usually, new questions arise, so new scenarios are tested.

Once an acceptable solution is found, implementation begins. After successful implementation, a new problem can be identified and we return to the model-building phase. The first step in data analysis is to make sure that the data you have is correct. After that, the data needs to be "cleaned" into a usable format, during which one learns the data limitations and the complexity of the problem. Performance measures are then developed so that the metrics will reflect the direct effect that changes have on the problem.

Creating the simulation to mirror real life is not an exact science. The model should be built as simply as possible because complexity decreases accuracy. The data limitations need to be assessed along with the limitations of artificially recreating the real-life system. More likely than not, the modeler will have to go back several times to data collection and analysis during the building of the model.

Stakeholder involvement is also a key element in any successful project. Stakeholders are more accepting of the model when the analyst has visibly been learning their work. Simulation is not an easy concept to understand. Most people label it as a "black box." Providers will not trust something that they do not understand. Simple graphs create a foundation for understanding and a gradual path for change. Leadership will strongly challenge simulation studies if the results do not coincide with their hypotheses, and do not shape results to the department's expectations.

Example Project

Situation

An outpatient clinic at an academic medical center offers comprehensive evaluations and consultations to patients undergoing an anesthesia-related, low- to medium-risk, planned surgery or procedure. Implementation of surgical process improvement initiatives across various surgical specialties led to an increase in demand for the clinic services. The administration believed that insufficient consultation rooms would hinder their ability to expand services.

Objective

Determine the capacity requirements, both facility and personnel, needed to support the expected growth in patient volume.

Analysis

Preliminary investigational process review was conducted through staff interviews and patient shadowing in order to understand the processes and patient flow at the clinic. Discrete event simulation was used to model the current state of the system. Inputs into the model included scheduled patient appointments, duration of each process step, and staff work schedules.

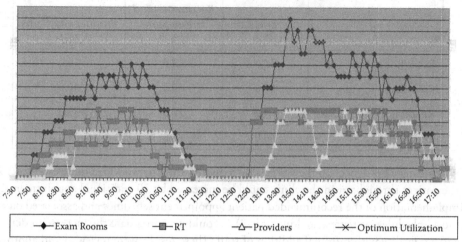

Figure 31.2 Current state of outpatient clinic.

The simulation model of the current system, Figure 31.2, indicated the existence of under-utilized capacity. This initial current state model was used as a framework to investigate possible improvements in the system.

Multiple future state scenarios were developed to evaluate the impact of potential changes on scheduling patterns and capacity reallocation on patient wait time and resource utilization. The most optimal future state was determined, Figure 31.3, based on the utilization of consultation rooms and clinical staff.

Results

The simulation model results indicated that there were a sufficient number of rooms at the outpatient clinic to meet the increase in demand. However, imbalance in patient scheduling across the

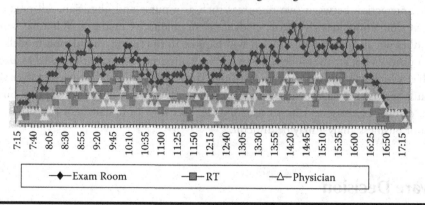

Figure 31.3 Future state after simulation of outpatient clinic.

Table 31.1 Potential Gains identified from Simulation Model

	Current State (%)	Recommended Future State (%)	Productivity Gains (%)
Exam Rooms	47.0	63.0	16.0
Providers	70.0	80.0	10.0
Respiratory Therapists	64.0	77.0	13.0
Throughput	56.0	86.0	54.0

day was causing a bottleneck in the system. By redistributing the workload more evenly across the day, the patient throughput in the clinic could be increased by 30 additional appointments.

Implementation of the recommended patient appointment schedules and associated change in staff work schedules, as represented in Table 31.1, could accommodate the increase in demand in the existing facility with minimal addition of staff. These results were reviewed and approved for implementation by a multidisciplinary team comprised of the clinical staff—providers, respiratory therapists, and administrators.

Advantages and Disadvantages of Simulation

As stated previously, apart from the ability to do a what-if analysis before making a huge investment, simulation has several advantages to offer. Simulation provides the ability to study data that may be very difficult to capture, for example, in the model discussed above, the data regarding the patient idle time or staff underutilized time. Also, simulation provides time-compressed data, which means simulation models can provide forecasted data regarding the behavior of the system for the next few years by artificially replicating the system.

Along with the stated value of simulation, there are some limitations to this methodology as well. It is important for the model to be usable and easy to build; certain assumptions have to be made that may not always reflect what happens in real life, for example, resources in the system cannot dynamically change their decision making as the environment changes. It fails to properly assess the interaction between two resources such as a nurse and physician. All predictions are wrong, but simulation does give better evidence than qualitative methods. What has happened in the past does not necessarily reflect what will happen in the future. Simulation models are often hard to transition. So, for the model creator, it is very important to make the model as user friendly as possible, which can be very time-consuming. The creator has great ownership over the model that is built because he/she knows and understands all the intricate detail put in place. Simulations require a certain expertise to run, so teaching the user how to update it or transitioning it to a manager or business analyst may be difficult.

Software Decision

It is important to keep in mind that simulation is not just about the computer program, but also the methodology that comes along with it. Software needs to be used so that the modeler can invest more of their time on the framework and use of methodology to help hospital leadership make meaningful decisions.

Several vendor products are available in the market for building simulation models. Although ARENA is the most widely used software, many other software packages that are specific to healthcare are also available, such as MEDMODEL, SIMUL8, and so on. Most of the simulation programs perform the standard tasks and are easy to use. Some of the preprogrammed modules available within these simulation programs, like queue management, resources seizure, locations, data tracking and reporting, and event tasks, reduce the time an analyst spends on programming. Most analysts prefer to purchase easy-to-use software programs, however, it is important to keep in mind that this might impede the flexibility of the program to conduct desired analysis. Some key considerations to keep in mind when purchasing simulation software include user familiarity, purpose of using the tool, (researchers prefer flexibility while a business analyst might prefer ease of use and animation capabilities), statistical analysis capabilities, appropriate probability distributions, and debugging features.

Future of Simulation in Healthcare

Clearly, the growth and application of discrete event simulation and advanced methodologies like agent-based simulation in healthcare is evident. Simulation will move from the hands of researchers to more operations engineers and managers to facilitate day-to-day decision making. The application areas are growing from a clinical, operational analysis focus to health policy, IT in healthcare, and public health focus. Lack of data is a big challenge in building robust simulation models in healthcare. Sometimes collecting the level of data required can be a time-consuming process and is not the best option. Although with multiple initiatives across the nation on data capture and standardization, there are going to be opportunities for management engineers to use these data and apply methodologies like simulation to make meaningful decisions. It is also our responsibility as healthcare systems engineers to use this methodology in a meaningful way to inform the care providers and decision makers using accurate statistical analysis in order to change the "black box" mentality of care providers that exists today.

Bibliography

Benneyan, James C. "An Introduction to Using Computer Simulation in Healthcare: Patient Wait Case Study," *Journal of the Society for Health Systems* 5, no. 3 (1997): 1–15.
Law, Averill M. *Simulation Modeling and Analysis*, 4th ed., New York: McGraw-Hill, 2007.
Lowery, Julie C. "Introduction to Simulation in Healthcare." In *Proceedings of the 28th Conference on Winter Simulation*, 78–84. Washington, DC: IEEE Computer Society, 1996.

ADDRESSING CURRENT CHALLENGES

Chapter 32

Industrial Engineers in Public Health

Michael L. Washington

Contents

Introduction

Researchers note that the public health system needs improvements. More specifically, Mays et al. (2004) state that the public health system needs "better information on how to organize, finance, and deliver public health services to achieve improvements in the population health" (p 183). They also state that one key element in improving the public health system is to increase the pipeline of public health systems researchers and that these researchers must be able to develop analytical methods and tools to help answer questions of policy and practice.

The National Academy of Engineering Committee on Engineering and the Health Care System (2005) issued a report titled *Building a Better Delivery System: A New Engineering/Health Care Partnership* that identifies industrial engineering as a discipline that improves health services, in that a better relationship needs to be developed between healthcare and engineering to improve healthcare systems. For decades, engineers have been using analytical tools to improve many sectors all over the world. One way to improve the public healthcare system would be to merge the research tools of industrial engineering with the knowledge of epidemiology to improve policy decisions, logistics, and delivery capabilities. While generally unknown, this idea is not new. Industrial engineers have been involved in improving the healthcare system since 1913 (Salvendy, 2001).

History of Industrial Engineering

In general, people have little knowledge of industrial engineers. Therefore, in order to understand the benefits they can provide to the public health system, and the tools and techniques they use, a description of an industrial engineer is needed. The operational definition of an industrial engineer or industrial and systems engineer (ISE) is (Salvendy, 2001, 5):

> An ISE is one who is concerned with the design, installation, and improvement of integrated systems of people, material, information, equipment, and energy by drawing up specialized knowledge and skills in the mathematical, physical, and social sciences, together with the principles and methods of engineering analysis and design to specify, predict, and evaluate the results to be obtained from such systems.

Traditionally, industrial engineers have concentrated on improving the work environment in areas like manufacturing, transportation, and distribution. Ergonomics, the study of ways to improve job satisfaction, employee health and safety, and job performance, is a specific industrial engineering concentration that involves healthcare. Since the 1970s, more industrial engineers, or individuals using industrial engineering–related tools, have entered the healthcare arena as consultants and management engineers in hospitals and other healthcare settings (Benson and Harp 1994; Butler 1995; Davies 1994; Isken and Hancock 1998; Liyange and Gale 1995; Mahachek 1992; Saunders, Leblanc, and Makens, 1989; Tomar et al., 1998; Washington 1997; Whitson 1997). Although most industrial engineers in healthcare commonly work in acute health-care settings, their skills can and have been applied in public health systems.

In 1913, Frank Gilbreth used motion-study techniques to improve surgical procedures. Lillian Gilbreth, Frank's wife, published articles in the 1940s on the use of industrial engineering tools in hospitals. The growing use of industrial engineering techniques in hospitals led to the development of the Hospital Management Systems Society (now called the Healthcare Information and Management Systems Society) in 1961, which started at the Georgia Institute of Technology in Atlanta, Georgia. Also in Atlanta, the Institute of Industrial Engineering created a hospital section in 1964 that eventually led to the birth of the Society for Health Systems (Salvendy 2001). The Georgia Institute of Technology has the largest industrial engineering department in the world and they developed the first academic program in health systems in 1958 (Sainfort 2004).

The National Academy of Engineering and the Institute of Medicine state that barriers exist in using some engineering tools (e.g., statistical process controls; queuing theory; quality function deployment; failure-mode effects analysis; mathematical modeling; discrete event computer simulation; linear, nonlinear, and mix-linear programming; neural networks; optimization techniques (e.g., tabu and scatter search); market models; and agency theory) in healthcare. As stated in the National Academy of Engineering and the Institute of Medicine report (2005, 3):

> [R]elatively few health care professionals or administrators are equipped to think analytically about health care delivery as a system or to appreciate the relevance of systems-engineering tools. Even fewer are equipped to work with engineers to apply these tools. The widespread use of systems-engineering tools will require determined efforts

on the part of health care providers, the engineering community, state and federal governments, private insurers, large employers, and other stakeholders.

Researchers at the Centers for Disease Control and Prevention (CDC) have a history of collaborating with and hiring industrial engineers to solve some public health problems. This chapter will discuss three historical projects* within the CDC utilizing industrial engineer skills. The studies are (1) a binary-integer linear program to schedule childhood vaccinations while minimizing parental costs, (2) a public vaccine-need forecasting model, and (3) and a discrete-event computer simulation of a sexually transmitted disease (STD) clinic to analyze its capacity to administer more hepatitis B (HBV) vaccinations.

Linear Programming

The widespread use of vaccines has been one of the most successful public health interventions of the twentieth century. Vaccination has resulted in the eradication of smallpox; elimination of poliomyelitis in the Americas; and control of measles, rubella, tetanus, diphtheria, *Haemophilus influenzae* type b, and other infectious diseases in the United States and other parts of the world (CDC 1999a).

Because of the biotechnology revolution, another problem developed as more childhood vaccines became available and the childhood vaccine schedule became more complex: determining how to administer vaccines in the most economical manner, while limiting the number of injections per visit. Jacobson et al. (1999) and Weniger et al. (1998) created a binary-integer linear program model to determine the minimum cost of vaccinating a child against selective vaccine-preventable diseases based upon a few constraints. Under the January to December 1998 Advisory Committee on Immunization Practices (ACIP) Recommended Childhood Immunization Schedule for the United States (Figure 32.1), which was the current schedule at the time of the study, the possibility existed for a child to receive up to six vaccinations during one visit. Healthcare researchers and practitioners had experienced difficulty in determining the most economical clinical visit schedule for parents and which vaccines to administer during a visit (Weniger et al. 1998).

The pilot project only included four vaccine manufacturers. Vaccines included in the model were diphtheria-tetanus-acellular pertussis (DTaP), *Haemophilus influenzae* type b (Hib), HBV, and a combination vaccines of DTaP-Hib and Hib-HBV. Vaccines that were on the 1998 schedule but not included in this pilot study were polio, measles-mumps-rubella, and varicella. The objective function of the model was to minimize the cost of administering the vaccinations, which only included the cost of the vaccine, vaccine preparation, injection, and clinical visit. Constraints during the pilot project were adhering to the 1998 ACIP Recommended Childhood Immunization Schedule for the United States up to age five, limiting injections per visit to no more than three, and not permitting excess vaccinations (receiving more than was recommended).

Results from the pilot project found the minimum cost of vaccinating a child to be $490.32. Results are shown in Table 32.1 (Jacobson et al. 1999; Weniger et al. 1998). Other scenarios were

---

* The historical examples presented in this chapter are intended for demonstration purposes only, in order to show the utility of industrial engineering in public health. Interested readers are encouraged to visit http://www.cdc.gov/hepatitis/B/index.htm and http://www.cdc.gov/vaccines/ for the most up-to-date information about hepatitis and vaccine-preventable diseases.

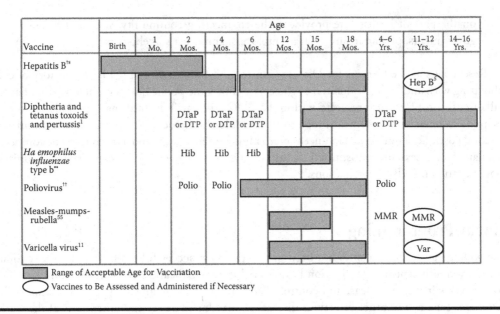

Figure 32.1 ACIP Recommended Childhood Immunization Schedule, United States, January–December. (From Centers for Disease Control and Prevention (CDC).) (1998). "Notice to Readers Recommended Childhood Immunization Schedule: United States, 1998." *The Morbidity and Mortality Weekly Report* **47, no. 1 (1998): 8–12. Used by Weniger et al. in 1998 linear programming paper.)**

considered: first HBV vaccination given in the second month, second-lowest cost, maximum cost, and all manufacturers represented in the vaccines being administered.

This project was a pilot study; however, the researchers conducted more research and developed a more detailed and complete working model on the Internet (http://vaccineselection.com). The pilot project expanded to include other recommended vaccines. Although updates to this website ended with the 2007 immunization schedule, it was the start of other industrial engineers creating tools to assist in immunization scheduling, in which the tools used some form of linear and nonlinear programming and the ACIP recommendations:

■ Catch-Up Immunization schedulers (https://www.vacscheduler.org/) based on the 2013 Childhood and Adolescent Immunization Schedule
■ Adolescent Immunization Scheduler (http://www.cdc.gov/vaccines/schedules/Schedulers/adolescent-scheduler.html) based on the 2013 Recommended Adolescent Immunization Schedule
■ Adult Immunization Scheduler (http://www.cdc.gov/vaccines/schedules/Schedulers/adult-scheduler.html) based on the 2012 Recommended Adult Immunization Schedule

Forecasting

During the late 1990s and early 2000s, better vaccine forecasting was needed. Six Georgia Institute of Technology industrial engineering students developed regression models for four immunization programs to predict vaccine needs by using historical data and interviewing appropriate scientists and administrators. Because this was a pilot project, the students only considered the most

Table 32.1   Linear Program Model Calculating the Minimum Cost of Vaccinating a Child with a Hepatitis B Birth Dose

Visit (months)	Vaccine (manufacturer)	Total Vaccine Price ($)	Injection Cost ($)	Clinic Visit Cost ($)	Total Cost ($)
0–1	HepB(B)	9.72	15.00	40.00	64.72
2	DTaP-Hib (A)	22.24	15.00	40.00	77.24
4	HepB (B), DTaP-Hib (A)	31.96	30.00	40.00	101.96
6	DTaP-Hib	22.24	15.00	40.00	77.24
12–18	HepB (B), DTaP-Hib(A)	31.96	30.00	40.00	101.96
60	DTaP (A)	12.20	15.00	40.00	67.20
Total Cost		**130.32**	**120.00**	**240.00**	**490.32**

| Only 2 manufactures are represented (A and B). |
| Total vaccine prices used are from the US Federal contract purchase prices (including excise taxes) effective as of September 4, 1997. |

Source: Data from S. H. Jacobson, E. C. Sewell, R. Deuson, and G. B. Weniger, "An Integer Programming Model for Vaccine Procurement and Delivery for Childhood Immunization: A Pilot Study," *Health Care Management Science* 2 (1999): 1–9; B. G. Weniger, R. T. Chen, S. H. Jacobson, E. C. Sewell, R. Deuson, J. R. Livengood, and W. A. Orenstein, "Addressing the Challenges to Immunization Practice with an Economic Algorithm for Vaccine Selection." *Vaccine* 16, no. 19 (1998): 1885–1897.

purchased childhood vaccines by doses for modeling. Vaccines selected for modeling were Hib, HBV, measles-mumps-rubella (MMR), and DTaP. Each vaccine was modeled separately for each program. Independent variables used in the models included modified estimates of numbers of children less than one year of age, total vaccine purchased from the preceding year, and a deterministic trend.

Compared with the forecasting methods used by the US CDC National Immunization Program (now the National Center for Immunization and Respiratory Diseases) in 2000, the regression models underestimated projects' vaccine needs 20% less frequently, and overestimated projects' vaccine needs 26% less frequently (Happ et al. 2000). This project, based on limited data, was a step in forecasting public vaccine needs.

Simulation

The CDC recommends those who seek evaluation of treatment for an STD be vaccinated against HBV (CDC 2009). An STD clinic in California offered the first of three HBV vaccines to those who wanted it during the initial visit. Unfortunately, they had difficulties getting clients to return for their second and third doses. The clinic wanted to enhance a program to encourage these clients to return and receive their final two HBV vaccinations. As a pilot project, a study was conducted to see how computer simulation could provide insight on the potential clinic flow of an STD clinic if the clinic started a campaign to have more clients return for their second and third HBV vaccinations. From the computer simulation, administrators wanted to answer the following questions:

1. Would the clinic have the capacity to serve more clients? If more clients returned for their second and third doses, there would be more clinic visits than would normally occur, which would be an increased burden on the staff.
2. Would campaigning for more clients to return for their second and third doses disrupt the current client flow?

Six clinic employees were directly involved with clients. Their titles and responsibilities were as follows:

■ 1 Clerk: The clerk was responsible for greeting clients, distributing paperwork, and data entry.
■ 2 Nurse Practitioners: Nurse practitioners provided clinical evaluations (e.g., histories and exams) and education, and they prescribed treatment.
■ 2 Registered Nurses (RNs): RNs administered vaccinations, drew blood and collected other specimens, and provided education. Nonclient care duties performed by RNs were preparing and cleaning rooms, laboratory activities, paperwork, and obtaining supplies.
■ 1 Counselor: For clients seeking consultation about HBV, HIV, and other STDs, a counselor was available.

The clinic provided services to 30 to 70 clients per day, and was, at that time, offering HBV vaccines to unvaccinated clients and return clients. Clients visiting for their second or third dose of HBV vaccination were labeled "Return HBV" in the model. The clinic averaged a little more than five Return HBV clients a day. Six other client categories existed. More detailed information about these client categories can be obtained from the author.

Arena® version 3.5 by Systems Modeling (now Rockwell Software) was the software used to model patient flow. The layout of the clinic is shown in Figure 32.2. The model was modified for what-if scenarios concerning only the number of Return HBV clients visiting the clinic. Scenarios included increasing the number of Return HBV clients incrementally to four times the current level. The RNs were the staff of interest, since they administer vaccinations.

During preimplementation operations, the RN utilization rate was about 13% (Figure 32.3). This was low, and increasing the number of Return HBV clients was not expected to disrupt the RNs' daily routine. After quadrupling the current Return HBV level, the utilization rate increased to about 22%. The utilization rate was still low, and almost 40% lower than the next lowest resource utilization rate.

Personnel other than RNs were affected by the increase of Return HBV clients. When the number of Return HBV clients increased, the clerk utilization rate increased from 58% to 70%. The increase was due to the clerk retrieving or creating files for extra Return HBV clients. The counselor and nurse practitioner utilization rates stayed about the same because the extra Return HBV clients do not visit them.

Since extra Return HBV clients were occupying the RN's and the clerk's time, other clients might have to wait to see the RN and clerk, thus increasing other clients' average length of stay (ALOS) in the clinic. Although the overall ALOS did not change much, the ALOS for the Return HBV and Category 3 clients increased by more than ten minutes. Return HBV, Category 1, and Category 3 clients' ALOS showed a gradual linear increase as the number of Return HBV clients

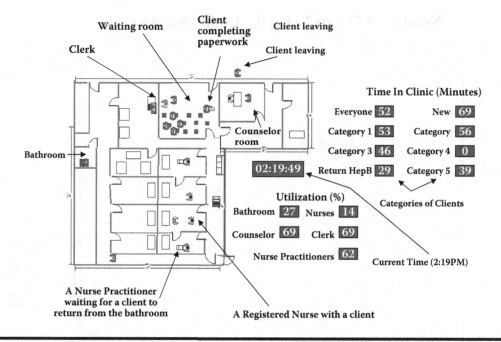

Figure 32.2 **Picture of the computer animation model of a California sexually transmitted disease clinic.**

increased. The ALOS for the Category 2 clients also increased by more than ten minutes; however, that statistic was not very reliable since an average of 0.75 Category 2 clients a day visited the clinic.

If more HBV vaccinations are provided by the clinic to clients returning to complete their vaccination series without any additional changes, the clinic should be able to handle four times as many Return HBV clients as are currently served. Before this analysis, clinic administrators suspected that RNs were underutilized. At the time of this study, administrators planned to assign RNs more duties, such as additional client education. If more than four times the current level of Return HBV clients arrive, the clinic administrators might consider hiring an extra part-time clerk.

Conclusion

Although industrial engineers have contributed to improving processes within the manufacturing industry, a need to use more engineering tools exists in the public health arena. Although this chapter only discussed three specific applications, researchers are using numerous analytical methods and engineering tools to solve public health problems. Some past and potentially new examples of industrial engineering tools used in public health include:

- mathematical modeling and simulation of disease processes;
- material handling, transportation, storage location, and storage techniques vaccines, medicine and other medical supplies;
- a bar-coding system to monitor vaccine usage information, and to easily record the vaccine information in medical records;

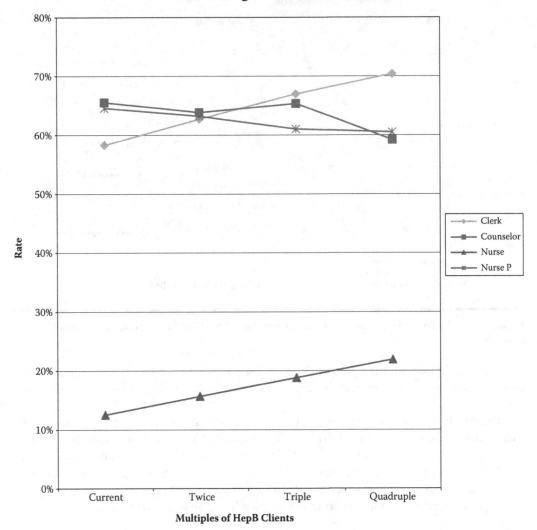

Figure 32.3 Results from the computer simulation model showing the personnel utilization rate as the number of clients using the clinic increases.

- cost–benefit analyses and Markov modeling to assess the continuation of routine vaccination of children;
- computer simulation to determine where and how much vaccines and medication to stockpile against a bioterrorist attack;
- decision theory to determine the best drug treatment for STD clients;
- facility layout to recommend physical changes to an existing or new clinic;
- statistical process control to identify disease outbreaks, medical errors, and potential bioterrorism attacks.

Numerous opportunities for industrial engineers (and other disciplines like operations research and economics) exist in public health and the pipeline for quality health services researchers can become larger if public health officials examine these disciplines for answers. Conversely, engineering disciplines might need to look into the public health sector to apply their skills when one considers the decline of jobs in the manufacturing sector.

References

Benson, R., and Harp. N. (1994). "Using Systems Thinking to Extend Continuous Quality Improvement. *Quality Letter for Healthcare Leaders* 6 (6): 17–24.

Butler, T. W. (1995). "Management Science/Operations Research Projects in health Care: The Administrator's Perspective." *Health Care Management Review* 20 (1): 19–25.

Centers for Disease Control and Prevention (CDC). (1998). "Notice to Readers Recommended Childhood Immunization Schedule: United States, 1998." *The Morbidity and Mortality Weekly Report* 47 (1): 8–12.

Centers for Disease Control and Prevention (CDC). (1999a). "Achievements in Public Health, 1900–1999: Impact of Vaccines Universally Recommended for Children, United States, 1990–1999." *The Morbidity and Mortality Weekly Report* 48 (12): 243–248.

Centers for Disease Control and Prevention (CDC), Division of Viral Hepatitis and National Center for HIV/AIDS, Viral Hepatitis, STD, and TB Prevention. CDC DVH-Hepatitis B FAQs for the Public, http://www.cdc.gov/hepatitis/B/bFAQ.htm (accessed January 19, 2013).

Davies, R. (1994). "Simulation for Planning Services for Patients with Coronary Artery Disease. *European Journal of Operational Research* 72 (2): 323–332.

Happ, M., Kao, W., Parikh, R., Shlyahov, V., Tariyal, S., and Tulley, C. (2000). A Study of Vaccine Forecasting and Awards Methodology. Senior Design Project, Georgia Tech.

Isken, M. W., and Hancock, W. M. (1998). "Tactical Staff Scheduling Analysis for Hospital Ancillary Units. *Journal of the Society for Health Systems* 5 (4): 11 –23.

Jacobson, S. H., Sewell, E. C., Deuson, R., and Weniger, G. B. (1999). "An Integer Programming Model for Vaccine Procurement and Delivery for Childhood Immunization: A Pilot Study." *Health Care Management Science* 2: 1–9.

Liyanage, L., and Gale, M. (1995). "Quality Improvement for the Campbelltown Hospital Emergency Service". *Proceedings of the IEEE International Conference on Systems, Man and Cybernetics*, Vol. 3, Vancouver, BC, Canada, 1997–2002.

Mahachek, A. R. (1992). "An Introduction to Patient Flow Simulation For Health-Care Managers." *Journal of the Society for Health Systems* 3 (3): 73–81.

Mays, G. P., Halverson, P. K., and Scutchfield, F. D. (2004). "Making Public Health Improvement Real: The Vital Role of Systems Research." *Journal of Public Health Management and Practice* 10 (3): 183–185.

National Academy of Engineering and the Institute of Medicine. (2005). *Building a Better Delivery System: A New Engineering/Health Care Partnership*. Washington (DC): National Academies Press (US).

Sainfort, F. (April 6, 2004). "Using Operations Research to Improve Health Care Delivery Systems." Presentation to CDC Health Systems Research Work Group, Atlanta, GA.

Salvendy, G., ed. (2001). *Handbook of Industrial Engineering: Technology and Operations Management*. New York: John Wiley & Sons, Inc.

Saunders, C. E., Leblanc, L. J., and Makens, P. K. (1989). "Modeling Emergency Department Operations Using Advanced Computer Simulation Systems." *Annals of Emergency Medicine* 18 (2): 134–140.

Tomar, R. H., Lee, S., Wu, S. Y., Klein, R., Klein, B. E., Moss, S. E., Fryback, D. G., Tollios, J. L., and Sainfort, F. (1998). "Disease Progression and Cost of Insulin Dependent Diabetes Mellitus: Development and Application of a Simulation Model." *Journal of the Society for Health Systems* 5 (4): 24–37.

Washington, M. L., and Khator, S. K. (1997). "Computer Simulation in Health Care." *Proceedings of the Quest for Quality and Productivity in Health Services Conference*, St. Louis, MO, USA, 201–210.

Weniger, B. G., Chen, R. T., Jacobson, S. H., Sewell, E. C., Deuson, R., Livengood, J. R., and Orenstein, W. A. (1998). "Addressing the Challenges to Immunization Practice with an Economic Algorithm for Vaccine Selection." *Vaccine* 16 (19): 1885–1897.

Whitson, D. (1997). "Applying Just-in-Time Systems in Health Care." *Industrial Engineering* 29 (8): 32–37.

LOOKING TO THE FUTURE

Chapter 33

On Leaving a Legacy

Duke Rohe and Jean Ann Larson

Contents

In order to make a difference in your profession, you must be a whole person. It is not just your educational degrees or job titles that give you credibility and make others want to work with you and be led by you. You cannot ask people to do that which you will not do. Remember Gandhi's wise words: "Be the change you want to see in the world."

It matters not if you grow professionally if you are not growing personally. If you intend to make a dramatic difference in your organization, you have to learn how to embrace change in your own life. As uncomfortable or difficult as it may be, change has to begin in you before it can influence the change in others. Don't just live life; experience it. Listen to it. Learn from it. Apply its lesson. Share it. That's how to change your world.

A Few Thoughts to Consider

Don't Follow Wise Men! Follow What Wise Men Follow.

Seek out what is important and intriguing to them. Sit at the feet of their understanding and see how it applies and affects you. Learn; do not mimic it, but employ it in your own unique way. Develop your spin on it from a new perspective. Drill down deeper than most are willing to explore to use it in different ways. Author your fingerprint version of it, which causes even its originator to marvel. Many great innovations have come from a new perspective or way of applying other knowledge.

> The ultimate creative act is to express what is most authentic and individual about you.
>
> **—Eileen M. Clegg**

Don't Keep It to Yourself

Share, share, share. Your new motto ought to be, "You give, you live; you don't, you won't." We were all creatures designed for giving. By sharing, giving, or teaching what you know to others, you will find that you will often learn as much about the topic and yourself as the person you are helping. Think how gratifying it has been to give help or offer an apt word to one in need. The same applies to the work you do. What are the lessons learned, the unique application or improvements made from which others might gain? Take time to fashion it in a way that others can pick it up, understand, and use it. Tool-i-size it. Find ways to broadcast it throughout your institution, throughout your profession, even throughout the world. Seed the world with your thoughts and ideas. You never know when your little seed becomes a spark that leads to more innovative solutions. Now you've done your share to make a difference in healthcare.

> Anything that is of value in life only multiplies when it is given.
>
> **—Deepak Chopra**

Grow Every Day, Every Way, Any Way

Be open to learning. Change is what causes us to transition our thinking, which ignites learning and growth. How have you grown since last week? What did you learn to do or not to do? If you can't answer that, then you are a great candidate for greater growth. In fact, we can always learn more—go deeper, get broader. Seek out other perspectives. Vary your route to and from your office. Talk to strangers and learn from them. We have all the time in the world, yet so little time to use it. Discover who you are, what you like, what you avoid. All of these things offer great material to learn a new thing about you. Keep a list of what you want to learn more about. Learn what intrigues you, develop it, and then articulate it in a manner that is authentically you.

> It is not the strongest of the species that survives, nor the most intelligent, but the one most responsive to change.
>
> **—Charles Darwin**

Your Work Is the Signature of Your Reputation

How you do what you do and how you treat others reflect your values. When others think of you, what comes to mind: friendly, helpful, genuine, and considerate? When others reflect on your work, what do they think: timely, informative, supportive, thorough, efficient, effective? What you do or don't do says a lot about you. Your work is your signature, so it ought to be your best. Not perfect, just the best you can do with the resources available. Anything less and you are cheating yourself.

> Work is something made greater by ourselves and in turn that makes us greater.
>
> —**Maya Angelou**

Dare to Interact with the World

This is the scariest and the coolest thing you could ever do. Imagine your work helping thousands around the world. Charles Platt began this by hosting the HME listserv. He started it in 1999, before most social media sites were even a twinkle in their inventor's eye. Now it averages 60 posts a month and has 3,000 members. That's enabling interaction. Duke, at a challenge from coauthor Jean Ann, endeavored to share an improvement tool or piece a week over the past 15 years. The weekly effort has expanded to the development of six tool sites and a wiki for various professions and sending CDs of tools to requestors internationally. Once you decide to interact with the world, it changes you. You have a dual purpose in your everyday work, which is to make changes and simultaneously translate it into tools and knowledge that may benefit others. You become the Solomon of proverbs, the Deming of profound knowledge, and the source of your profession's growth. It's no longer an effort; it's a passion.

> Don't be too timid and squeamish about your actions. All life is an experiment. The more experiments you make, the better.
>
> —**Ralph Waldo Emerson**

What's in the Wake Behind You?

When you look back through time, who are the benefactors of you being there? What have they gained? Believe it or not, your presence moving forward through life leaves a wake behind of those it has touched. If the wake is just you and yours, the wake is limited. If it includes those in your profession, your spiritual friends, your special interest groups, the wake gets higher and broader. Those affected are themselves changed by degree and are different because of it.

> Carve your name on hearts, not tombstones. A legacy is etched into the minds of others and the stories they share about you.
>
> —**Shannon L. Alder**

Take Time to Recharge and Reflect

Sometimes, the best learning occurs during quiet times. Through periodic pausing and listening to life, you can learn from it. What you do and what you say make learning material. Suspend life's motion long enough to see where it is coming from and where it is taking you. Only then can you choose what to do with it. Life doesn't want to change you; it just wants you to be able to choose to change. Change happens regardless of you. What matters is your response. Choose to reflect, learn, and recharge.

> Life can only be understood backwards; but it must be lived forwards.
>
> **—SørenKierkegaard**

It Is Not Just What You Do; It Is How You Do It and How You Treat Others

Excellence is a great pursuit. Not one of perfection, but one of being perfected. It encompasses all of who you are. Your manner of helpfulness, attentiveness, assurance, and reliability are an important and integral part of what you do.

> I've learned that people will forget what you said, people will forget what you did, but people will never forget how you made them feel.
>
> **—Maya Angelou**

Be Patient—with Yourself and Others

Patience is the power to set impulse aside until you understand its control over you. To become more patient, challenge your impatience. On the way home from work, purposely get in the slow lane of traffic and remain there. Pretend that those in front of you who are driving slowly are protecting you from getting a speeding ticket. Endeavor to remain peaceful as you travel home. Stop the urge to change lanes when the cars beside you pass you by. You are just going to relax, listen to music, and enjoy the ride. You are not going to let anything steal your peace. This exercise may have to be repeated several times, but it will teach you how to pursue peace over impatience. Also, remember that with people and relationships, going slow *is* fast. You cannot hurry up another's season of growth. If you try to rush with colleagues or loved ones, mistakes and regrets happen that will cause you to spend more time fixing!

> The greatest power is often simple patience.
>
> **—E. Joseph Cossman**

Failure Builds Character

You learn more from failure than from success. Failure is overrated and overweighted. It attempts to measure your worth by what you do instead of who you are. Surely failure is painful, but that's where you learn about yourself. How you caused it, how you managed it, how you grew from it. Failure is a tremendous teacher. In fact, who you are today was built from the failures you learned from your yesterdays. So fail faster. As Thomas Edison was quoted to have said, "I have not failed. I've just found 10,000 ways that won't work." And remember:

> In the middle of difficulty, lies opportunity.
>
> **—Albert Einstein**

Find Your Divine Purpose

And then figure out a way to share your gifts with others throughout your life—regardless of your title or organization. Whether you know it or not, you are here on this earth for a purpose. Your job is to become the best *you* that you can be and to make the world a better place. Find what divinely inspires you and let it influence what you say and do. Politics may try to separate church and state, but no one can separate the spirit from the mind. They are the two wings of flight. You are truly a child of God. Learning is not completed until you express your true self. Everyone has a gift that can help others. Discover it, develop it, distribute it in full belief, and it will make a difference—especially in you.

> Sometimes, you have to step outside of the person you've been and remember the person you were meant to be. The person you want to be. The person you are.
>
> **—H. G. Wells**

Everyone You Meet Is Afraid of Something, Loves Something, and Has Lost Something

Your job is to make sure that you both bring out the best in each other. The greatest gift you can give to yourself is to be a gift to another. Be the listening ear, understanding heart, supporting arm, encouraging word that meets the need of another. Just as there are process flows that need attention, there are relationship flows that require time and attention to bring out the best in them.

> Treat people as if they were what they ought to be, and you help them to become what they are capable of being.
>
> **—Goethe**

> The greatest good you can do for another is not just to share your riches but to reveal to him his own.
>
> **—Benjamin Disraeli**

Leverage Thyself

So how do you leverage yourself with your colleagues, clients, and customers? How can one person make such a positive impact that it is felt in his department, conceivably in his hospital or company, inconceivably in all of healthcare? It first starts in the heart then grows in the mind. We all want to make a difference, why not a *big* difference? Extraordinary people are just ordinary people who do extraordinary thinking.

> Our deepest fear is not that we are inadequate, Our deepest fear is that we are powerful beyond measure. It is our light, not our darkness that most frightens us. We ask ourselves, who am I to be brilliant, gorgeous, talented and fabulous?
>
> **—Marianne Williamson**, *A Return to Love*

Make yourself so valuable in terms of knowledge and help that your organization would grieve if you left. Become the source of how to speed change along. Be great, not at just delivering what is asked for, but at providing what is sorely needed to be successful. Be generative in capturing new knowledge not related to your field and bending it to revolutionize your organization. Be different than your peers in many ways. Consider new mental models. Network within, between, and outside organizations in healthcare. Tie your heart to the value you provide the folks who ultimately serve your ultimate customer. Become a servant leader to those that may admire your ways. Remember that you stand on the shoulders of those you have learned from, so the credit is never solely yours.

> If I have seen further, it is by standing on the shoulders of giants.

—Isaac Newton

Grow yourself by listening to life as it unfolds new challenges that only you can learn from. Be an eternal learner who always wants something just beyond your grasp. Be so optimistic that there is a treasure under every rock; even in stumbling there is growth in getting up. Have a hope that is beyond human accomplishment and see how it surprises you. Be the wake of joy to those you pass each day. Even the memory of you brings a smile. Seek out and sit with great mentors and grasp even what they don't yet know; then share it with the world. Explore the world of *different* so that you don't have to remain the same. Turn everything into an expedition that transforms problems into challenges, goals into summits, and work into adventure. Dare to climb the highest peaks: the ones within. Know what you share, share what you know. Pretend you are the only one who can rid this world of waste, and the expedience with which you transfer this know-how to others, adds to the bottom line of serving their customers. Know that there are only a few things that are important, so get to know them well. Also, never forget that you leave a legacy whether you intend to or not—so make it one that is worthwhile.

> The greatest use of life is to spend it for something that will outlast it.

—William James

Index

Page references in *italics* refer to figures.
Page references in **bold** refer to tables.

Printed in the United States
by Baker & Taylor Publisher Services

Printed in the United States
by Baker & Taylor Publisher Services